# POVERTY AND THE LONE-PARENT: THE CHALLENGE TO SOCIAL POLICY

For my parents

# Poverty and the lone-parent: the challenge to social policy

JANE MILLAR
*School of Social Sciences*
*University of Bath*

**Avebury**

**Aldershot · Brookfield USA · Hong Kong · Singapore · Sydney**

Published by

Avebury

Gower Publishing Company Limited
Gower House
Croft Road
Aldershot
Hants GU11 3HR
England

Gower Publishing Company,
Old Post Road,
Brookfield,
Vermont 05036,
U.S.A.

British Library Cataloguing in Publication Data
Millar, Jane
    Poverty and the lone-parent family: the
    challenge to social policy.
    1. Great Britain. Non-contributory welfare
    benefits. Requirements of single-parent
    families
    I. Title
    368.4

ISBN 0-566 05770 0

Laserset by Computype, 241 Hull Road, York YO1 3LA

Printed and Bound by Athenæum Press
Newcastle upon Tyne

# Contents

# List of tables

# Acknowledgements

I should like to thank Jonathan Bradshaw who supervised the thesis on which this book was based. David Piachaud also provided valuable comments. Thanks to Sue Medd and Vivienne Taylor, who did all the typing and re-typing. The ESRC provided financial support for the study.

Jane Millar

# Introduction

In Britain the number of families headed by a lone parent has risen steeply over the past few decades. Currently there are estimated to be almost one million lone parents caring for about one and a half million dependent children. These families make up about 13 per cent of all families with children. Nine in ten are women and two-thirds become lone parents because of marital breakdown. This situation is not unique to Britain. Lone parents made up about 10 per cent of all families with dependent children in the EEC in the early 1980s, about 12-13 per cent in Canada and in Australia, about 20-25 per cent in Sweden and in the United States. Thus, throughout the western industrialised countries lone-parent families form a substantial—and growing—proportion of all families.

This change in family structure is one of the most important challenges facing social policy today. Twenty-five years ago the vast majority of all children were brought up by two parents in a family where the father went out to work and provided for the family financially while the mother stayed at home and cared for her husband and children. Today's children still usually live with two parents but changing patterns of employment and of family life mean that children are now much more likely to experience a wide variety of different family types. Changing employment patterns mean that many children have employed mothers as well as employed fathers; or conversely, because of rising unemployment, live in families where neither parent is employed. Changing family patterns, in particular because of marital breakdown, mean that many children will spend some part of their

1

childhood in a lone-parent family, usually living with their mother; and many of these children will go onto live in a 're-constituted' family (ie with a natural parent and a step-parent).

Bringing up children is both time consuming and expensive. It has been estimated that basic child care tasks fill 'round about fifty hours a week' and that, meeting only very basic minimum needs, a child of eight costs about £14.00 a week (May 1985 prices) to feed, clothe, take on an occasional outing and buy an occasional present (Piachaud, 1985). These tasks are usually shared between two parents, but in lone-parent families one person must take on both the child care and the financial provider roles. The difficulty of doing this is reflected in the very widespread and longstanding association between poverty and lone parenthood—in both this and many other countries lone mothers have a very high risk of poverty, three or four times above the average.

Lone-parent families are a challenge to social policy in a number of different ways. Seeking ways to provide adequate support for lone-parent families raises questions about the relative roles of the state, fathers and mothers in providing for children; questions of equity in provision between different family types; questions about the structure of employment and gender inequalities in the labour market. Underlying all this is the question of whether it is possible to break the link between poverty and lone parenthood without, in the process of doing so, severely undermining or even destroying the 'family' itself.

The main aim of this study is to analyse the living standards of lone-parent families; and in the light of this to evaluate current income support policy towards such families and consider ways in which policy could develop in the future. The point of focusing on living standards is that an analysis of the living standards of lone-parent families helps us to understand more clearly the outcomes of current policy, and the extent to which there is a gap between the needs of lone-parent families and the provisions of current policy. This evaluation of current income support policy is further extended by setting the British material in the wider context of policy developments in other countries.

The analysis of living standards which forms the major part of the research is based on a secondary analysis of data from the Family Finances Survey (FFS) and Family Resources Surveys (FRS). These two linked studies were carried by OPCS on behalf of the Department of Health and Social Security between 1978 and 1980. The sample consists of about 3,000 families with dependent children, all of whom had, when initially interviewed, family incomes of less than 140 per cent of supplementary benefit levels. They were therefore all 'low-income' families and both lone parents and two-parent families were included in the sample. Very detailed information on both income and expenditure were collected, as well as more general information relating to the living standards of the families.

The book is divided into eight chapters. Chapters One and Two set the scene: Chapter One describes the numbers and trends in lone parenthood in this and other countries; and Chapter Two looks at the development of income support policy in the UK towards lone parents up to the early 1980s. Chapters Three to Six cover the analysis of the FFS/FRS material which was carried out on both a cross-sectional and a longitudinal basis. The topics covered include the level and sources of income; expenditure; access to assets; savings and debts; the relative importance of child benefit and means-tested benefits; receipt of supplementary benefit over time; and the persistence of poverty. Chapter Seven contains the comparative analysis looking at employment, maintenance and social security policy towards lone parents in the EEC countries, the Nordic countries and in other English-speaking countries such as Australia, Canada and the United States. The final chapter summarises the main findings from the FFS/FRS analysis, and considers policy options.

A final introductory comment is required on the terminology. It was around the mid to late 1960s that the term 'one-parent family' came into usage. Deven (1987) suggests that the Finer Committee (which was appointed in 1969 and reported in 1974) was very influential in establishing this terminology. Prior to this such families had usually been designated by terms such as 'broken families', 'unmarried mothers' or 'fatherless families'. Lefaucheur (1987) describes a similar process in France where the terminology changed from 'families privées de père' (father-deprived families) and 'familles dissociées' (broken families) to 'parent isolèe' and 'familles monoparentales'. This renaming was not simply a reflection of the need to find a term for an increasingly numerous family type, it also reflected a change in attitude towards such families, which in turn was at least in part a reflection of changing views about the 'family'. The description of such families as 'broken', for example, already assumes that it is the two-parent family which is 'complete' and therefore superior. Such a view of the family was indeed particularly dominant during the 1950s. The 'family' consisting of two adults and their children was then seen as the best, the most 'functional' unit for both individuals and society; and a clear sexual division of labour within the family was strongly re-inforced by such influential theories as that of 'maternal deprivation'. Families not conforming to this norm were therefore seen as likely to be a source of problems. In the 1960s, however, this rather optimistic view of the family increasingly came under attack and the 'dysfunctional' nature of the family was stressed, for example in the work of R. D. Laing and in feminist critiques of the family. This affected the way lone-parent families were viewed—if the 'traditional' family was not necessarily benign, then other types of family were not necessarily malign. The focus of research therefore started to shift from seeing lone-parent families as a problem to seeing such families as having problems.

The adoption of the term 'one-parent family' therefore provided a neutral term which reflected a change in attitude and a shift away from moral judgements. This is not, however, to say that lone parents have now escaped from moral censure. Indeed in recent years the 'new right' have once again stressed the value and importance of the 'traditional' two-parent family, particularly as a defence for the individual against the power of the 'state' (eg Mount, 1983). Rhodes Boyson's recent description (in a speech in 1986) of single mothers as 'evil' may represent an extreme view but the ideology of the family which generates such a view is a very important influence on the social policy of the present government (David, 1986; Campbell, 1987).

The term 'one-parent family' represented a less judgemental way of describing such families, nevertheless it has some disadvantages which are perhaps becoming clearer as time goes on. The name 'one-parent family' focuses attention on the custodial parent only and draws attention away from the absent parent. But, except in the case of widows and widowers, the other parent *does* exist and is still a parent. It is not the case that when a two-parent family separates what follows is one lone-parent family and one lone individual—both remain parents. The child/ren may indeed live part of the time with one parent, part of the time with the other (eg school terms with one parent, holidays with the other); or if the child/ren live full-time with one parent the other may still be involved emotionally and financially. And even if the 'absent parent' is really totally absent, he (or less commonly she) still remains the parent. He also remains the parent even if the other parent re-marries. As Trost (1987, p. 63) has pointed out remarriage does not mean that 'the one-parent family disappears and becomes a two-parent family . . . the *family* does not change, the *household* does'. But both in research, and more crucially, in policy there has been a tendency to 'forget' the absent parent, whose invisibility is increased by this focus on the 'one-parent' family. The problem is that while 'one-parent family' has come into the language as a commonly understood term, we still lack a name for the parent who is missing. We therefore know very little about these invisible 'absent' parents, which in turn means policy is sometimes based on assumptions rather than facts—as in the introduction of the 1984 Matrimonial and Family Proceedings Act. In preference to 'one-parent family' the term used here is 'lone-parent family' or, where appropriate, lone mother and lone father. The implication is not quite so singular as 'one parent' and the usage is smoother. This study of course focuses on lone-parent families—we have no information about the absent parent—but it is important to remember the existence of that parent.

In 1988, as part of the changes to social security following the 1986 Act, supplementary benefit was renamed income support and family income supplement became family credit. These changes are discussed in Chapter Eight here. The research reported here refers to the situation prior to these changes and therefore the old terminology is retained.

# 1 Lone parenthood— demographic background

One parent bringing up a child or children alone is far from being a new phenomenon. Of the various ways to become a lone parent—death of a partner, birth of a child to an unmarried mother, separation, desertion, and divorce—only formal divorce is relatively recent. In the past the main route into lone parenthood was through the death of a partner, today it is through marital breakdown, regulated by the legal system. In policy terms, therefore, lone parents are both a 'new' and an 'old' problem. This chapter uses demographic data to explore how the 'problem' of lone parents has changed over the years. It is divided into three main sections. The first looks at numbers and trends in Britain over the past 20 to 25 years and describes the extent to which living with one parent only is increasingly becoming a common experience for children. The second section puts the current situation in historical perspective, going back to nineteenth century census data and earlier parish records, to describe the incidence of lone parenthood in the past. The final section compares the current situation in Britain with that in other industrialised countries around the world.

## NUMBERS AND TRENDS

Lone-parent families are usually defined as families consisting of a mother or father living without a spouse, and not cohabiting, together with her or his never-married dependent children (ie children aged under 16, or under 19 and in full-time education). Cohabiting couples and families where one

6

partner is temporarily absent are not included as lone-parent families. Lone-parent families may form a single household on their own or may be living as part of a larger household (for example an unmarried mother with her child living in her parents' household).

The definition is relatively straightforward but actually identifying such families is rather more difficult. As described above, lone parenthood is a status that people come into in a variety of different ways. They also leave in a variety of ways—through marriage, re-marriage, cohabitation, placing children for adoption, death (of the parent or child), and the child leaving home. Some of these changes in status are fairly unambiguous but others, such as marital separation or the beginning and end of cohabitation, may not be. All these complications make it difficult to accurately identify and count the number of lone-parent families.

The estimates that are available are usually based on a combination of census data, data from social surveys such as the General Household Survey and administrative statistics. Each have some drawbacks. Administrative statistics (on benefit receipt, illegitimate births, divorce) obviously do not record all lone-parent families and among those counted not all will be lone parents—for example many 'illegitimate' births are to cohabiting couples.[1] The accuracy of survey data is affected by both non-response and by small sample sizes. The census data provides the most accurate count of the population but it is not always possible to accurately identify lone parents from the census because of the way household relationships are recorded which means that both undercounts and overcounts are possible. The undercount happens because some single mothers are 'hidden' in larger households, where the relationship between the mother and the child is not recorded (instead the relationship of each separately to the 'head' of the household is recorded). The overcount happens because some cohabiting couples may be recorded as unrelated adults, with one or perhaps both being recorded as lone parents. Leete (1978) and Haskey (1986a) provide detailed discussions of the various data sources and their advantages and disadvantages for estimating the number of lone-parent families.

By using all these various sources in combination it is, however, possible to make estimates of the total number of lone-parent families and to look at trends in recent years. Table 1.1 shows the estimated total of lone-parent families in Britain for various years between 1961 and 1984. Over that period the number of lone-parent families approximately doubled—from 474,000 in 1961 to 940,000 in 1984. Taking five year periods (ie 1961 to 1966; 1966 to 1971; 1971 to 1976; 1979 to 1984) then the highest rate of increase was between 1971 and 1976, reflecting the immediate impact of the 1969 Divorce Reform Act, which came into operation in 1971. The most recent figures suggest there may have been

7

some slowing down in the rate of increase—between 1979 and 1981 the number of lone-parent families rose by 7.1 per cent but by only 1.1 per cent between 1982 and 1984. However some of this apparent overall decline is accounted for by the fall in the number of lone fathers, in fact the number of lone mothers increased by 3.3 per cent between 1982 and 1984. At the current rate of increase it is estimated that there will be about 1.5 million lone parents by 2005/6 (DHSS 1985a). Lone parents are estimated to make up about 13 per cent (or almost one in seven) of all families with dependent children, up from about 8 per cent in 1971.

Table 1.1

Number of lone-parent families by sex, Great Britain, 1961–1984

| Year | Lone mothers | Lone fathers | Total | Increase 1961 = 100 |
|------|--------------|--------------|---------|---------------------|
| 1961 | na | na | 474,000 | 100 |
| 1966 | na | na | 499,000 | 105 |
| 1971 | 500,000 | 70,000 | 570,000 | 120 |
| 1976 | 660,000 | 88,000 | 750,000 | 158 |
| 1979 | 748,000 | 92,000 | 840,000 | 177 |
| 1980 | 766,000 | 104,000 | 870,000 | 184 |
| 1981 | 801,000 | 99,000 | 900,000 | 190 |
| 1982 | 828,000 | 102,000 | 930,000 | 196 |
| 1984 | 855,000 | 85,000 | 940,000 | 198 |

*Sources:*  1961 and 1966, NCOPF (1982).
1971 and 1976, Leete (1978).
1979–1982, Hansard, 3rd April 1985, written answers, col.636.
1984, Haskey (1986a).

All based on Census, GHS and/or FES data.

Between 1971 and 1984 the total number of lone-parent families increased by about 65 per cent. However, as is clear from Table 1.2, the rate of increase between 1971 and 1984 was not the same for the various different types of lone parents. The numbers of widowed and separated women remained about the same. The number of single (that is, unmarried) mothers more than doubled. The number of lone fathers increased only slightly, with the majority of this increase probably accounted for by marital breakdown. Marital breakdown certainly accounted for the largest increase, which was in the number of divorced lone mothers. By 1984 there were more than three times as many of these families as there had been in 1971.

These differential rates of increase have had the effect of changing the composition of the lone-parent family population. Women continue to make up the vast majority—about nine in ten—of all lone parents. However, the proportion who are widows fell from 21 per cent in 1971 to 12 per cent in 1984, while the proportion who are divorced women rose from 21 per cent to 40 per cent.

Table 1.2

The number and marital status of lone parents, Great Britain, 1971 and 1984

| | 1971 | | 1984 | | Percentage rise |
| Marital status | Number | Percent | Number[1] | Percent | 1971 to 1984 |
|---|---|---|---|---|---|
| Single women | 90,000 | 16 | 200,000 | 21 | +122 |
| Widowed women | 120,000 | 21 | 110,000 | 12 | − 8 |
| Divorced women | 120,000 | 21 | 380,000 | 40 | +217 |
| Separated women | 170,000 | 30 | 170,000 | 18 | 0 |
| Lone fathers | 70,000 | 12 | 80,000 | 9 | + 14 |
| Total | 570,000 | 100 | 940,000 | 100 | + 65 |

1.    Estimated from total and proportions

*Sources:*   1971, Leete (1978)
        1984, Haskey (1986a)

## Children in lone-parent families

Lone-parent families tend to be smaller than two-parent families with an average of 1.6 children compared with 1.8. Therefore, although 13 per cent of all families are headed by a lone parent, only 11 per cent of all children live in these families. These figures, however, refer to the situation at one point in time. What they do not show is the proportion of families who have ever been headed by a lone parent or the proportion of children who have spent some part of their childhood living with one parent only. This way of considering the incidence of lone parenthood gives a much clearer picture of the ways in which the type of families children live in can and do change throughout their childhood.

Following a group of children through their lives from birth gives a good indication of the dynamics of family life. Information on British children is available from three such studies. The first, the 1946 birth cohort, was originally planned as a study of maternity services and not as a longitudinal study. The children were however subsequently followed up at age four (Douglas and Blomfield, 1958), age 11 (Douglas, 1964) and 16 (Douglas, Ross and Simpson, 1968) with the educational experiences of the children being the main focus of these studies. Children born 'illegitimate' were excluded from the study and in fact it is only for the four year-old children that any detailed information was published on family status. At that time (1950) 3.8 per cent of the children were living in a lone-parent family—1.4 per cent were living with a widowed mother and 2.4 per cent with a divorced or separated parent, usually the mother (Douglas and Blomfield, 1958, p. 114). The second birth cohort study started in 1958 when all the children born in a week in March of that year (about 15,000) were selected for the National Child Development Study (NCDS). These children were followed up at the age of seven (in 1965) when 3.1 per cent were living in a lone-parent family, again at the age of 11 (in 1969) when this had risen to 5.5 per cent and finally at the age of 16 (in 1974) when the figure was 8.4 per cent. In addition to these families headed by a lone parent, some of the children also lived in reconstituted or step-families: 2.7 per cent at age seven, 4.1 per cent at age 11 and 5.0 per cent at age 16. Thus the proportion living with both natural parents fell at each stage of the study from 92 per cent to 89 per cent to 84 per cent (Ferri, 1976; Fogelman, 1983).

Looking back from the age of 16, it is possible to chart to what extent these were the same families and how many children had ever lived in a lone-parent family. In the NCDS at age 16, 8.4 per cent of the children were living with only one parent but 12.2 per cent of the children had been with only one parent at some time in their childhood. This parent was much more likely to be a lone mother than a lone father, and lone fathers were much less likely to have had the sole care of very young children.

The Child Health and Education Study (CHES) is a more recent survey which followed up, in 1975, the children from the 1970 British Births Survey. Of these children, 4.8 per cent were born to an 'unsupported' mother, that is, a woman not currently married or cohabiting, but not necessarily an unmarried woman. At the age of five, 5.8 per cent were living in a lone-parent family, usually with their mother. This 5.8 per cent includes both those who had been living in such families since birth (1.7 per cent) and those who were subsequently doing so (4.1 per cent). A further 2.8 per cent of the children were living in re-constituted or step-families. The CHES results (re-produced in Table 1.3) clearly illustrate the extent to which children move between different family circumstances even before they reach school age: of these five year old children, one in ten had not lived with both natural parents since birth, but had spent at least some time in a lone-parent family (Burnell and Wadsworth, 1981).

Table 1.3

## Changing families from birth to age five: Child Health and Education Study 1970–1975

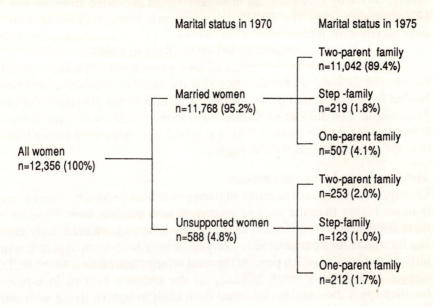

Marital status in 1970       Marital status in 1975

Two-parent family
n=11,042 (89.4%)

Married women
n=11,768 (95.2%)

Step -family
n=219 (1.8%)

One-parent family
n=507 (4.1%)

All women
n=12,356 (100%)

Two-parent family
n=253 (2.0%)

Unsupported women
n=588 (4.8%)

Step-family
n=123 (1.0%)

One-parent family
n=212 (1.7%)

*Source:* Burnell and Wandsworth (1981), p.17.

Some preliminary results are also available from the 1980 follow-up of these children when they were aged 10 (CHES 1982). By that time, 15.6 per cent were not living with both natural parents, including 7.1 per cent living with their mother only and 0.7 per cent with their father. Clearly the likelihood of living in a lone-parent or a re-constituted family will increase with the age of the child, simply because there will be more time available for older children to have experienced these changes. But putting together the NCDS and the CHES results suggests that, as well as the number of lone-parent families increasing, children are becoming more likely to experience family disruption at younger ages. In 1970, 8.6 per cent of the five year olds were not living with both natural parents compared with 5.9 per cent of the six year olds in 1965. In 1980, 15.6 per cent of the 10 year olds were not living with both natural parents compared with 9.6 per cent of the 11 year olds in 1969.

Figures from the General Household Survey also show the extent to which children spend at least part of their childhood in lone-parent families. In 1982 80 per cent of children aged under 18 were living with both natural parents, 10 per cent with a lone mother and 7 per cent in a re-constituted family (OPCS, 1984). This suggests that almost a fifth of children aged under 18 have spent at least some part of their childhood in a lone-parent family. Looking forward from birth rather than backward from the age of 18, estimates from the OPCS Longitudinal Study suggest that only three-quarters of children born in the 1970s will live with both natural parents throughout all their childhood up to age 16 (Brown, 1986).

Thus measuring the incidence of lone parenthood to include not only the current lone-parent families but also the families who have ever been headed by a lone parent gives a different picture of the prevalence of lone parenthood. The number of children (and parents) with some experience of living in (or as) a lone-parent family is obviously likely to be rather higher than the cross-sectional figures suggest.

### The duration of lone-parenthood

Clearly, if the number of families who have ever been headed by a lone parent is much higher than the number of current lone parents, then for some of these families the experience of lone parenthood must have been fairly short. But for others lone parenthood is likely to be very long-term. Again it is the birth cohort studies which provide the most information on this. In the NCDS sample only a fairly small minority of the children ever in lone-parent families spent their entire childhood from birth to age 16 living with only their mothers (2.4 per cent). However, 27.9 per cent of the children were living with a lone mother and a further 3.2 per cent with a lone father at two or more of the four interviews. Bearing in mind that we have no information about what happened between the interviews, this implies that about 31 per cent of the children spent at least four to five years in a lone-parent family. Ferri's (1976) study of the lone-parent families when these children were aged 11 found that three-quarters of the children who had been living with their mothers alone at age seven were still with their mothers alone at age 11. In the CHES sample of the children who were in lone-parent families at age five, 29 per cent had been in such families since birth; or to put it the other way round, of the children born to unsupported mothers in 1970, 36 per cent were still living with their mothers alone five years later. The social security statistics also indicate that for some lone parents being a lone parent is likely to be a relatively long-term experience. In 1983, there were 108,000 lone mothers on supplementary benefit who had been in receipt of benefit for at least five years (DHSS, 1986).

Looking at re-marriage rates also gives some indication of the duration of lone parenthood. Among divorced women aged under 35 at the time of divorce about half re-marry within three years of divorce (OPCS 1985a), but re-marriage rates have been declining and second marriages are more likely than first marriages to end in divorce (Haskey, 1983a, 1983b; Leete and Anthony, 1979). About half of widows aged under 40 re-marry within four years of widowhood (Haskey, 1982); and of teenage mothers themselves born in the mid 1950s almost half (46 per cent) who had 'illegitimate' child as a teenager went on to have a legitimate birth before the age of 25 (Werner, 1984). These figures tentatively suggest that the median duration of lone parenthood could be in the region of three to five years. Similar results were found in an analysis of the DE Women and Employment Survey data (Ermisch, Jenkins and Wright, 1987).

THE HISTORICAL CONTEXT

Given the increase in the number of lone-parent families in recent years it is not surprising that lone parenthood is often thought of as something 'new'. However, looking over the longer term gives a rather different view. Indeed going back to before the twentieth century then it might be expected that there would have been more lone-parent families than there are today. Higher rates of mortality (for all age groups) would have meant a much higher risk of widowhood for both women and men—while still in the child-rearing years. Illegitimacy rates did not start falling until the mid-nineteenth century; and, although divorce was not readily available this does not mean that marital breakdown did not happen. Arguably the easier availability of divorce in the twentieth century has simply meant that marital breakdown is more visible, not necessarily that it is more likely.

It is of course difficult to get accurate figures to compare past and present. But the information that is available suggests that lone parenthood was at least as common, if not more so, in the past as it is today. Anderson (1983) has calculated that the proportion of marriages broken at various marriage durations by death in the nineteenth century is close to the proportion now broken by death and divorce together. Census statistics seem to indicate a similar picture. From the Census Historical Tables (OPCS, 1982) it is possible to make an estimate of the number of women who were potentially lone mothers during the nineteenth century. These tables give, from 1861 onwards, data on age and marital status. No details about children are available but confining the analysis to women aged 25 to 49 includes the age group most likely to have children. As Table 1.4 shows there is a steady decline over the years in the proportion of widowed women (although the effect of the 1914-18 war is apparent in the figure for 1921). In 1861 8.1 per cent of women aged between 25 and 49 were widows, in 1901 the figure was 7.3 per cent, in 1951 it was 3.2 per cent and in 1981 1.5 per cent. In 1921 (when divorce was first recorded separately in the census) 0.1 per cent of women in this age group were divorced, this rose to 1.4 per cent in 1951 and to 7.3 per cent in 1981. Thus the proportion of women potentially lone mothers through either widowhood or marital breakdown was very similar in 1861 (8.1 per cent) and 1981 (8.9 per cent).

Table 1.4

Widowed and divorced women as a proportion of all widowed, divorced and married women aged 25–49, Great Britain 1861–1981

| Census year | All widowed divorced and married women n(000s) | Widowed women | | Divorced women | | Widowed plus divorced women | |
|---|---|---|---|---|---|---|---|
| | | n(000)s | % | n(000s) | % | n(000s) | % |
| 1861 | 2323.8 | 203.8 | 8.1 | | | 203.8 | 8.1 |
| 1871 | 2608.8 | 236.4 | 8.3 | | | 236.4 | 8.3 |
| 1881 | 2952.1 | 262.2 | 8.2 | | | 262.2 | 8.2 |
| 1891 | 3582.6 | 276.3 | 7.7 | | | 276.3 | 7.7 |
| 1901 | 3921.3 | 286.4 | 7.3 | | | 286.4 | 7.3 |
| 1911 | 4866.2 | 274.6 | 5.6 | | | 274.6 | 5.6 |
| 1921 | 5418.7 | 388.8 | 7.2 | 5.9 | 0.1 | 394.7 | 7.3 |
| 1931 | 5764.3 | 322.3 | 5.9 | 14.4 | 0.3 | 336.7 | 6.2 |
| 1951 | 6932.5 | 222.9 | 3.2 | 95.4 | 1.4 | 318.3 | 4.6 |
| 1961 | 6832.7 | 158.4 | 2.3 | 98.3 | 1.4 | 256.7 | 3.8 |
| 1971 | 6768.1 | 128.1 | 1.9 | 163.4 | 2.4 | 291.5 | 4.3 |
| 1981 | 7048.2 | 104.9 | 1.5 | 513.6 | 7.3 | 618.5 | 8.9 |

*Source:* OPCS (1982a) Census Historical Tables, 1801–1981.

For the period before the nineteenth century census some estimates of the proportion of families headed by a lone parent can be made from parish listings. These do not, of course, give a nationally representative sample and the amount of information in them varies from parish to parish. However they do usually include information on the number (although not the age) of children. Snell and Millar (1987) used these records to make estimates of the proportion of single-family households headed by a lone parent between 1551 and 1851. In total the records from 70 communities were used, and these showed a wide variation in the proportion of single-family households headed by a lone parent (ranging from none to as high as 60 per cent). The overall proportion for all the communities over the whole period was 19 per cent. This is in fact higher than the current proportion of families with children headed by a lone parent (13 per cent). Of all the lone parents in the listings 32 per cent were men (compared with only 9 per cent today). This undoubtedly reflects the fact that many of these lone-parent families in the

14

past would have come about because of the death of one partner, and therefore both more widows and more widowers would be heading lone-parent families. The widowed father bringing up his children alone because the mother has died in childbirth is quite a familiar figure in Victorian novels (as, of course, is the 'fallen' unmarried mother).

In a similar analysis, but looking only at widows, Smith (1984) using parish records for the period 1671 to 1820 calculated that 12.4 per cent of all women aged 16 and above were widows. This is in fact lower than the contemporary figure (14.4 per cent according to the 1981 census) but today widows are almost always older women (78 per cent aged over 65). In the 'pre-industrial' period Smith calculates that about 20 per cent of the widows were aged between 16 and 44 and 45 per cent were aged between 45 and 64. Thus many more of those widows would have had children and Smith suggests that widows with children would have been less likely to re-marry than those without children.

Thus all the evidence suggests that lone parenthood is not a new phenomenon. Anderson (1983, p. 4) points out:

> The problem of marital break up is not, then, new; but we view it against a historical background when it was temporarily lower and we lack so far the institutions and attitudes which were available in the past to handle what was, clearly, statistically, an equally or even more serious problem.

TRENDS IN OTHER COUNTRIES

Lone parenthood is not therefore new, and furthermore nor is the current situation unique to this country. This is obvious from a comparison of the available statistics, even though the possible comparisons are not always exact. Information is not always available and even when it is there are often different definitions of both the status of a lone parent (should cohabiting couples be included, or married but temporarily separated couples —prisoners' wives, for example, or the wives of men who are employed elsewhere for long periods?) and of a child (is a child aged under 16, under 18, under 20 or is a child any unmarried person living with his or her parents?). In fact, for the countries shown in Table 1.5, it is the latter part of the definition which is the source of most variation. Dependent children are most commonly defined as aged under either 15, 16, or 17 but some countries include those aged up to 24 or 25 and some count all never-married children regardless of age. (Footnote 2 gives both the sources for Table 1.5 and details of how children are defined—insofar as this is available.)

The figures in Table 1.5 are not, therefore, directly comparable but they are the most recent available and give a good indication of the proportion of

Table 1.5
## Proportion of families with children headed by a lone parent: various countries

| Country | Year | Lone-parent families as a % of all familes with children | Approximate % of lone-parent families headed by a woman |
|---|---|---|---|
| **EEC countries** | | | |
| Belgium | 1977 | 9.4 | 78 |
| Denmark | 1984 | 19.8 | na |
| FR Germany | 1982 | 11.4 | 84 |
| France | 1982 | 9.4 | na |
| Greece | na | na | na |
| Ireland | 1981 | 7.1 | 80 |
| Italy | 1981 | 3.5 | 74 |
| Luxembourg | 1970 | 13.3 | 81 |
| Netherlands | 1983 | 10.0 | 90 |
| UK | 1984 | 13.0 | 91 |
| **Nordic countries** | | | |
| Finland | 1984 | 13.0 | na |
| Iceland | 1984 | 16.2 | na |
| Norway | 1984 | 17.8 | na |
| Sweden | 1983 | 19.0 | na |
| **Eastern Europe** | | | |
| Czechoslovakia | 1980[1] | 11.4 | 89 |
| Hungary | 1984 | 19.5 | 82 |
| Poland | 1984 | 12.6 | 91 |
| Yugoslavia | 1971 | 14.5 | 80 |
| **Outside Europe** | | | |
| Australia | 1985 | 14.3 | 88 |
| Canada | 1981 | 16.6 | 83 |
| United States | 1984 | 25.7 | 89 |

1. Czech Socialist Republic. Equivalent figure for Slovak Socialist Republic is 8.6 per cent.

*Sources:* See footnote 2.

families with children headed by a lone parent in various countries around the world. As is immediately clear the situation in Britain, where 13 per cent of all families with children are headed by a lone parent, usually a lone mother, is far from being unique. Within the EEC countries the proportion of lone-parent families ranges from 3.5 per cent in Italy up to 19.8 per cent in Denmark. Outside of the EEC the incidence of lone parenthood appears to be in general even higher. In the Nordic countries lone parents form a significant minority of all families with children, the same is true in Eastern Europe and in non-European, English-speaking countries such as Canada, the United States and Australia. In the United States as many as a quarter of all families with children (aged under 18) are headed by a lone parent. And, as in Britain, this cross-sectional figure will tend to under-estimate the total incidence of lone parenthood. American research (Bumpass, 1984) suggests that as many as half of the most recent cohort of children will spend sometime in a lone-parent family before they reach the end of their childhood; and that half of all children experiencing the divorce of their parents will spend five years living in a lone-parent family before the re-marriage of their parent. In the United States black families are much more likely to be headed by a lone mother than white families (57 per cent and 18 per cent respectively in 1985) and the duration of lone parenthood is also much longer for the black families (Bane and Ellwood, 1984; Duncan and Rodgers, 1987). The duration of lone parenthood is also likely to vary, perhaps quite substantially, from country to country. For example, in Ireland where civil divorce is not available, those who become lone parents through marital breakdown are likely to stay as lone parents because they cannot obtain a divorce and so cannot re-marry. The situation is similar in Italy.

Lone-parent families are therefore a significant family type throughout the industrialised world and almost always it is women who make up the vast majority of lone-parent families. In most countries the number of such families has increased fairly dramatically in recent years. It is difficult to get figures to look at trends over time but some indication of the way the number of such families has increased is given by looking at the changes in the divorce rates and in the rates of births to unmarried mothers. Neither of these are necessarily a good guide to the number of lone-parent families —not all divorces involve dependent children, some divorces are followed quickly by re-marriage or cohabitation (which may also precede formal divorce) and not all 'illegitimate' births will lead to the formation of a lone-parent family. However, looking at trends in these figures over time gives some indication of the changes in the size of the potential lone-parent family population. As Table 1.6 shows, there are substantial variations in divorce and 'illegitimacy' rates between the EEC countries. The 1982 figures for the number of 'illegitimate' births show France, the UK and especially Denmark to have very high rates relative to the other countries, and Belgium and Italy to have the lowest rates. However, all countries have seen a substantial rise in births to unmarried mothers since 1970. Every country has had an increase of at least about half, with the increases for the Netherlands, Ireland and Denmark being particularly high. Divorce rates in 1982 range from zero and less than 1.0 per 1,000 marriages in Ireland and Italy to 12 per 1,000 marriages in the UK and Denmark. With the exception of Ireland and Italy, where legal divorce is non-existent or very restricted, all other countries have seen at least a doubling of the divorce rate since 1960, with the UK, Belgium and the Netherlands having had particularly high increases. Thus while there are variations in the incidence of divorce and 'illegitimacy' across Europe, the common trend is for these both to have been on the increase throughout the Community.

Table 1.6

Divorce and illegitiamcy rates: Europe 1960, 1970, and 1982

| Country | Divorce rate per 1000 existing marriages | | Illegitimate births per 1000 live births | | |
| --- | --- | --- | --- | --- | --- |
| | 1960 | 1982 | 1960 | 1970 | 1982 |
| Belgium | 2.0 | 6.4 | 21 | 28 | 41 (1980) |
| Denmark | 5.9 | 12.4 | 78 | 110 | 332 |
| FR Germany | 3.6 | 7.8 | 63 | 55 | 85 |
| France | 2.9 | 7.2 | 61 | 68 | 142 |
| Greece | – | – | – | – | – |
| Ireland | – | – | 16 | 27 | 50 |
| Italy | – | 0.9 | 24 | 22 | 46 |
| Luxembourg | 2.0 | 4.9 | 32 | 40 | 60 |
| Netherlands | 2.2 | 9.0 | 14 | 21 | 59 |
| UK | 2.0 | 12.1 | 52 | 80 | 115 |

*Source:* Eurostat (1984).

These increases in divorce and 'illegitimacy' are likely to have changed the marital status structure of the lone-parent family population to some extent. In the UK for example, in 1971 16 per cent of lone parents were unmarried women, 21 per cent were widows and 51 per cent were divorced or separated women but by 1984 the proportions had changed to 21 per cent, 12 per cent and 58 per cent respectively. Thus the proportion of widows had fallen substantially, although the actual numbers of widows with children remained more or less unchanged. Table 1.7 shows the number, proportion and marital status of lone parents in six countries, comparing the early to mid 1970s with the early to mid 1980s. The countries shown (West Germany, France, the Netherlands, the UK, Australia and the United States) were mainly chosen because the detailed information required was available in each case. They do however also illustrate very clearly the way in which marital breakdown has—over the past 15 or so years—replaced widowhood as the main route into lone parenthood. This is the case both in countries

Table 1.7

Trends over time in the number and type of lone-parent families: various countries

| Country | Year | Number (000s) | % of all families with children | Family type (%) Widowed | Divorced | Separated | Single |
|---|---|---|---|---|---|---|---|
| Fr Germany | 1970 | 750 | 8.7 | 39 | 33 | 16 | 13 |
|  | 1982 | 930 | 11.4 | 25 | 43 | 18 | 13 |
| France | 1968 | 720 | 8.7 | 54 | 17 | 21 | 8 |
|  | 1982 | 890 | 9.8 | 31 | 39 | 15 |  |
| Netherlands | 1971 | 220 | 10.0 | 63 | 16 | 12 | 6 |
|  | 1983 | 280 | 10.0 | 23 | 59 | 5 | 13 |
| UK[1] | 1971 | 570 | 8.0 | 24 | 24 | 34 | 18 |
|  | 1984 | 940 | 13.0 | 13 | 44 | 19 | 24 |
| Australia | 1975 | 170 | 8.5 | 27 | 21 | 41 | 11 |
|  | 1982 | 300 | 14.1 | 14 | 37 | 30 | 19 |
| US White | 1970 | 2600 | 10.1 | 24 | ——73—— | | 3 |
|  | 1984 | 5500 | 20.0 | 9 | ——76—— | | 15 |
| US Black | 1970 | 1150 | 35.7 | 16 | ——69—— | | 15 |
|  | 1984 | 2800 | 59.2 | 6 | ——44—— | | 49 |

1. Marital status of lone mothers.

*Source:* See footnote 2

where the total number of lone-parent families has increased substantially (eg Australia and the United States) and countries where there has been very little increase in the total number (eg the Netherlands and France). In 1971 in the Netherlands 63 per cent of the approximately 220,000 lone parents were widowed; 15 per cent were divorced, 12 per cent were separated and 6 per cent were single. By 1983 there were an estimated 280,000 lone parents of whom 23 per cent were widowed, 59 per cent were divorced, 5 per cent were separated and 13 per cent were single. A similar picture is found for the other countries shown. In all cases (with the one exception of black families in the US) divorced and separated lone mothers form the majority of the lone-parent family population. The proportion of lone-parent families headed by an unmarried mother has also increased in all the countries shown. However, an unknown proportion of these unmarried mothers will have become lone mothers on the ending of a consensual union. Cass and O'Loughlin (1984) estimate that about a quarter of the unmarried Australian lone mothers are in fact separated de facto wives.[3] In Britain couples are now more likely than in the past to live together, although this cohabitation usually precedes rather than replaces marriage (Eldridge and Kiernan, 1985), and many will marry when children are born. However evidence from the OPCS Longitudinal Study (Brown, 1986) suggests that de facto two-parent families may be more likely to separate than married two-parent families. According to the 1981 census about 60 per cent of jointly registered illegitimate children aged under ten were living with both natural parents compared with 90 per cent of legitimate children.

Thus the UK is far from being unique as regards the incidence of lone parenthood, the way in which this has increased over recent years, and the shift from widowhood to marital breakdown as the main cause of lone parenthood.

## SUMMARY

About one in seven of all British families are headed by a lone parent, usually a lone mother. About a quarter of all British children will spend at least some period living with one parent only before they reach the age of 16. Over the past twenty to twenty-five years the number of lone-parent families in Britain has about doubled. A similar situation is apparent in most other industrialised countries—lone-parent families form a significant, and increasing, proportion of families in countries as socially, economically and demographically diverse as, for example, Sweden and Ireland. Across all countries the vast majority of lone parents are women.

This demographic change is one of the most significant challenges currently facing social policy. This is not so much because of the actual numbers of such families. Indeed if we take a longer historical look then the evidence suggests that lone-parent families were probably more numerous in the past than today; the first half of the twentieth century probably represents the period when the prevalence of such families was at its lowest. More important than the numbers of such families is the fact that most lone-parent families now come into being as a result of marital breakdown. In this respect the recent increase in the number of lone-parent families represents a 'new' problem for social policy and one which raises very fundamental questions about the role of the state in relation to the 'family'.

## Notes

1. Of all 'illegitimate' births 63 per cent are jointly registered by two parents. About three-quarters of these parents have the same address (Brown 1986).

2.  Sources for Tables 1.5 and 1.7 and definition of child (given in brackets after each country):

Belgium (unmarried, age not clear), Luxembourg (unmarried, age not clear): EEC (1982).

FR Germany (under 18), France (under 25), Italy ('minor'children), Netherlands ('non-adult'), Czechoslavakia (under 15), Hungary (under 15), Poland (under 24), Yugoslavia (not clear): various articles in Deven and Cliquet (eds.) (1986).

Ireland (under 15): Millar (1986).

Denmark (under 17), Finland (under 15), Ireland (under 15), Norway (under 20), Sweden (under 17): Statistical Reports of the Nordic Countries (1987).

UK (under 16 or under 19 for students): Haskey (1986a).

Canada (unmarried, regardless of age): Abowitz (1986).

United States (under 18): Nichols-Casebolt (1986), Australia (under 16 or under 24 for students): Robinson and Griffiths (1986).

3.  It is also likely to be the case that the relatively high proportions of unmarried mothers in the Nordic countries (for example estimated to be 24 per cent of all lone parents in Denmark in 1980, almost 50 per cent in Sweden in the late 1970s) is accounted for, at least in part by the fact that cohabitation is fairly common in these countries. Marriage rates fell sharply in Sweden in the late 1960s and marriage has, to some extent, been replaced by cohabitation. In the 1970s about 30 per cent of Swedish women aged 20-24 were living in consensual unions (compared with 5 per cent in the UK) and approximately 34 per cent of births in Sweden are 'illegitimate' (Ermisch, 1983).

21

# 2 The development of income support policy

Having looked at the trends in the number of lone-parent families and described how marital breakdown has become the main route into lone parenthood, this chapter describes the development of income support policy for lone parents up to the early 1980s. The FFS/FRS data which forms the main basis for this study refers to the period prior to 1980. We therefore consider here the development of policy up to 1980, and describe the situation in the 1980s in Chapter Eight.

## POLICY TOWARDS LONE PARENTS

Women (and children) have always made up a large proportion, probably the majority, of those in receipt of state benefits. Under both the Old and New Poor Laws lone mothers—mostly widows, but also unmarried mothers and 'deserted' wives—formed a very significant category of claimants (Thane, 1978; Snell and Millar, 1987). The unemployed (or the 'able-bodied poor') of course commanded the most attention from policy-makers, nevertheless it would still be a substantial undertaking to give a full historical account of how income support policy for lone parents has developed, a task that is not the focus of this study. Instead we briefly trace the development of some of the key elements of current income support policy for lone parents, and consider the factors that have been and remain barriers to the development of policy.

There are three features in particular that stand out in current policy. The first is the different treatment accorded to widows as compared with other groups of lone parents. Only widows are covered under the national insurance scheme. All other groups of lone parents—widowers, unmarried mothers, divorced and separated parents—must, if they require state income support, rely on the 'safety net' of supplementary benefit. Secondly, unlike other claimants under pension age lone parents with the care of dependent children are not required to register for employment when they claim supplementary benefit. There is therefore no compulsion, or indeed expectation, that lone parents should seek paid work. Thirdly, although lone parents may not be expected to support themselves through employment, there is an expectation that someone else should provide support. This expectation can be seen in both the 'liable relative' and the 'cohabitation' rules attached to supplementary benefit. The 'liable relative' rules mean that someone *outside* the household is expected to provide support for lone parents—a circumstance that applies to no other group of claimants. Under the cohabitation rule a couple 'living together as man and wife' are treated as if they were a married couple, that is their resources are 'aggregated' and they are assessed as one and not two units. Thus a man living with a lone mother is expected to provide financial support for both her and her children. These rules mean that implicitly the main alternative to state income support for lone mothers is not seen as employment but as financial dependence on a man.

These three features of income support for lone parents—the different treatment for widows, the absence of any requirement to seek employment and an assumption of financial dependency—are all very closely related such that it is difficult to disentangle their development one from another. The different—and more favourable—treatment for widows has been a longstanding feature of income support policy for lone parents, going back to the time of the Poor Law. The local administration and control of the Poor Law meant that there was very considerable variation across the country in the provisions made; but even with such local variation in policy there was a clear hierarchy in the way lone mothers were treated. At the bottom, the least 'deserving' was the unmarried mother, who was very rarely given any outdoor relief and also treated very punitively within the workhouse. The separated woman (or deserted wife) came next in the hierarchy—here the main concern was over potential 'collusion' between the husband and wife; and therefore claims from deserted women were treated with suspicion. In 1871 a circular from the Local Government Board recommended that no deserted wives be given outdoor relief for the first twelve months of the desertion, in order to discourage such collusion (Finer and McGregor, 1974). The most deserving of all lone mothers was the widow, and it was widows who were the most likely to be granted outdoor relief.

Why should widows have been seen as more 'deserving' of support than other lone parents? One reason was to do with the way family obligations were defined. That family members should have financial obligations towards each other has always been a feature of state income support policy and under the Poor Laws this obligation was defined quite widely (to include, for example, grand-parents and adult children towards their parents). Although it is common to think of family support obligations as somehow 'natural' and fundamental to the character of families, in legal terms the obligation to maintain in family law derives from the Poor Law rather than the other way around. As Eekelaar and Maclean (1986a, p. 2) point out 'family support obligations . . . found their first legal expression in the public law provisions relating to the poor'. Finding 'liable relatives' was originally mainly a mechanism for keeping down the costs to the state of providing income support. If someone else had financial responsibility for a claimant then that claimant could either be refused state assistance or the costs of that assistance could be recouped. This was one of the main differences between widows and other lone mothers—widows were more deserving at least in part because there was no-one else available to take financial responsibility for them.

However the idea that widows—or any other groups of women—would have or have had someone to take financial responsibility for them rests on certain assumptions about the family, and the relative roles and obligations of different family members. It was under the New Poor Law that these became more explicit and located in a particular ideological view of the family. As Thane (1978, p. 29) points out the 1834 Act was based quite clearly on certain views about the causes of poverty and also about the role of the family:

> These policy-makers of 1834 identified the unemployed male
> 'able-bodied' worker as the central problem of poverty at that time . . .
> They took for granted the universality of the stable two-parent family,
> primarily dependent upon the father's wage, and the primacy of the
> family as a source of welfare.

Thus, if the family was the primary source of support and the man's earnings the main source of support within the family, then women who lost that support would have some call upon the state to replace it. However there were limits to the obligation of the state to provide such support and the development of income support policy for lone parents is essentially the story of how these limits were defined and how this definition changed over time. The limits were initially wider for widows than for other lone parents probably because there was no alternative person to provide support, but even

24

for widows there were other limits to the support. First there were moral judgements about whether individuals were 'deserving' of support. As late as 1914 the Local Government Board circular *Relief to Widows and Children* (quoted in Finer and McGregor, 1974, p. 1215) made the following distinctions:

> The special investigators appointed by the Royal Commission on the Poor Laws divided the mothers of out-relief families into four classes:
>
> I.   Women really above the average, capable and trustworthy, able to give their children an excellent training, to plan their future well-being, and to sacrifice a present gain for a future good.
>
> II.  Women of lower morale, good in intention, but less able to carry out their intentions, to look forward or to cope with their responsibilities. Often these are the women whose health has failed, whose force of character has not given them the power to rise above it.
>
> III. The slovenly and slipshod women of weak intentions, and often of weak health, not able to make the most of their resources.
>
> IV.  The really bad mothers, people guilty of wilful neglect, sometimes drunkards or people of immoral character.

Secondly, alongside these moral judgements there was the even more fundamental question of 'whether the primary role of the unsupported working-class mother was motherhood or work' (Thane, 1978, p. 36). This was a central and largely unresolved issue which persisted throughout the period of the operation of the New Poor Law. As Thane points out, the ideology of the New Poor Law with its focus on the 'stable two-parent family, primarily dependent upon the father's wage', should have tipped the balance towards motherhood—particularly for widows. But in practice the local Poor Law Guardians appear to have been very reluctant to provide sufficient support to allow even widows to be full-time mothers. It was not until 1914 that the principle that a widow with young children should be given sufficient support to enable her not to have to seek employment was accepted in national policy. Despite this, however, there continued to be considerable local variation in the treatment of widows (and also of course other lone mothers).

In 1925 widows pensions were introduced for the first time, as a national insurance benefit intended as a replacement for the lost breadwinner's earnings. Thus, by this time (towards the end of the Poor Law) the limits to the support for widows had been greatly extended beyond what other lone parents could expect. They were now treated as a separate group, they received a benefit as a right and without having to satisfy any moral judgements as to their deservingness, and they were not obliged (in theory at least) to support themselves through employment. For other lone parents there was however little change—moral judgements were still made, there was still pressure for them to find employment and there was still the search for the 'liable relative' who could provide support instead of the state.

The Beveridge proposals, and the legislation that followed, did little to change this. Under these proposals married women were to gain their rights to social insurance through their husbands and therefore within the insurance scheme their status was that of a financial dependent. This made the claim of widows to a social insurance benefit quite clear-cut—the pension was as a replacement for the lost earnings of the man on whom the widow had been dependent when married. On the same argument, however, it also meant that separated or divorced women would have a claim for the replacement of the lost earnings of their husbands. Beveridge was willing to accept this but only up to a point. There were two basic problems—first was the question of fault; if the marriage had broken down because of the woman's actions then how could she have a claim against something she herself had caused? The second problem was the question of 'alternative remedies'—she already would have a claim against her husband for maintenance and therefore a national insurance benefit would in effect duplicate this. Beveridge went through various different proposals in the drafts of his report (Harris, 1977), but in the final report he recommended that divorced/separated women should be treated in much the same way as widows with a 'temporary separation benefit' to be paid for 13 weeks (as was the recommendation for the widows benefit) to be followed by entitlement to a 'training allowance' or 'guardians benefit'. Unmarried mothers were to receive no special treatment, and would therefore have access only to assistance benefit.

As to whether lone mothers should or should not take paid employment Beveridge was quite clear that widows without dependent children should be expected to work and support themselves, but for those with children the benefit should be sufficient:

> to meet subsistence needs, even if the widow does not undertake any gainful occupation while she is looking after the children. Some widows in such a position may nevertheless be able to work and earn and may desire to do so. The right principle appears to be to treat such earnings . . . by making a reduction of the benefit which allows the widow to retain a proportion, but not the whole, of her earnings in addition to full benefit. (p. 65)

Even if the Beveridge proposals had been enacted it would still not have been the case that all lone parents would have been treated alike. The division inherent in the Beveridge proposals was between, on the one hand, widows and separated and divorced women who could prove they were not at fault and, on the other hand, all the rest—unmarried mothers, widowers, separated and divorced women unable to prove they were not at fault. The former category would have received an insurance benefit sufficient so that they would not have to take paid employment, the latter would have been dependent on assistance. The state would have still attempted to recoup the costs of supporting separated women from their husbands. However, these Beveridge proposals were not enacted and effectively the provisions for lone parents remained much the same after the 1946 and 1948 legislation as before: widows retained their separate status, others were dependent on national assistance. Ambiguity remained as to whether or not lone mothers should or should not be expected to be in employment. As Lewis and Piachaud (1987, p. 36) note

> the pendulum swung in favour of treating women with dependent children and no husbands as mothers rather than workers at different times for different groups of women . . . After World War II the attention given to maternal bonding theory contributed to all women with children, including deserted wives and unmarried mothers, being treated as mothers first and workers second.

This is perhaps too simple a picture, certainly Marsden's (1973) research, carried out in the mid 1960s (just before national assistance was replaced by supplementary benefit), found that unmarried mothers were very likely to be put under pressure to find jobs while this was not the case for other groups of lone mothers. Marsden concluded that there was a degree of 'discrimination' against the unmarried mother. Nevertheless it was the case that all lone mothers were entitled to receive benefit and even unmarried mothers could not be refused benefit if they would not take a job.

The Finer report, which appeared in 1974, was the next major attempt to reform benefit provisions for lone parents. By that time of course the situation was rather different from what it had been in the 1940s—there were many more lone-parent families; the 1969 Divorce Reform Act allowed divorce on the sole grounds of 'irretrievable breakdown' so the idea of matrimonial fault was less important; and employment among mothers of dependent children was on the increase. The Finer Committee considered not just social security provisions for lone parents but also the administration of family law and maintenance provisions under family law. As regards social security the central recommendation was for the 'guaranteed maintenance allowance'. The key features of this benefit were first, all lone parents would be eligible, second, the benefit would be non-contributory and divided into two parts. The child component would be non-means-tested

27

while the adult component would be reduced for earnings, tapering out at about the level of average male earnings. Thirdly, the benefit would replace maintenance payments for divorced and separated lone mothers and the state would both assess and collect such payments from the absent partner. Thus the Finer Committee was proposing that all lone parents be treated alike regardless of both sex and marital status; that lone parents should be given a 'real choice' as to whether to take employment or not; and that private maintenance should in effect become the state's responsibility.

The Finer proposals were not implemented. Much of the criticism centred on the fact that the proposed GMA was to be means-tested, with the attendant problems of take-up and the poverty trap (for example articles by Field, Ward and Townsend in the edition of *Poverty* devoted to Finer in 1975). The government response appears to have been very low key with more attention given to the proposal for a family court than to the social security proposals. Barbara Castle's diary for the period (Castle, 1980) suggests that the Finer proposals got rather lost because the main preoccupation at the time was with the proposed introduction of child benefit. One of the main problems from the government point of view appears to have been the cost involved, and Barbara Castle writes that the proposed addition to child benefit for lone parents plus a higher level of disregarded earnings for those on supplementary benefit was the 'most' that could be done for lone parents. Both of these were introduced: child benefit increase (later one-parent benefit) as a flat-rate addition to child benefit for lone parents in 1975 and also in 1975 a disregard of £6.00 for lone parents as opposed to £2.00 for unemployed claimants and £4.00 for their partners.

## UNRESOLVED QUESTIONS

The key features of income support policy for lone parents were therefore effectively in place before the second world war and the modern 'welfare state' has had little success in developing provision for this group. Indeed, writing in 1975 (in a comment on the Finer proposals) George noted that 'social security provision for one-parent families is the most striking example of how little progress has been made in the past 50 years' (p. 6). As this brief outline of the way in which income support policy for lone parents has developed suggests, the same issues and problems seem to have come up time and time again without being adequately resolved. Indeed a number of barriers or unresolved questions seem to stand in the way of policy development and these barriers still centre round much the same issues.

First, there is a fear that adequate support for lone-parent families would undermine 'the family'—that such support leads to an increase in the number of 'broken' families and that more adequate support would therefore mean

28

that the number of such families would increase still further. This view is sometimes expressed in terms of the question of equity, the argument being that extra support for lone-parent families would place them in a more favourable position than two-parent families and that this would be unfair to the latter. Implicit in this argument is the corollary that support for lone parents would not only be unfair but also act as an inducement to the creation of such families and undermine the incentive for lone parents to re-marry.

Secondly, there is considerable uncertainty about the justification for providing such support, particularly for non-widowed lone mothers. Within the context of a sexual division of labour where men are assumed to provide the family income through paid employment and women to provide unpaid labour in the home, the loss of the 'breadwinner' through death creates a relatively unambiguous need for income support for the surviving spouse (if she is a woman—in general widowers do not have the same benefit entitlements as widows). However the loss of the 'breadwinner' through events other than death does not tend to be recognised as such a clear-cut situation of deserving need. The absent parent is still in theory available to provide support. Although as we shall see all the evidence shows that in practice this support is rather limited, nevertheless it could be argued that the state should not simply step in and release fathers from their responsibilities towards their children (and thereby, going back to previous point, perhaps encouraging them to do so). There is thus no clear view as to what the relative roles of the custodial parent, the non-custodial parent and the state should be. The lack of debate on these issues has meant that policy has developed in different, and sometimes conflicting, directions.

The justification for providing support on the grounds of loss of the 'breadwinner' in any case seems to have been progressively weakened, even for widows. The increase in labour market participation rates among married women (especially mothers) has to some extent eroded the traditional 'breadwinner' and 'housewife' roles and this can be seen as reducing the need for compensation for the loss of the man's earnings. Widows benefits are essentially based on an assumption of women's financial dependency on men within marriage. The fairly limited moves towards 'equal treatment' of men and women in social security (mainly in response to the 1978 EEC Directive on Equal Treatment) has not extended to individual entitlement to all benefits, nevertheless the *principle* that benefits should be based on the assumption of women's financial dependency seems to be increasingly unacceptable and out of step with the reality that most women are in paid employment for most of their lives.

Thirdly, there is still some ambiguity in state income support policy as to whether or not lone mothers should be expected to support themselves through employment. The view that mothers, and especially the mothers of young children, *should* stay at home to care for their children was very influential in Britain in the 1950s and 1960s and had a very major impact on social policy (many writers have discussed this, see, for example, Wilson, 1977; Gittins, 1985; David, 1986; Pascall, 1986). For lone mothers the assumption is that they are mothers first and workers second. Thus lone mothers on supplementary benefit are not required to register for work and are effectively guaranteed long-term support for as long as the children are dependent. This assumption—that the primary responsibility of lone mothers is to provide care for their children rather than be in the labour market—was central to the Finer report which stated (p. 279) that 'we regard it as most important that mothers, particularly when they have very young children, should not feel under any pressure to take paid employment'. One of the key principles put forward in the report was that income support for lone parents should 'allow a genuine choice about whether or not to work' (p. 269). More recently the tapered earnings disregard for lone parents on supplementary benefit was proposed (in the *Social Assistance* review) on the grounds that lone parents 'should be encouraged by a higher disregard to maintain a link with the employment field, to which they will eventually return' (DHSS, 1978, p. 65). It was not therefore intended as much to encourage employment during the period of lone parenthood as to facilitate employment later, when the children no longer require care.

These unresolved questions—about the basis or justification for support for lone parents, about the relative roles of public support and private maintenance and about the role of self-support through employment—are all closely interrelated and it is impossible to understand why policy has developed in the way it has, or how policy might develop in the future, without reference to these issues. The final chapter returns to these points.

## POVERTY AND LONE PARENTHOOD

That income support policy towards lone parents has not been an outstanding success can be seen by the longstanding association between poverty and lone parenthood. This is apparent in all studies of poverty going back to the work of Rowntree in York at the turn of the century (Rowntree, 1901). Table 2.1 shows the position of lone parents in four of the main poverty studies up to the mid 1970s. In none of these studies were lone parents the main focus of the research, but in all of them—despite the fact that they were based on very different concepts of poverty and consequently very different methodologies—it was found that lone parents, especially lone mothers, had a very much higher than average risk of poverty.

The high risk of poverty for lone parents is also apparent from the government figures on 'low-incomes families' which were until recently

30

produced every two years from Family Expenditure Survey data and social *Study* ?
security administrative statistics. These figures have always shown
lone-parent families to be a greater risk of poverty than two-parent families.
The most recent figures for 1985 (DHSS, 1988) show 62 per cent of
lone-parent families to be either in receipt of supplementary benefit or to
have incomes below supplementary benefit level compared with 10 per cent
of two-parent families. The slightly different analysis presented in the recent
Green Paper in the Reform of Social Security (DHSS, 1985a) showed that 7
per cent of families (in the sense of tax units) in the lowest quintile of
equivalent income were lone-parent families (as against the 4 per cent of all
families which were lone-parent families); and that 41 per cent of all lone
parents had incomes in the lowest quintile. In the Family Finances Survey
(Knight, 1978), on which this study is based, lone-parent families were found
to be substantially over-represented in the low-income sample.

Table 2.1

Poverty among lone-parent and two-parent families: various UK poverty
studies

| Risk of poverty | Lone-parent family/households | Two-parent family/households | All families/ households |
|---|---|---|---|
| Abel-Smith and Townsend | | | |
| 1953–54 | 24% | 6% | 10% |
| Townsend | | | |
| 1969 | 25% | 4% | 7% |
| Fiegehen et al. | | | |
| 1971 | 19% | 3% | 7% |
| Layard et al. | | | |
| 1975 | 58% | 19% | 26% |

*Sources:* Abel-Smith and Townsend, 1965, table 9
(expenditure below 140 per cent national assistance)
Townsend, 1979, table 7.11 and table 22.3
(income below100 per cent supplementary benefit)
Fiegehen at al., 1977, table 5.6
(income below 100 per cent supplementary benefit)
Layard et al., 1978, table 3.3 and table 8.1
(income below 140 per cent long-term rate of supplementary benefit)

Thus, there is a great deal of evidence detailing the extent and risk of
poverty or low income among lone parents. There has also been some recent
research on various aspects of living on benefits, of employment, and of

maintenance and divorce. However there has been no recent research which takes a broad look at the circumstances of lone-parent families examining not only the level and sources of income of such families, but also the consequences of this in terms of their living standards. The Family Finances and Family Resources Surveys, on which this book is based, in fact provide the first opportunity for carrying out such a study since the late 1960s/early 1970s; and the first opportunity for considering explicitly the adequacy of the income levels on which so many lone-parent families live.

## SUMMARY

This chapter has described the main features of income support policy for lone parents and how these developed. Three elements of current policy—the different treatment for widows, the absence of a requirement to seek paid work, and an assumption of financial dependency—were identified and it was argued that the origins of these go back to the Poor Laws. Attempts to treat all lone parents alike and to introduce a specific benefit for them have failed in the past because there has been no consensus about the justification for support for lone parents, about the relative roles of public support and private maintenance and about the role of self-support through employment. These questions remain unresolved.

The chapter concluded with a brief discussion of poverty research in relation to lone parents. From all the evidence it is clear that lone-parent families—especially lone mothers—are at particular risk of poverty. The FFS/FRS data however provides an opportunity to extend our knowledge of the living standards of lone parents and therefore of the practical outcome of current income support policy. The next chapter describes the FFS/FRS study—the methodology, the sample and the data collected—and discusses in more detail its strengths, and its weaknesses, for examining the situation of lone parents.

# 3 The Family Finances and Family Resources Surveys

This chapter describes the background to the Family Finances and Family Resources Survey (the FFS and FRS) the sample design, the questionnaires, the response rates achieved and the representativeness of the sample. The second section discusses the advantages and disadvantages of these data for analysing the living standards of lone-parent families, and the final section describes the basic characteristics of the families, and how family type changed between the FFS and the FRS.

SAMPLE DESIGN

In 1978 the Department of Health and Social Security commissioned the Office of Population Censuses and Surveys to carry out the FFS. The impetus for the study came from a recognition within DHSS of the limitations of existing data-sets for examining the situations of one of their main client groups—low-income families. The main source of data already available was the Family Expenditure Survey. This contains very detailed income and expenditure data but, because it is representative of all households, the number of low-income families included in the sample is too small for any detailed analysis. The FFS was therefore designed to be a 'FES for low-income families' intended to provide information on

> the family composition and spending patterns of low-income families,
> some indication of the allocation of certain expenditure categories within

33

the family, the take-up of income-tested benefits, the 'poverty trap' and the relative cost of expenditure items covering the whole family within large and small families. (Knight, 1981, p.1)

In consultation with DHSS, OPCS were responsible for the survey design, the fieldwork, the data-coding and the production of a methodological report (Knight, 1981) which provides the basis for the description of the sample design given here. After the interviewing for the FFS had started the DHSS customers decided that the study would be of even more value if it incorporated a longitudinal element so that the duration of low incomes could also be investigated. It was therefore decided that the same families should be followed up one year later and re-interviewed for the FRS. The FFS and the FRS covered Great Britain only, but a parallel survey was also carried out in Northern Ireland (Graham and Marshall, 1983).

The aim of the study was to investigate the circumstances of low-income families with dependent children. It was therefore necessary to decide how such families should be defined. Families with dependent children were defined according to the standard social survey definition of families with one or two parents and children aged either under 16, or 16 but under 19 and in full-time education. The definition of 'low income' was that of a current net income minus housing costs of below 140 per cent of the ordinary rates of supplementary benefit.

The use of supplementary benefit as the yardstick against which to measure low income was in part determined by the fact that DHSS—as sponsors of the study—were particularly interested not only in supplementary benefit recipients (for whom they have administrative responsibility) but also in those families living on incomes close to supplementary benefit levels.[1] In addition a simple measure of cash income used as a cut-off point for defining a low income would take no account of differences in family size and in the number of people dependent upon that income. Some measure of 'equivalent' income, to control for differences in family size, was therefore needed. Measuring income relative to supplementary benefit takes this into account because the scale rates vary with the number and ages of the children as well as with the number of adults. The cut-off point for low incomes was set at 140 per cent rather than 100 per cent of supplementary benefit in order to take account of the fact that supplementary benefit recipients can have incomes above the basic rate if they receive the long-term rate, or if they receive additional payments or if they have some disregarded income.[2] Thus if the cut-off point had been set at 100 per cent some families in receipt of supplementary benefit would have been excluded from the sample.

34

The aim, therefore, was to interview families with children whose net incomes fell below 140 per cent of the basic rates of supplementary benefit. Estimates from the 1975 Family Expenditure Survey suggested that about 18 per cent of all families with children would fall into this low-income group. Also in order to achieve adequate sub-samples of particular groups (ie those with incomes below 100 per cent and lone parents) for separate analysis, estimates of the proportions of such families were made from the 1975 Family Expenditure Survey and this indicated that the survey should aim to achieve successful interviews with 3,200 families. This is equivalent to approximately 0.045 per cent of the total number of families with dependent children in 1979; and approximately 0.29 per cent of the estimated total of 'low-income' families (DHSS, 1983). However one sub-group which would not be adequately represented in a sample size of 3,200 families was large families (defined as those with four or more dependent children). It was therefore decided that these families should be over-sampled by being given a chance of selection of three times their normal probability.

The content of the survey was dictated by the requirement that this was to be a reproduction of the FES for low-income families. The questionnaire was therefore exactly the same as that used in the FES, and the families were also asked to keep the two-week expenditure diary. Because detailed information on expenditure was to be collected and because expenditure is subject to seasonal variations (for example, in fuel bills) the interviewing was to be spread out over a 12 month period (as is the case for the FES).

In order to achieve a representative sample of low-income families with children, a multi-stage stratified research design was used. This was initially based on child benefit records and a door-step sift was used to identify the low-income families. Interviewing was spread out over 12 months which introduced a further complication in relation to the calculation of income relative to supplementary benefit. The supplementary benefit scale rates were at that time up-rated each year in November, and would progressively fall in real terms throughout the year according to the rate of inflation, reaching their lowest point just before the next up-rating (assuming prices are rising and not falling). However earnings may increase at any time during the year. If the cut-off of 140 per cent of supplementary benefit were held constant throughout the year this would have meant that the number of families eligible for inclusion in the sample would have fallen from the first to the fourth quarter, and families who would have been eligible in the first quarter might have become ineligible by the time of the final quarter. Thus a constant cut-off line would have meant that the composition of the sample would have changed during the course of the year. In order to avoid this the cut-off point was raised each quarter on the basis of the rises in the retail price index (excluding housing) in the preceding quarters. Thus the cut-off points were as follows:

| | |
|---|---|
| 1st quarter (October to December 1978) | 140.0 per cent |
| 2nd quarter (January to March 1979) | 141.7 per cent |
| 3rd quarter (April to June 1979) | 145.6 per cent |
| 4th quarter (July to September 1979) | 149.7 per cent |

Finally it should be noted that although the sample was of 'families' drawn from child benefit records not all the families lived alone in separate households. Where families lived in larger households—sharing with other adults and/or children—all the members of the household were included in the interviews and all the adults were asked to keep expenditure diaries.

The two stages involved in getting to the sample mean that the representativeness of the sample could have been affected by non-response at either the first stage of sift interviews or at the second stage of the main interviews. The response to the sift interviews was 75.2 per cent, and at the main FFS interview it was 82.2 per cent giving an overall response rate of 61.6 per cent. The only significant difference between the achieved sample and the eligible sample was that the former tended to under-represent one child families, and this was corrected by an adjustment to the weighting. Thus in addition to the weight of 0.333 given to families of four or more children to counteract their over-representation in the sample, families with one child were given a weight of 1.1827.

**The Family Resources Survey**
The aim of the FRS was to re-interview all the families successfully interviewed at the FFS one year later (within two weeks of the date exactly 12 months after). If families had separated then the rule was to follow the family with the children. The FRS did not include the expenditure diaries, otherwise the information collected at the FRS was the same as at the FFS with the addition of some questions specifically intended to cover topics of particular interest for low-income families, such as debts, financial hardship and other qualitative measures of deprivation.

The response rate at the FRS was 84.2 per cent which gives an overall response of 51.9 per cent (that is 84.2 per cent of the 61.6 per cent successfully interviewed at the FFS). Non-respondents at the FRS had, of course, been interviewed at the FFS and therefore it is possible to make quite detailed comparisons of their characteristics with those of respondents. The two groups were compared in the following characteristics: family type; household type; sex of head of family; age of head of family; number of dependent children; age of youngest child; tenure and employment status of head of the family. The same comparisons were made separately for lone-parent families. The only significant (at 5 per cent) differences for the sample as a whole were in household type and in the number of dependent children, with the non-respondents more likely to live in multi-unit households and to have large families than the respondents. There were no significant differences between the respondents and the non-respondents in the lone-parent family group.

Table 3.1 shows the number of families, both weighted and unweighted at the FFS and the FRS. These are the sample numbers on which this analysis is based.

### Table 3.1

### FFS sample by type and response at FRS

| | FFS | | FRS | | % of FRS |
| | weighted | (unweighted) | weighted | (unweighted) | re-interviewed at FRS |
| Status at FFS | n | n | n | n | % |
| --- | --- | --- | --- | --- | --- |
| Family type | | | | | |
| Lone parent | 1032 | (1121) | 864 | (938) | 83.7 |
| Two parents | 1594 | (2050) | 1345 | (1713) | 84.4 |
| Household type | | | | | |
| Single-unit | 2102 | (2566) | 1790 | (2168) | 85.2 |
| Multi-unit | 524 | (605) | 419 | (483) | 80.0 |
| Family and household type | | | | | |
| Lone parent | | | | | |
| – single unit | 795 | (878) | 669 | (739) | 84.2 |
| – multi-unit | 237 | (243) | 195 | (199) | 82.3 |
| Two parents | | | | | |
| – single-unit | 1307 | (1688) | 1121 | (1429) | 85.8 |
| – multi-unit | 287 | (362) | 224 | (284) | 78.1 |
| Total | 2626 | (3171) | 2209 | (2651) | 84.1 |

*Notes:*   'Weighted' refers to the sample weighted according to the following weights:

| 1 child | — | 1.1827 |
| 2 or 3 | — | 1.0000 |
| 4 or more | — | 0.3333 |

'Unweighted' refers to the numbers actually interviewed and are shown in all tables in brackets. For all the analysis it is the re-weighted sample numbers which are used.

## SECONDARY DATA ANALYSIS

The widespread use of secondary data analysis—defined by Hakim (1982, p.4) as 'any further analysis of one or more data sets which yields findings or knowledge additional to those presented in the original report'—is comparatively recent in British social policy research. The considerable expense involved in carrying out large scale surveys and the time required for the analysis of such data combined with the more readily available computer technology and the easier access to survey data through the ESRC data archive have meant that researchers have increasingly turned to secondary analysis. The advantages of secondary analysis of existing data-sets are obvious. First it is clearly considerably cheaper to work with data already collected than to mount a large scale survey from scratch. The savings apply not only to the cost of actually carrying out surveys but also to the time involved—several years can elapse from the initial planning of a survey, through to carrying out the fieldwork, the analysis and finally the appearance of the results. The costs involved mean that increasingly only government departments have sufficient resources to be able to carry out such work. Secondary analysis by independent researchers of survey data originally carried out by government departments can therefore provide something of a counter-balance to the danger that the research questions and debate might be increasingly dictated by the concerns of the government.

However there are disadvantages to secondary analysis. In any secondary analysis the questions that can be posed and the topics that can be investigated are imposed by the data rather than the other way around. The organisation of the data and the classifications used (eg definitions of households, families, social class, employment status and so on) also impose constraints, although these can sometimes be overcome (see Overton and Ermisch, 1984, for example, for their description of defining 'minimal household units' and using these to analyse household formation from GHS data). There is also the problem of 'missing' data—not in the sense of failure to respond but in the sense of failure to ask. Before going on to the main analysis it is therefore useful to consider some of the limitations of the FFS/FRS data for an analysis of the situation of lone-parent families.

### Lone parents and the FFS/FRS

As described above the questionnaire for the FFS was the same as that used in the FES. Very detailed information was therefore collected on income and expenditure but at the same time using the FES interview schedule meant that there were a number of omissions from the data which would obviously have been included if the survey had been specifically designed to investigate the circumstances of lone parents. The most glaring of these was the failure to ask respondents any detailed questions about their marital status. The lone parents were not therefore asked if they were single, widowed, divorced or separated nor was any information collected on how long they had been living as lone parents. It has been possible to identify widows through the questions that were asked about receipt of benefits, including widows benefits, which is likely to provide a fairly good proxy for the identification of widows as most widows do receive such a benefit (Richardson, 1984). Nor were any detailed questions asked about receipt of maintenance—although the number of women in receipt of maintenance payments can be identified there is no information on how long such payments had been made, whether they were regular or whether they were intended for the maintenance of the woman as well as for the children.

On the face of it there are fairly serious limitations and mean that it has not been possible to compare the risks of poverty and the living standards of different types of lone-parent families (single, widowed, separated and divorced). On the other hand the main aim of the study was to investigate the living standards of low-income lone parents and not, for example, to consider the financial consequences of marital breakdown. Arguably, also, for non-widowed lone mothers (who were the vast majority of the lone parents in the FFS) marital status is a less important determinant of living standards than other factors such as the number and age of the children for whom they are caring.[3] Nevertheless this is a limitation to the study and one that is very surprising given that those within DHSS responsible for planning the survey must have been aware that a significant proportion of the families in the sample would be lone-parent families (in light of all the evidence already available on the extent of poverty among such families).

Another constraint on the analysis arises from the fact that, although information was collected at three levels (the individual, the family and the household) there is little information available on the distribution of resources *within* the families and households. This would be a more significant limitation if the focus of the study was the two-parent rather than the lone-parent families. However such information would have been very useful for considering two particular groups: the lone parents who were sharing a household and the lone parents who became part of a two-parent family during the course of the study. For the latter group the lack of information on the distribution of resources within families means that it is not possible to fully explore the consequences of a change in marital status for the living standards of the women and their children—it is possible to look at how total *family* income changed but it is not possible to know exactly what this meant in terms of the access of the 'ex-lone mothers' to this income. As research has shown (Pahl, 1980; Land, 1983; Charles and Kerr, 1986) all members of one family do not necessarily have the same standard of living.

Returning to the lone parents who shared a household, in most of the detailed results reported in this book these families have been excluded. In the original analysis of incomes and living standards these 'multi-unit' households were considered separately from those living alone because of the different issues and questions raised. For reasons of space, none of this analysis is reported here. 'Single-unit households' have been defined as those consisting only of the parent(s) and dependent children (ie under 16 or 16-19 and in full-time education). All other households, including those that consist of one 'family', have been defined as 'multi-unit households'. Thus households consisting of three generations (grandparent(s), parent(s) and child(ren)) and those consisting of a family with both dependent and non-dependent children are multi-unit households. The reason for adopting these definitions is that the single-unit families, so defined, are the basic unit for tax and social security purposes and therefore the unit of interest for policy. (It should be remembered that the sample was one of families drawn from the child benefit register and that where the selected families lived in larger households the other members of the household were also interviewed.) The majority (80 per cent) of the sample consisted of single-unit households.

In addition to the constraints imposed by the type of questions asked and not asked of the respondents it is also important to note the constraints imposed by the nature of the sample itself—and in particular by the definition of low income used in the sample selection. As described earlier in this chapter low-income families were defined as families with a net family income after meeting housing costs of below 140 per cent of the ordinary rates of supplementary benefit. This is the same definition of 'low-income' as used in the official DHSS estimates of the numbers of low-income families, and it is not uncommon in poverty research—often being used as an indicator of those 'in or on the margins of poverty' (eg Townsend, 1979; CPAG/Low Pay Unit, 1986). It is not, however, an uncontroversial definition of poverty—as has often been pointed out, it takes for granted what actually needs to be determined, namely that supplementary benefit is itself adequate to prevent poverty (Nicholson, 1979; Veit-Wilson, 1985). However from the point of view of this study—where the aim is to examine the living standards of lone parents in relation to the level and the type of social security benefits available to them—then a definition of low income in relation to supplementary benefit is entirely appropriate. Thus this study focuses upon those families living at or below the state's 'minimum' income level.

However a further point must be made about the sample definition and this concerns the deduction of housing costs from the measure of income used. The reason for doing this was because housing costs are not taken into account for supplementary benefit purposes. The deduction of housing costs from income in poverty research is, in fact, quite a common procedure (see Layard et al., 1979, pp.10-11 for a discussion of the problems raised by housing costs). However the deduction of housing costs from net income might be expected to have affected the composition of the sample and led to a sample that was more heterogeneous in its experience of low incomes than would otherwise have been the case. This is because some of the families in the sample would have been included only because they had relatively high housing costs. These would usually be families who were buying their own homes and hence relatively high mortgage costs. Arguably the low disposable incomes of these families should be seen differently from those of the other families given that they were acquiring a major asset in the form of their own homes. The low incomes of such families could therefore be seen as a consequence of a particular and temporary stage in their life-cycle. In terms of the comparisons between the lone parents and the two-parent families, it was the latter group rather than the former who were more likely to include these 'owner-occupier poor'. Using imputed (based on the mean level) rather than actual housing costs then 7 per cent of the lone parents and 14 per cent of the two-parent families had incomes outside the scope of the sample (ie above 140 per cent of supplementary benefit). Thus altogether relatively high housing costs probably accounted for the inclusion of about 11 per cent of the families. These were usually two-parent families (75 per cent compared with 61 per cent of the sample as a whole); employed (83 per cent compared with 47 per cent of the sample as a whole); and owner-occupiers with mortgages (80 per cent compared with 23 per cent of the sample as a whole). The proportion of families affected is fairly small but it should be borne in mind that this was a factor affecting the composition of the sample.

A final point about the nature of the sample is that it contained very few lone fathers (only 41 re-weighted cases). This is not surprising because lone fathers are less likely to be poor than lone mothers (although this does not mean that they do not face problems and difficulties—see for example George and Wilding, 1972; Greif, 1985). The focus of this study is therefore on lone mothers rather than lone fathers. The lone fathers are included where possible but the sample number means that they cannot be included in any detailed analysis.

**Access to the data**
Secondary analysts rarely have access to all the data from a large-scale survey, a more usual procedure (where data is obtained from the ESRC Date Archive, for example) is for the researcher to request that part of the data which is required for a particular analysis. In the case of this study, which was based in the Social Policy Research Unit at York University, the

FFS/FRS data tapes were already at the University where a number of projects analysing the FFS/FRS data were under way.[4] These projects had been commissioned by the DHSS and the data being used had been supplied by the Statistics Branch of DHSS. The majority of the data collected was available on these tapes. What was not available, however, was the OPCS measure of income relative to supplementary benefit—the relative net resources measure as used in the sample selection. In fact it was not until this study had been underway for over a year that we were able to obtain this data.[5] However as this study required a number of different measures of income and also needed to know how different components of income contributed to the total it would, in any case, have been necessary to calculate these income measures rather than relying on the summary measure used by OPCS. A comparison of the two measures showed that there was in fact very little difference between them in the distribution of income relative to supplementary benefit for the single-unit households. For 84 per cent of all the families (88 per cent of the lone mothers) the two measures were within five points of each other. However one consequence of calculating our own measure rather than relying on the OPCS measure was that a small number of the families had, according to our measure, net incomes of above 140 per cent of supplementary benefit. Overall this affected 7 per cent of the families (3 per cent of the lone mothers, none of the lone fathers and 9 per cent of the two-parent families). A detailed examination of these cases did not reveal any systematic reason for this but only rarely did the measure put these families above 150 per cent. These families have been included in the analysis. These differences illustrate the extent to which so-called 'hard' data can in fact vary quite substantially according to the different definitions and measures used.

## THE CHARACTERISTICS OF THE FAMILIES

The estimate of the number of low-income families for 1979 (DHSS, 1981) showed that, at that time, about half of all lone-parent families were estimated to be either in receipt of supplementary benefit or to have net incomes below 140 per cent of the ordinary rate of supplementary benefit. Thus the FFS sample of lone-parent families is representative of about half of the total population of lone-parent families. The most immediate, striking difference between these low-income lone parents and all lone parents is that it is lone mothers rather than lone fathers who are more likely to be found in the low-income group. In the FFS sample, 94 per cent of the lone parents were women compared with 89 per cent of all lone parents at that time (OPCS, 1981), confirming the finding of other studies that lone mothers are more likely to experience poverty than lone fathers (eg, Finer, 1974; Layard et al.,

1978). Although the FFS collected no information on marital status it is possible to identify widows by receipt of widows benefit and, again in line with the findings of other studies, widows were under-represented in this low-income sample in comparison with the general population. Only 7 per cent of the FFS lone mothers were in receipt of a widows benefit while, at that time, about 17 per cent of all lone mothers were widows (OPCS, 1981). Thus the type of lone parents most likely to experience poverty are women who are unmarried or who are divorced or separated from their husbands.

As regards characteristics the lone mothers and the lone fathers were rather different. As Table 3.2 shows, in terms of age the FFS lone mothers were very similar to all lone mothers, with slightly more younger women in the FFS sample than in general (38 per cent aged under 29 compared with 30 per cent). On the other hand, however, the FFS lone fathers included a much wider spread of age-groups than is found amongst lone fathers in general, with both more younger men (14 per cent aged under 19 compared with 6 per cent) and more older men (12 per cent aged over 60 compared with 7 per cent).

Table 3.2

Age by sex: FFS lone parents and all lone parents

| | Lone mothers | | Lone fathers | |
| | FFS | All[1] | FFS | All[1] |
| Age | % | % | % | % |
| --- | --- | --- | --- | --- |
| 16–24 | 20 | 15 | 2 | 1 |
| 25–29 | 18 | 15 | 12 | 5 |
| 30–39 | 37 | 37 | 31 | 21 |
| 40–49 | 18 | 21 | 26 | 41 |
| 50–59 | 17 | 10 | 18 | 25 |
| 60 + | 1 | 1 | 12 | 7 |
| Total | 100 | 100 | 100 | 100 |
| Median age | 33 | 34 | 41 | 45 |
| Base (no. interviewed) | 972 | 966 | 59 | 119 |
| | (1062) | | (59) | |

1. General Household Survey, 1978/79 combined, Table 2.12. *General Household Survey 1979.*

43

Families with only one dependent child were less common among the FFS lone parents than among lone parents in general and large families were more common. Of the FFS lone mothers 25 per cent had three or more children compared with 17 per cent of all lone mothers. Again the differences were more pronounced among the FFS lone fathers, 41 per cent of whom had three or more children compared with 21 per cent of all lone fathers. Lone fathers only rarely have the care of pre-school age children, but the children of the FFS lone fathers did tend to be younger than in general (52 per cent with a youngest child aged under ten compared with 32 per cent). Amongst the lone mothers, the FFS mothers were slightly more likely than lone mothers in general to have a youngest child of under school age (38 per cent compared with 31 per cent). This would be expected given that they themselves were slightly younger and had larger families than lone mothers in general.

Table 3.3

Number of dependent children and age of youngest child by sex: FFS lone parents and all lone parents

|  | Lone mothers | | Lone fathers | |
| | FFS | All[1] | FFS | All[1] |
| Number of dependent children | % | % | % | % |
| --- | --- | --- | --- | --- |
| 1 | 43 | 53 | 40 | 48 |
| 2 | 32 | 31 | 19 | 31 |
| 3 | 17 | 11 | 37 | 18 |
| 4 or more | 8 | 6 | 4 | 3 |
| Total | 100 | 100 | 100 | 100 |
| Mean no. of children | 1.9 | 1.7 | 2.0 | 1.8 |
| | FFS | All | FFS | All |
| Age of youngest child | % | % | % | % |
| 0–4 | 38 | 31 | 7 | 5 |
| 5–9 | 32 | 31 | 45 | 28 |
| 10 plus | 30 | 38 | 48 | 68 |
| Total | 100 | 100 | 100 | 100 |
| Base (no. interviewed) | 972 (1062) | 959 | 59 (59) | 119 |

1. General Household Survey, 1978/79 combined, Table 2.11. *General Household Survey 1979*.

As regards tenure, as Table 3.4 shows, the FFS lone parents were much more likely than all lone parents to be local authority tenants (72 per cent compared with 56 per cent) and therefore less likely to be owner-occupiers (13 per cent compared with 32 per cent). Within the FFS sample the lone mothers were more likely to be local authority tenants than the lone fathers (81 per cent compared with 72 per cent).

## Table 3.4

### Tenure: FFS lone parents and all lone parents

|  | FFS Lone mothers % | FFS Lone fathers % | All % | All lone parents[1] % |
| --- | --- | --- | --- | --- |
| Tenure |  |  |  |  |
| Owner-occupier |  |  |  |  |
| – outright | 3 | 4 | 4 | 12 |
| – mortgage | 10 | 9 | 9 | 20 |
| Rented |  |  |  |  |
| – local authority | 81 | 72 | 72 | 56 |
| – private unfurnished | 3 | 8 | 8 | 8 |
| – private furnished | 2 | 3 | 3 | 3 |
| Rent free | 0 | 4 | 4 | – |
| Rented with job | 0 | 0 | – | 2 |
| Total | 100 | 100 | 100 | 100 |
| Base (no. interviewed) | 972 (1062) | 59 (59) | 1032 (1121) | 1015 |

1. General Household Survey, 1977/78 combined, Table 3.43. *General Household Survey 1978.*

For both lone mothers and lone fathers a very striking difference between these low-income lone parents and all lone parents was in the proportion who were in paid employment. Only 23 per cent of the FFS lone mothers were in employment compared with 48 per cent of all lone mothers at that time (Table 3.5). The FFS lone mothers were less likely than lone mothers in general to be in either full-time or part-time employment, but most of the difference was accounted for by the very small proportion of the FFS lone mothers who were in full-time employment (only 4 per cent compared with 22 per cent of all lone mothers). The main factor affecting the labour market participation rates of mothers (whether married or not) is the age of their youngest child—women with care of pre-school children are the least likely to be employed (Martin and Roberts, 1984). For the FFS lone mothers, as for all lone mothers, this pattern is apparent with only 13 per cent of the women with the care of a pre-school child being in employment compared with 33 per cent of the women whose youngest child was aged ten or above. Within each age group (of children), however, the FFS lone mothers were less likely to be employed than lone mothers in general.

Table 3.5

Whether employed by age of youngest child: FFS lone mothers and all lone mothers

| | Age of youngest child | | | | | | | |
| | FFS lone mothers | | | | All lone mothers[1] | | | |
| | 0–4 | 5–9 | 10+ | All | 0–4 | 5–9 | 10 | All |
| Employment | % | % | % | % | % | % | % | % |
| --- | --- | --- | --- | --- | --- | --- | --- | --- |
| Employed: | | | | | | | | |
| full-time | 2 | 3 | 8 | 4 | 11 | 22 | 31 | 12 |
| part-time | 11 | 21 | 26 | 19 | 10 | 34 | 31 | 25 |
| all employed | 13 | 24 | 33 | 23 | 21 | 56 | 64 | 48 |
| Base (no. interviewed) | 365 | 316 | 289 | 972 (1062) | 137 | 127 | 162 | 426 |

1. General Household Survey, 1979, Table 5.7. *General Household Survey 1979.*

Amongst the FFS lone fathers, 21 per cent were employed and a further 3 per cent were self-employed. Of those who were in employment two-thirds were in full-time jobs. According to data from the 1979 Family Expenditure Survey (Popay et al., 1983) about 70 per cent of all lone fathers had earnings as their main source of income and thus the proportion of the FFS lone fathers in paid employment was considerably below that of all lone fathers. Unfortunately the number of lone fathers in the FFS is too small for a breakdown of employment status by family responsibilities, nor is comparable data available for all lone fathers. However the fact that these lone fathers had 'heavier' family responsibilities than lone fathers in general (larger families and younger children) suggests that these lone fathers were particularly likely to be constrained in their employment by their child-care responsibilities. The FFS lone fathers were much more likely than the FFS lone mothers to say that they were 'unemployed' (52 per cent compared with 5 per cent) which is almost certainly because men are more likely than

46

women to see their 'normal' role as being in paid work. Thus as many as 76 per cent of the lone fathers would be defined as 'economically active' compared with only 28 per cent of the lone mothers.

## Comparisons with the FFS two-parent families

This section compares the characteristics of the lone-parent families in the FFS with those of the two-parent families. Table 3.6 summarises the results. The two-parent families were twice as likely as the lone-parent families to have four or more dependent children. They were also more likely to have a youngest child of under school age, and this was true whatever the number of children with the exception that the lone-parent families were more likely to have only one child of below school age (19 per cent compared with 12 per cent). The tenure patterns were quite different, with substantially more owner-occupiers with mortgages amongst the two-parent families and fewer tenants. (As discussed above this was in part a result of the definition of income used in the sample selection.) Slightly more of the two-parent families than of the lone-parent families lived in single-unit households. In both family types the vast majority of those who shared lived with older non-dependent children.

Amongst the two-parent families there were very few families where both parents were employed (6 per cent or 8 per cent including the self-employed), which one would expect as families with two earners would be unlikely to be in a low-income sample. The mothers in the two-parent families were in fact less likely than the lone mothers to be employed either full-time (2 per cent compared with 4 per cent) or part-time (12 per cent compared with 19 per cent). However over half of the fathers in the two parent families were employed (50 per cent full-time, 2 per cent part-time and an additional 8 per cent self-employed). Therefore about twice as many of the two-parent families compared with the lone-parent families received some income from employment.

Thus, there were a number of differences between the low-income lone-parent and two-parent families. However, in general lone-parent families and two-parent families have different characteristics and therefore this is perhaps not too surprising. Of more interest is to examine whether the low-income two-parent families differ from all two-parent families in the same way as the low-income lone-parent families differed from all lone-parent families, and therefore to consider whether the same type of characteristics were associated with low incomes for both family groups.

The factors identified for the lone-parent families where similar comparisons can be made for the two-parent families were that compared with all lone parents the FFS lone parents tended to be slightly younger and had larger families more often containing a youngest child of under school

47

### Table 3.6
### Summary of characteristics of FFS lone parents and two-parent families

| Characteristics | Lone-parent families % | Two-parent families % |
|---|---|---|
| **Number of dependent children** | | |
| 1 | 43 | 25 |
| 2 | 31 | 36 |
| 3 | 18 | 22 |
| 4 or more | 8 | 16 |
| **Age of youngest child** | | |
| 0–4 | 36 | 51 |
| 5–9 | 33 | 28 |
| 10+ | 31 | 21 |
| **Tenure** | | |
| Rented : local authority | 72 | 56 |
| : private (unfurnished) | 8 | 6 |
| : private (furnished) | 3 | 1 |
| Owner-occupiers : mortgage | 9 | 32 |
| : outright | 4 | 3 |
| Rent free | 4 | 2 |
| **Household structure** | | |
| Single-unit | 77 | 82 |
| Living with parents | 6 | Ø |
| Living with older non-dependent children | 13 | 15 |
| Other | 4 | 2 |
| **Employment status**[1] | | |
| Employed : full-time | 6 | 50 |
| : part-time | 19 | 2 |
| Self-employed | Ø | 8 |
| Unemployed and seeking work | 7 | 30 |
| Other | 68 | 10 |
| **Median age of mother** | 33.0 | 32.8 |
| | | |
| Proportion of sample | (39%) | (61%) |
| Base (no. interviewed) | 1032 | 1594 |
| | (1121) | (2050) |

1. In two-parent families employment status of father.
Ø   Less than 1%

age. They were also less likely to be owner-occupiers and less likely to be in employment. Comparing the low-income two-parent families with all two-parent families (using information from the 1979 GHS) then again the low-income families were larger (38 per cent with three or more dependent children compared with 20 per cent) and more often contained a youngest child of under school age (51 per cent compared with 37 per cent). The median age of the family head (usually the man) was fairly similar at 36 for the low-income fathers compared with 38 for all two-parent family heads. Local authority tenants were over-represented amongst the low-income two-parent families (56 per cent compared with 30 per cent), as were private tenants (7 per cent compared with 4 per cent) and owner-occupiers were under-represented (35 per cent compared with 62 per cent). Comparing the employment status of all fathers under 64 with dependent children and the low-income fathers shows the former were much more likely to be in work (94 per cent compared with 60 per cent). But a striking difference between all two-parent families and the low-income two-parent families was that the latter were substantially less likely to have two earners (8 per cent compared with 51 per cent) and this, of course, is not applicable to lone-parent families.

Thus, in general, whether there were one or two parents in the family similar family characteristics were associated with low incomes. Large families which include young children were most likely to be found in the low-income group for both family types. However there was a significant difference between the lone parents and the two-parent families in that the latter were much more likely to have some income from employment.

### Changes in family status between the interviews
As Table 3.7 shows about one in ten of the FRS sample were living in a different type of family at the FRS than they had been at the FFS: about 3 per cent had become lone-parent households, 5 per cent had become two-parent households and 2 per cent no longer had dependent children.

Changes in family type more often involved women than men (Table 3.8). Of both the lone fathers and the two-parent families at the FFS, 6 per cent had changed family type compared with 16 per cent of the lone mothers. Of the newly-formed lone-parent households at the FRS, the majority were headed by a woman. Thus the most frequent change in family status was from lone parenthood to a two-parent family, which would be expected for this sample given the fact that lone-parent families were substantially over-represented in the FFS.

Table 3.9 compares the characteristics of women who remained lone mothers with the women who had been lone mothers at the FFS but were living in a two-parent family at the FRS. (The number of men making such a change is too small for a similar comparison.) The two groups of women

## Table 3.7

### Changes in family type between the FFS and FRS

| Family type at FRS | Famiy type at FFS | | |
| | Lone-parent family | Two-parent family | All |
| | % | % | % |
| --- | --- | --- | --- |
| Lone-parent family | 33.1 | 2.7 | 35.8 |
| Two-parent family | 5.0 | 57.5 | 62.5 |
| Lone-parent family : no children | 1.0 | 0.0 | 1.0 |
| Two-parent family : no children | 0.1 | 0.9 | 1.0 |
| All | 39.2 | 61.0 | 100.0 |
| Base (no. interviewed) | 864 | 1345 | 2209 |
| | (938) | (1713) | (2651) |

were different in a number of respects. The 'ex-lone mothers' were particularly likely to be young women, with only one or two dependent children, the youngest being of under school age. Thirty per cent of these women had only one pre-school age child (compared with 17 per cent of those who stayed lone mothers). They were also more likely than those who remained lone mothers to have been living in someone else's household, to have been in receipt of supplementary benefit and were less likely to be widows.

## Table 3.8

### Family type at the FFS by family type at the FRS

| Family type at FRS | Family type at FFS | | | |
| | Lone mother | Lone father | Two-parent family | All |
| | % | % | % | % |
| --- | --- | --- | --- | --- |
| Lone mother | 84 | 0 | 4 | 33 |
| Lone father | 0 | 94 | 1 | 2 |
| Two-parent family | 13 | 6 | 96 | 62 |
| Lone mother: no children | 3 | 0 | 0 | 1 |
| Lone father: no children | 0 | 0 | 0 | 0 |
| Two-parent family: no children | 0 | 0 | 1 | 1 |
| Total | 100 | 100 | 100 | 100 |
| Base (no. interviewed) | 813 | 47 | 1345 | 2209 |
| | (814) | (49) | (1713) | (2651) |

50

## Table 3.9
### Characteristics of lone mothers and ex-lone mothers

| Characteristics at FFS | Lone mother at both % | Lone mother to two-parent family (ex-lone mother) % |
|---|---|---|
| **Age of woman** | | |
| Under 24 | 18 | 39 |
| 25–29 | 18 | 27 |
| 30–34 | 21 | 15 |
| 35–39 | 18 | 11 |
| 40 plus | 26 | 7 |
| Total | 100 | 100 |
| **Number of dependent children** | | |
| 1 | 41 | 41 |
| 2 | 32 | 42 |
| 3 | 19 | 9 |
| 4 plus | 8 | 8 |
| Total | 100 | 100 |
| **Age of youngest child** | | |
| Under 5 | 36 | 63 |
| 5 to 9 | 42 | 32 |
| 10 plus | 22 | 5 |
| Total | 100 | 100 |
| **Household status** | | |
| Single-unit household | 78 | 83 |
| Head of h/h in multi-unit h/h | 16 | 5 |
| Not head of h/h in multi-unit h/h | 7 | 12 |
| Total | 100 | 100 |
| **Tenure** | | |
| LA tenant | 72 | 71 |
| Private tenant | 11 | 11 |
| Owner occupier   : mortgage | 9 | 9 |
| : outright | 3 | 3 |
| Rent free | 5 | 5 |
| Total | 100 | 100 |
| **Proportion :**   in employment | 23 | 19 |
| in receipt of SB | 77 | 86 |
| in receipt of maintenance | 28 | 31 |
| in receipt of widow's benefit | 9 | 2 |
| **Base (no. interviewed)** | 685 (749) | 107 (118) |

Table 3.10 compares the characteristics of the women in the two-parent families at the FFS who became lone mothers and those whose status did not change. In most respects these two groups were similar. However younger women were more likely to have become lone parents and the 'new' lone mothers were particularly likely to have come from families where the man was unemployed and in receipt of supplementary benefit. Of the 'new' lone mothers, 49 per cent had been living with an unemployed husband at the FFS compared with 29 per cent of the women whose marital status did not change. Thus families 'headed' by an unemployed man were much more likely to have separated those headed by an employed man (6 per cent compared with 2 per cent excluding 'new' widows). Some of this difference would have been accounted for by the fact that the younger men were more likely to be unemployed than the older men, and it was the younger families who were more likely to have separated. However, if age is controlled for this difference between the employed and the unemployed families is still apparent. As all the FFS families were in the same narrow band of income, this suggests that unemployment itself (rather than just the low income associated with it) is a contributory factor in marital breakdown. (See also Daniel, 1981.) About 9 per cent of the women who became lone mothers were receiving a widows benefit at the FRS—most of these were women who had been married to retired men at the FRS.

Table 3.11 shows all the changes in both family and household status. The original group of lone mothers were the most likely to have had some change (27 per cent). These changes were usually either the result of lone mothers becoming part of a two-parent family (12 per cent) or because the dependency status of children had changed. Thus, of the 8 per cent who went from a single-unit to a multi-unit household, 68 per cent were defined as multi-unit households at the FRS because of the presence of older children, 11 per cent had gone to live with their parents, 7 per cent with other relatives and 15 per cent with non-relatives. This latter small group (about one per cent of all lone mothers at the FFS) are possibly women who had started co-habiting by the time of the FFS although it is not possible to be certain about this from the data available. Of the 3 per cent of lone mothers who moved from multi-unit to single-unit households, about two-fifths had been living with their parents at the FFS, and about a third had had older children living with them at the FFS who had apparently left home by the time of the FRS. For the lone fathers and the married couples, changes in the dependency status of children were more common than changes in marital status, and accounted for most of the changes in household status. Of the women who became lone mothers from two-parent families, the majority did not change household status, but about 10 per cent apparently went to live with their parents.

## Table 3.10

### Characteristics of married and ex-married mothers

| Characteristics at FFS | Two-parent family at both (married) % | Two-parent family to lone mother (ex-married) % |
|---|---|---|
| **Age of woman** | | |
| Under 24 | 16 | 36 |
| 25–29 | 23 | 17 |
| 30–34 | 23 | 22 |
| 35–39 | 16 | 11 |
| 40 plus | 22 | 15 |
| Total | 100 | 100 |
| **Number of dependent children** | | |
| 1 | 25 | 16 |
| 2 | 38 | 44 |
| 3 | 22 | 29 |
| 4 plus | 16 | 12 |
| Total | 100 | 100 |
| **Age of youngest child** | | |
| Under 5 | 53 | 59 |
| 5 to 9 | 32 | 34 |
| 10 plus | 16 | 6 |
| Total | 100 | 100 |
| **Household status** | | |
| Single-unit household | 84 | 82 |
| Head of h/h in multi-unit h/h | 16 | 16 |
| Not head of h/h in multi-unit h/h | 0 | 2 |
| Total | 100 | 100 |
| **Tenure** | | |
| LA tenant | 55 | 67 |
| Private tenant | 11 | 9 |
| Owner occupier : mortgage | 33 | 18 |
| : outright | 3 | 4 |
| Rent free | 2 | 3 |
| Total | 100 | 100 |
| Proportion : in employment (woman) | 15 | 10 |
| in employment (man) | 62 | 37 |
| in receipt of SB (man) | 24 | 42 |
| Base (no. interviewed) | 1297 (1622) | 53 (64) |

## Table 3.11

### Changes in family and household type by family type at the FFS

| Family/household type at FRS | Family type at FFS | | | |
| | Lone mother | Lone father | Two-parent family | All |
| | % | % | % | % |
|---|---|---|---|---|
| No change | 73 | 81 | 87 | 81 |
| Family type only : | | | | |
| Lone parent to two-parent (or vice versa) | 12 | 4 | 3 | 7 |
| No dependent children | 2 | 0 | 1 | 1 |
| Household type only : | | | | |
| Single- to multi-unit | 8 | 9 | 5 | 6 |
| Multi- to single-unit | 3 | 4 | 2 | 3 |
| Changes in both family and h/h | 2 | 2 | 2 | 2 |
| Total | 100 | 100 | 100 | 100 |
| Base (no. interviewed) | 813 (814) | 47 (49) | 1346 (1713) | 2209 (2651) |

## SUMMARY

The FFS was designed to be representative of low-income families with children. About 3,000 such families were interviewed and detailed information on income and expenditure was collected. The same families were re-interviewed one year later for the FRS. Of the FFS families almost a third were headed by a lone parent—most commonly a lone mother.

Looking at the characteristics of these low-income families shows that, as might be expected given the higher risk of poverty for lone mothers than for lone fathers, it is the latter rather than the former who stand out as being the most atypical group. However all the FFS families—whether lone mothers, lone fathers or couples—shared certain characteristics. In comparison with families in general they were more likely to have greater families responsibilities (younger children and larger families), they were also more likely to be local authority tenants and to be unemployed or out of the labour market.

Even during the relatively short time period of one year a number of the families experienced some change—sometimes more than one—in their status which would be likely to have some impact on their living standards. The lone mothers were the most volatile group with over a quarter (27 per cent) having a change in either marital status or household type or both. The younger lone mothers were the most likely to cease to be lone parents and equally younger couples were more likely to have separated than older couples. Families where the man was unemployed were especially likely to have experienced marital breakdown.

## Notes

1. Knight (1981) in the methodological report of the FFS discusses the decision to measure income relative to supplementary benefit as follows (p.4):

> There is no special validity in this method above other methods. It draws on a set of benefit rates whose level at the time might be said not only to reflect current political decisions but to be a product of past decisions too. They are however benefit rates of particular importance in being those to which the State would bring up the incomes of families in many circumstances. Indeed it is the fact that the main circumstances in which benefit rates do *not* set a floor to family income is when the family head is in full-time work, which makes the use of these benefit rates particularly appropriate for determining the scope of a survey commissioned by the Department that administers the benefit. Among its concerns will be even-handed treatment of those in and out of work, including problems of incentives to work created by a benefit not available to those in work.

2. The '140 per cent' line was first used by Abel-Smith and Townsend (1965) and they gave precisely the same reasons—that many recipients of supplementary benefit (or national assistance as it was then called) actually had incomes higher than the basic scale rates. The FFS was carried out in 1978/79 before the 1980 Social Security Act which abolished the discretionary 'exceptional needs payments' and 'exceptional circumstances additions' in favour of the 'additional requirements' and 'single payments' which are paid as a right to claimants in specified circumstances. However, it is still of course true that there are quite substantial variations in the incomes of supplementary benefit recipients (Millar, 1985).

3. However, as is apparent from the later analysis here and from other studies (Eekelaar and Maclean, 1986a and 1986b) maintenance can be an important source of income when received in addition to earnings. As information was available on receipt of maintenance it was possible to examine its importance to family income. What was not possible was to say what proportion of divorced/separated women were receiving maintenance.

4. These included analyses of the living standards of unemployed families (Bradshaw et al., 1983; Cooke, 1987); the economies of scale in large families (Godfrey and

Baldwin, 1983); the fuel expenditure of families (Wicks and Hutton, 1986) and debt (Hutton, 1986; Parker, 1986).

5.    Thanks to Ruth Hancock at the LSE, who was also analysing the data on behalf of DHSS (examining labour supply and the incentive effects of means-tested benefits) but who had obtained the data-tape from OPCS.

# 4 Incomes and living standards

This chapter looks in detail at the incomes and living standards of the lone parents at the time of the FFS. The first section of the chapter describes the composition of gross income and considers the relative importance of the various different sources of income—earnings, benefits and maintenance—to the total. The second section examines the level of income relative to supplementary benefit, describes the length of time the families had been living on a low income, and considers the value of income in kind. The third section of the chapter focuses on other indicators of living standards—expenditure, access to assets and savings and debts.

As described in Chapter Three for most of the detailed analysis the single-unit and multi-unit households were considered separately. In this chapter only the single-unit households are included. These comprise 77 per cent of all the lone-parent families in the FFS sample and 82 per cent of the two-parent families.

## GROSS WEEKLY INCOME

The main sources of income available to the lone-parent families can be divided into earnings, social security benefits, maintenance and other income (mainly from pensions or investments). This section examines the contribution of each of these in turn to the total gross weekly incomes of the families.

**Earnings**

As Table 4.1 shows, about a quarter of both the lone mothers and the lone fathers received some income from earnings. However, this represented a larger proportion of the total for the men than for the women. Only 7 per cent of the women received more than half of their gross incomes from earnings compared with 17 per cent of the men. Amongst those with some income from earnings the mean amount received by the women was £17.37 compared with £37.64 for the men. This was because the women were more likely than the men to be in part-time jobs. Their average normal weekly hours were 17.6 compared with 30.7 for the men. Moreover, about half of the employed women were also receiving social security benefits. Of those in employment, 9 per cent received family income supplement, 48 per cent received supplementary benefit and 4 per cent received a widows benefit.

Table 4.1

Gross earnings as a proportion of gross weekly income at the FFS: lone parents in single-unit households

| Proportion of total made up of earnings | Lone mothers % | Lone fathers % |
|---|---|---|
| 0% | 76 | 77 |
| Up to 10% | 4 | 0 |
| 10% to 24.9% | 8 | 1 |
| 25% to 49.9% | 6 | 5 |
| 50% to 74.9% | 4 | 7 |
| 75% to 99.9% | 3 | 7 |
| 100% | 0 | 3 |
| Total | 100 | 100 |
| Mean: those in receipt only | £17.37 | £37.64 |
| Mean: all | £4.15 | £8.59 |
| Base (no. interviewed) | 754 | 41 |
| | (835) | (43) |

The employed lone mothers were concentrated in semi-skilled jobs (42 per cent), unskilled jobs (20 per cent), clerical work (15 per cent) and shops (12 per cent). In comparison with average hourly earnings at that time the earnings of the FFS lone mothers were equivalent to about 23 per cent of those of all women in part-time manual jobs; and to about 42 per cent of average male manual hourly earnings.

## Social security benefits

Table 4.2 shows the contribution of social security benefits to total gross income. Almost all the lone parents had some income from benefits because the vast majority received child benefit. For almost half (46 per cent) of the lone mothers social security benefits were their only source of income, and a further 28 per cent were dependent on benefits for at least 75 per cent of their income. Lone fathers were more likely than lone mothers to be entirely dependent on benefits—65 per cent had no other sources of income apart from benefits.

Table 4.2

Social security benefits as a proportion of gross weekly income at the FFS: lone parents in single-unit households

| Proportion of total made up of earnings | Lone mothers % | Lone fathers % |
|---|---|---|
| 0% | 0 | 3 |
| Up to 10% | 1 | 3 |
| 10% to 24.9% | 8 | 7 |
| 25% to 49.9% | 9 | 4 |
| 50% to 74.9% | 8 | 5 |
| 75% to 99.9% | 28 | 13 |
| 100% | 46 | 65 |
| Total | 100 | 100 |
| Mean: those in receipt only | £31.49 | £32.86 |
| Mean: all | £31.49 | £32.05 |
| Base (no interviewed) | 754 | 41 |
| | (835) | (43) |

The type of benefits received are shown in Table 4.3. The majority of the lone parents were in receipt of supplementary benefit (78 per cent of the lone mothers and 68 per cent of the lone fathers). For both the men and women benefits made up, on average, about 80 per cent of total gross income, and supplementary benefit about 50 per cent. Child benefit adds the only other large component—contributing about 17 per cent and 20 per cent to the incomes of the lone mothers and the lone fathers respectively. Child benefit increase (the flat rate supplement to child benefit paid to lone parents which was renamed one-parent benefit in 1981) was received by only a quarter of the lone mothers and a third of the lone fathers. (The next chapter

59

discusses the contribution of child benefit to income in more detail and also considers the take-up rates of mean-tested benefits.)

## Table 4.3

### Type of social security benefits received at the FFS: lone parents in single- unit households

| | Lone mothers | | Lone fathers | |
|---|---|---|---|---|
| Benefits | % with income from: | Average ppn. of total gross income | % with income from | Average ppn. of total gross income |
| Child benefit | 99 | .170 | 95 | .200 |
| Child benefit increase [1] | 24 | .010 | 34 | .020 |
| Supplementary benefit | 78 | .560 | 68 | .490 |
| Family income supplement | 4 | .004 | 5 | .003 |
| Widows benefit | 5 | .030 | – | – |
| Rent rebate/allowance | 9 | .010 | 12 | .006 |
| Rate rebate | 10 | .004 | 12 | .003 |
| Other[2] | 36 | .010 | 39 | .090 |
| Total | | .800 | | .840 |
| Base (no. interviewed) | 754 (835) | | 41 (43) | |

1. Now known as one-parent benefit
2. Including retirement pensions, unemployment benefit, attendance allowance, mobility allowance, etc.

## Maintenance and other sources of income

Table 4.4 shows the contribution of maintenance and other sources of income, such as investment and pension income, to the total. Women in receipt of a widows benefit have been excluded from the maintenance figures. At most three in ten of the lone mothers were receiving some maintenance and the mean amount received by these women was £12.25.[1] Of those who received maintenance payments, 62 per cent were in receipt of supplementary benefit. For these women, therefore, the maintenance received would not have increased their incomes because the amount of supplementary benefit would have been reduced accordingly. Other sources of income rarely contributed more than 5 per cent of the total for either the lone mothers or the lone fathers.

## Table 4.4

### Maintenance and other income as a proportion of gross income at the FFS: lone parents in single-unit households

| | Maintenance | Other income | |
| | Lone mothers[1] | Lone mothers | Lone fathers |
| Proportion of total | % | % | % |
|---|---|---|---|
| 0% | 68 | 78 | 82 |
| Up to 5% | 4 | 17 | 12 |
| 5% to 9.9% | 2 | 2 | 3 |
| 10% to 24.9% | 11 | 2 | 3 |
| 25% to 49.9% | 8 | 1 | 0 |
| 50% to 74.9% | 5 | Ø | 0 |
| 75% to 99.9% | 3 | 0 | 0 |
| 100% | 0 | 0 | 0 |
| | | | |
| Total | 100 | 100 | 100 |
| | | | |
| Mean: those in receipt only | £12.25 | £2.04 | £3.32 |
| Mean: all | £3.74 | £0.45 | £0.59 |
| Base (no. interviewed) | 717 | 754 | 41 |
| | (795) | (835) | (43) |

Ø    Less than 1 per cent
1.    Excluding those receiving widows benefit

**The main source of gross income**

Thus it is clear that social security benefits were the most important source of income for lone parents. The main source of income (ie equivalent to more than 50 per cent of the total) was benefits for 83 per cent of the lone fathers and earnings for the remaining 17 per cent. For the lone mothers benefits were the main source for 77 per cent and for 60 per cent it was supplementary benefit that was the main source. Only 7 per cent had earnings as their main source and the same proportion had maintenance as their main source.

Among the lone mothers, there were a number of significant differences according to the characteristics of the women. Older women and women who owned their homes outright were the most likely to have widows benefits as their main source of income. For those employed for more than 24 hours per week earnings were most likely to be the main source. Nevertheless even for these women benefits remained very important —16 per cent had supplementary benefit, and 11 per cent had other benefits, as their main source. A quarter of the women employed for less than 24 hours had no main source of income—relying on a fairly even mixture of benefits, maintenance and earnings. Young women with young children and women living in local authority housing were more likely than average to be dependent on supplementary benefit for their main source of income. Women who were owner-occupiers or lived rent free were the most likely to have maintenance as their main source of income and for the latter it is possible that the rent-free accommodation is part of the maintenance agreement, but the information necessary to establish this is not available.

The composition of gross income for the two-parent families was very different from that of the lone parents (Table 4.5). The lone parents were about twice as likely as the two-parent families to be dependent on social security benefits as their main source of income. The type of social security benefit received was also different : 11 per cent of the two-parent families had unemployment benefit as their main source of income but this was true for none of the lone parents. Only 18 per cent of the two-parent families had supplementary benefit as their main source compared with 69 per cent of the lone mothers. Thus, while the low incomes of the lone-parent families were mainly the result of dependence upon benefits, for the two-parent families the reasons why the families had low incomes were more complex. Unemployment was a significant factor, with 32 per cent of the men being unemployed. In addition low earnings brought a substantial number of families into the sample. The men in the two-parent families earned on

Table 4.5

Main source of income at the FFS by family type: single-unit households

| Main source of income | Lone mothers % | Lone fathers % | Two-parent families % |
|---|---|---|---|
| Social security benefits | 77 | 83 | 39 |
| Earnings: man | – | 17 | 57 |
| : woman | 7 | – | 2 |
| Maintenance | 7 | – | – |
| Other | – | – | 1 |
| No main source | 8 | – | 1 |
| Total | 100 | 100 | 100 |
| Base (no. interviewed) | 754 | 41 | 1307 |
|  | (835) | (43) | (1688) |

average about 72 per cent of average male full-time hourly earnings (based on 1979 New Earnings Survey). In addition in only 10 per cent of the families were both parents employed compared with 53 per cent of all two-parent families with dependent children (1979 General Household Survey). As discussed in Chapter Three it was also the case that slightly more of the two-parent than of the lone-parent families were brought into the sample mainly because of high housing costs.

In order to make comparisons with published Family Expenditure Survey data 'normal' gross weekly income was also calculated (ie instead of current social security benefits previous earnings are used in the income calculation for those who have been away from work for less than 13 weeks). Table 4.6 compares the composition of normal gross income in the FFS and FES samples. Although in general dependence on benefits is high for lone mothers, the low-income lone mothers were considerably more likely to have benefits as their main source compared with lone mothers in general (80 per cent compared with 48 per cent). However, similar proportions had maintenance as their main source, underlining the fact that few lone mothers receive sufficient maintenance payments to provide an adequate level of income. The greater than average degree of dependency upon benefits was also apparent for the low-income lone fathers and for the two-parent families.

Table 4.6

Sources of normal gross weekly income: FFS and FES compared

| Main source of normal income | Lone mothers | | Lone fathers | | Two-parent families | |
| | FFS % | FES % | FFS % | FES % | FFS % | FES % |
| --- | --- | --- | --- | --- | --- | --- |
| Earnings | 9 | 44 | 24 | 70 | 68 | 95 |
| Benefits | 80 | 48 | 76 | 30 | 29 | 4 |
| Maintenance | 6 | 7 | – | – | – | – |
| Other | – | 1 | – | – | 1 | – |
| No main source | 5 | – | – | – | 2 | ∅ |
| Total | 100 | 100 | 100 | 100 | 100 | 100 |

∅   Less than 1 per cent

*Source for FES:* J. Popay et al., *One-Parent Families.* Study Commission on the Family 1983, Table 2 based on 1979 Family Expenditure Survey.

In relation to living standards it is net (or disposable) rather than gross income which is the most important. Net income has been defined here as gross income less tax, nationl insurance contributions, housing costs and work expenses. In fact for these families the levels of net and gross income were very similar, which would be expected given that so many of the families received the majority of their income from social security benefits. As Table 4.7 shows the level of net weekly income was very similar for the lone mothers and the lone fathers. However, the lone fathers were more likely than the lone mothers to have relatively low levels of income (17 per cent below £20 per week compared with 10 per cent) as well as relatively high levels of income (23 per cent above £40 per week compared with 15 per cent).

Table 4.7

Total net weekly income at the FFS: lone parents in single-unit households

| Total net weekly income | Lone mothers % | Lone fathers % |
|---|---|---|
| Up to £10 | 1 | 5 |
| £10.01 to £20 | 9 | 12 |
| £20.01 to £30 | 45 | 44 |
| £30.01 to £40 | 30 | 16 |
| £40.01 to £50 | 12 | 20 |
| £50.01 plus | 3 | – |
| Total | 100 | 100 |
| Median weekly income | 28.88 | 27.50 |
| Mean weekly income | 30.36 | 31.45 |
| Base (no. interviewed) | 754 | 41 |
| | (835) | (43) |

The level of total net weekly income varied with family size, such that those with larger families tended to have higher levels of total net income. Such a variation would be expected given that about three-quarters of the lone mothers were in receipt of supplementary benefit, which includes additions for dependent children. In fact, the pattern was the same for both those in receipt of supplementary benefit and those not in receipt. Receipt of child benefit probably accounts for this in part—as we have seen, child benefit contributed on average as much as nearly a fifth of the total gross incomes.

In order to compare the levels of income of different groups (eg earners and non-earners) it is therefore necessary to control for differences in family size, otherwise any observed differences may be the result of differences in the number and ages of the children rather than reflecting real differences between the sub-groups. In order to do this we calculated total net weekly income as a proportion of the appropriate supplementary benefit short-term scale rate for 1978/1979. As Table 4.8 shows, not surprisingly (given the high level of receipt of supplementary benefit) the majority of the families had incomes very close to supplementary benefit levels. The lone fathers tended to have slightly lower relative incomes than the lone mothers; of the lone fathers 23 per cent had incomes of less than 90 per cent of supplementary benefit compared with 13 per cent of the lone mothers. A small number of lone mothers had incomes which exceeded 140 per cent of supplementary benefit although the sample was designed to include only those with incomes below that level. As discussed in Chapter Three slight differences in the definition of income used here and in the sample selection would account for this.

Table 4.8

Income relative to supplementary benefit at the FFS: lone parents in single-unit households

| Net income relative to SB | Lone mothers % | Lone fathers % |
|---|---|---|
| Up to 90% | 13 | 23 |
| 90.1% to 110% | 42 | 45 |
| 110.1% to 120% | 20 | 10 |
| 120.1% to 130% | 23 | 22 |
| 140.1% plus | 3 | 0 |
| Total | 100 | 100 |
| Base (no. interviewed) | 754 | 41 |
| | (835) | (43) |

Table 4.9 shows how the level of relative income varied according to the sources of income. Widows had higher relative incomes than average, but the women with highest mean values were those whose incomes included

both earnings and maintenance, whether or not they received supplementary benefit. The women with the lowest mean values were those dependent on supplementary benefit only, maintenance only, or both supplementary benefit and maintenance.

Table 4.9

Income relative to supplementary benefit at the FFS by source of income: lone mothers in single-unit households

| Source of income | Mean value (S.D.) | | Proportion of all lone mothers % | Base (no. interviewed) | |
|---|---|---|---|---|---|
| In receipt of widows benefit | 117.4 | (21.2) | 5 | 37 | (40) |
| Not in receipt of a widows benefit and: | | | | | |
| SB only | 104.1 | (15.3) | 50 | 380 | (428) |
| SB, no earnings, maintenance | 105.6 | (17.3) | 16 | 120 | (127) |
| SB, earnings, no maintenance | 120.3 | (14.5) | 8 | 64 | (73) |
| SB, earnings, maintenance | 123.9 | (10.9) | 3 | 23 | (27) |
| Maintenance only | 105.6 | (21.6) | 5 | 36 | (38) |
| Earnings only | 109.0 | (23.0) | 5 | 36 | (39) |
| Earnings and maintenance | 123.6 | (25.9) | 6 | 48 | (53) |
| All with SB | 106.9 | (16.6) | 78 | 588 | (657) |
| All with earnings | 119.6 | (20.2) | 24 | 178 | (201) |
| All with maintenance | 111.5 | (21.3) | 30 | 230 | (249) |
| All lone mothers | 107.8 | (21.2) | 100 | 754 | (835) |

Thus, it is clear that, even within this sample drawn from a restricted income range, there were variations in the level of income according to the source of income received. Those in employment were the best-off and those on supplementary benefit were the worst-off. Being able to combine different sources—especially earnings and maintenance—provided the highest income levels. Thus there were differences in the characteristics of those with the highest and lowest incomes. Table 4.10 compares the characteristics of the lone mothers with incomes below 95 per cent of supplementary benefit and above 124 per cent (the top and bottom quintiles). With the exception of the number of dependent children all the differences were statistically significant at at least the 5 per cent level. Those with the lowest incomes were most likely to be young women with young children living in local authority rented accommodation, not in employment and

## Table 4.10

### Characteristics of lone mothers in the top and bottom quintiles of income relative to supplementary benefit at the FFS: single-unit households

| Characteristics | Bottom 20 per cent (income below 95% of supplementary benefit) % | Top 20 per cent (income above 124% supplementary benefit) % |
|---|---|---|
| Number of dependent children | | |
| 1 | 39 | 41 |
| 2 | 34 | 37 |
| 3 | 17 | 18 |
| 4 plus | 9 | 4 |
| Total | 100 | 100 |
| Age of youngest child | | |
| 0–4 | 52 | 23 |
| 5–9 | 27 | 40 |
| 10 plus | 20 | 37 |
| Total | 100 | 100 |
| Age of mother | | |
| Under 20 | 4 | 0 |
| 20–24 | 29 | 9 |
| 25–29 | 20 | 20 |
| 30–39 | 32 | 46 |
| 40–49 | 11 | 17 |
| 50 plus | 4 | 8 |
| Total | 100 | 100 |
| Tenure | | |
| Rented    : local authority | 72 | 56 |
|       : private (unfurnished) | 9 | 9 |
|       : private (furnished) | 8 | 2 |
| Owner-occupier   : mortgage | 8 | 18 |
|       : outright | 0 | 6 |
| Rent free | 4 | 10 |
| Total | 100 | 100 |
| Proportion with income from | | |
| earnings | 10 | 57 |
| maintenance | 27 | 51 |
| widows benefit | 3 | 9 |
| supplementary benefit | 81 | 10 |
| Net income as a proportion of supplementary benefit (mean) | 80.2 | 133.9 |
| Median level of total net weekly income | £21.97 | £36.06 |
| Base (no. interviewed) | 150 | 150 |
| | (169) | (151) |

67

receiving supplementary benefit. Those with the highest incomes were most likely to be women aged over 30 with children at school and living in owner-occupied or rent free accommodation. They were more likely to be in paid work and/or receiving maintenance and were therefore less likely to be receiving supplementary benefit. The median net weekly incomes of those in the bottom quintile was £21.97 compared with £36.06 for these in the highest quintile, although the number of children in the families was very similar.

Just as the main sources of income of lone-parent families were different from those of two-parent families, so was the level of their incomes relative to supplementary benefit. As Table 4.11 shows, the two-parent families tended to have higher relative incomes than the lone-parent families. Of the former 41 per cent had net incomes above 120 per cent of supplementary benefit compared with 26 per cent of the lone mothers and 22 per cent of the lone fathers. Thus, not only were lone parents over-represented in this low-income sample, within it, they were more likely to have lower incomes.

Table 4.11

Income relative to supplementary benefit at the FFS by family type: single-unit households

| Income relative to SB | Lone mothers % | Lone fathers % | Two-parent families % |
|---|---|---|---|
| Up to 90% | 13 | 23 | 15 |
| 90.1% to 110% | 42 | 45 | 32 |
| 110.1% to 120% | 20 | 10 | 12 |
| 120.1% to 140% | 23 | 22 | 32 |
| 140.1% plus | 3 | 0 | 9 |
| Total | 100 | 100 | 100 |
| Mean value: income relative to SB | 107.8 | 97.6 | 110.7 |
| Mean value: cash | £30.17 | £29.43 | £43.98 |
| Base (no. interviewed) | 754 (835) | 41 (43) | 1307 (1688) |

The living standards of the families would be affected not only by the level of income relative to needs but also by the length of time they had been living on such income levels. There is no direct information on this from the

FFS but it is possible to examine this indirectly by two methods. First, by comparing 'current' income (as received at the time of the interview) and 'normal' income (including usual earnings in last job for those who have been out of work for less than 13 weeks at the time of the interview). For the vast majority (90 per cent) of the lone parents current and normal incomes were the same (again this is because the majority of the lone parents were supplementary benefit recipients). Among the two-parent families however 35 per cent had lower current incomes than normal incomes, implying that the length of time on low incomes was likely to have been shorter than for the lone parents.

Secondly, looking at weeks on benefit in the previous year, Table 4.12 shows that not only were the lone parents much more likely than the two-parent families to be benefit recipients, but they had also spent more time on benefit. The lone mothers were four times (60 per cent compared with 15 per cent) as likely as the two-parent families to have been in receipt of benefit for at least 12 months.

Table 4.12

Receipt of benefit in the 12 months preceding the FFS by family type: single-unit households

| Receipt of Sup. Ben. and/or Unemployment Benefit | Lone mothers % | Lone fathers % | Two-parent families % |
|---|---|---|---|
| No receipt in previous 12 months | 20 | 33 | 58 |
| Some, but not currently | 3 | 0 | 9 |
| Currently in receipt : up to 13 weeks | 6 | 8 | 8 |
| : 13 to 26 weeks | 4 | 8 | 4 |
| : 26 to 39 weeks | 4 | 2 | 4 |
| : 39 to 51 weeks | 4 | 0 | 2 |
| : 52 weeks | 60 | 48 | 15 |
| Total | 100 | 100 | 100 |
| Base (no. interviewed) | 754 (835) | 41 (43) | 1307 (1688) |

The comparisons made so far have all been in relation to the levels of income support implied by supplementary benefit. In order to examine how these families compared with the population in general Table 4.13 compares their gross total weekly incomes with average gross weekly earnings for men in 1979. On this measure there was a dramatic difference between the incomes of the FFS families and the earnings of men in general. None of the lone parents had gross weekly *incomes* which were as high as the gross weekly *earnings* of half of all full-time employed men (who did not necessarily have dependent children and who may have had other sources of income). Only 6 per cent of the lone mothers and none of the lone fathers had gross incomes which were as high as the gross earnings of nine-tenths of men in full-time work. As with the other measures we have used, the two-parent families were better off than the lone-parent families, although their situations relative to those of employed men in general were also poor.

Table 4.13

Gross weekly incomes as a proportion of male gross earnings 1979: single-unit households

| | Lone mothers | | Lone fathers | | Two-parent families | |
| | Median[1] | Lowest decile | Median | Lowest decile | Median | Lowest decile |
| Income relative to earnings | % | % | % | % | % | % |
|---|---|---|---|---|---|---|
| Up to 50% | 76 | 15 | 63 | 14 | 19 | 2 |
| 50.1% to 75% | 22 | 56 | 34 | 49 | 41 | 14 |
| 75.1% to 100% | 2 | 24 | 3 | 25 | 30 | 27 |
| 100.1% to 125% | Ø | 5 | 0 | 9 | 8 | 25 |
| 125.1% to 150% | 0 | 1 | 0 | 3 | 2 | 18 |
| 150.1% plus | 0 | Ø | 0 | 0 | 0 | 13 |
| Total | 100 | 100 | 100 | 100 | 100 | 100 |
| Base (no. interviewed) | 754 | | 41 | | 1307 | |
| | (835) | | (43) | | (1688) | |

Ø    Less than 1 per cent

1.    Median male gross earnings and lowest decile male gross earnings

   *Source: New Earnings Survey* 1979, Part A, Table 22. Full-time men, aged 21 and over, including those whose pay was affected by absence. Median £91.80, lowest decile £59.00.

## The costs of working

About seven in ten of the employed lone mothers had some deductions from their gross earnings (the number of employed lone fathers is too small for a similar analysis). A third (34 per cent) were paying national insurance contributions, and a slightly smaller proportion (30 per cent) were paying income tax. The most common of the other work expenses were travel costs, paid by almost half of the women and usually amounting to less than 20 per cent of their gross earnings. Only 15 per cent had some child-care costs but, for those who did pay for child-care, this represented the largest single expense. For 44 per cent of the employed women total work expenses were under a fifth of their gross earnings, and for 26 per cent work expenses were between a fifth and a half of gross earnings. In terms of their total gross incomes, about half (48 per cent) of the employed women spent up to a tenth of their gross incomes on work expenses, 9 per cent spent between a tenth and a fifth and 12 per cent between a fifth and a half.

Of the employed lone mothers 40 per cent paid either tax, national insurance contributions or both. Of these women 24 per cent received a rate rebate, 25 per cent a rent rebate, 18 per cent family income supplement and 19 per cent supplementary benefit. In all six out of ten of those with tax and/or national insurance payments were at the same time receiving some income from means-tested benefits, thus illustrating the extent to which low-income lone parents are likely to suffer the consequences of the 'poverty trap'.

In the two-parent families 14 per cent of the women were employed and gave details of their earnings. Of these women 12 per cent had child-care expenses (compared with 15 per cent of employed lone mothers). The amount paid was never more than £5.95 per week and on average they paid £1.86 per week (compared with £3.75 for lone mothers). About six in ten of the employed married women had husbands who were also in paid work—of their combined gross earnings child-care costs usually amounted to less than 5 per cent, with only a handful paying between 5 and 10 per cent of their combined earnings for child-care. Thus work expenses in relation to income were substantially higher for the lone mothers than for the two-parent families.

## Housing rebates

Most of the lone parents were receiving some help with housing costs. The women in receipt of supplementary benefit (78 per cent of all the lone mothers) would usually have had their housing costs met in full.[2] For those not in receipt of supplementary benefit help with housing costs was, at that time, available in the form of rent rebates (for local authority tenants), rent allowances (for private tenants) and rate rebates (for both tenants and owner-occupiers). As Table 4.14 shows, among the lone mothers not receiving supplementary benefit, the majority (69 per cent) of the local authority tenants were receiving some help with their housing costs. Council tenants generally pay their rent and rates together and therefore it is surprising that fewer reported receipt of a rate rebate than of a rent rebate. It may be that this is due to mis-reporting because council tenants often find it difficult to distinguish between the two rebates (Bradshaw and Beadham, 1984). Among those who reported receiving rebates, on average, about three-quarters of their housing costs were rebated. About half of the women in private unfurnished accommodation were receiving some help with housing costs, but none of those in private furnished accommodation were receiving any help despite having slightly higher levels of housing costs. The owner-occupiers could only be entitled to the less valuable rate rebates; so although just over half of those with mortgages were receiving rate rebates, on average, these amounted to only 17 per cent of their total weekly housing costs.

Table 4.14

Rent and rate rebates by tenure for lone mothers not in receipt of supplementary benefit at the FFS: single-unit households

| | | Tenure | | |
| | | | Owner-occupier | |
| Housing benefits | LA tenant | Private tenant - unfurnished | Mortgage | Outright |
| --- | --- | --- | --- | --- |
| Rent rebate/allowance | | | | |
| Proportion in receipt | 69% | 38% | – | – |
| Mean weekly value[1] | £5.15 | £4.07 | – | – |
| Rate rebate | | | | |
| Proportion in receipt | 55% | 33% | 53% | 38% |
| Mean weekly value | £2.04 | £1.12 | £1.63 | £1.47 |
| Rent and/or rate rebate | | | | |
| Proportion in receipt | 69% | 50% | 53% | 38% |
| Mean weekly value | £6.74 | £3.79 | £1.63 | £1.47 |
| Average proportion of total housing costs rebated | 73.9% | 52.1% | 16.8% | 58.3% |
| Base (no. interviewed) | 75 (86) | 18 (18) | 32 (33) | 16 (19) |

1. Among those in receipt in each case.

## Income in kind
The analysis so far has concentrated on cash income. However income in kind, in the form of fringe benefits from employment and the state benefits of free milk and free school meals are also relevant to the living standards

of the families. Receipt of fringe benefits from employment was in fact fairly limited: only 3 per cent of the lone mothers (12 per cent of those in employment) received any of these benefits (which included free meals, free food, free goods and free coal and coke). Five per cent of the two-parent families were receiving fringe benefits from employment.

The majority of the lone mothers (78 per cent) received some state benefits in kind. Of the lone mothers with children aged five and over, 63 per cent received free school meals for all their children at school,[3] and 81 per cent of those with children under five received free welfare milk. Families in receipt of supplementary benefit are entitled to these two benefits automatically. Of lone mothers in receipt of supplementary benefit 67 per cent were taking up their entitlement to free school meals and 88 per cent their entitlement to free welfare milk.

It is debatable whether the value of these benefits should be added to net weekly income. Although they improve living standards they are not disposable in the sense that the families have command over them. However, in order to make some assessment of the impact of income in kind Table 4.15 shows the effect of adding the imputed value (which in the case of free school meals includes the value of the exchequer subsidy) of these to the total net weekly income and then recalculating income relative to supplementary

Table 4.15

Income relative to supplementary benefit at the FFS including the imputed value of income in kind: single-unit households

| Income relative to SB | Lone mothers | | Lone fathers | | Two-parent families | |
|---|---|---|---|---|---|---|
| | Actual | Plus income in kind | Actual | Plus income in kind | Actual | Plus income in kind |
| | % | % | % | % | % | % |
| Up to 90% | 13 | 8 | 23 | 18 | 15 | 11 |
| 90.1% to 110% | 42 | 27 | 45 | 31 | 32 | 27 |
| 110.1% to 120% | 20 | 20 | 10 | 19 | 12 | 15 |
| 120.1% to 140% | 23 | 33 | 22 | 18 | 32 | 34 |
| 140.1% to 160% | 2 | 12 | 0 | 12 | 8 | 12 |
| 160.1% plus | 1 | 1 | 0 | 2 | 1 | 1 |
| Total | 100 | 100 | 100 | 100 | 100 | 100 |
| Mean value | £30.17 | £32.99 | £29.43 | £31.63 | £43.98 | £45.77 |
| Base | 754 | 754 | 41 | 41 | 1307 | 1307 |
| | (835) | (835) | (43) | (43) | (1688) | (1688) |

73

benefit. Adding the value of income in kind made quite a substantial difference, particularly for the lone fathers, 14 per cent of whom had incomes above 140 per cent of supplementary allowance when income in kind is included compared with none when only cash income is considered. Similarly among the lone mothers the proportion with income above 140 per cent rises from 3 per cent to 13 per cent when income in kind is included. Most of the increase can be attributed to the state benefits as so few received employment-related income in kind. The effect on the income of the two-parent families was smaller and adding income in kind bought the incomes of the lone-parent and two-parent families closer together. This was because the lone-parent families were both more likely to be receiving these benefits and the mean imputed value of the state benefits was higher for them (£3.51 compared with £2.94). Also, because their incomes were generally lower, adding the value of these benefits had a more significant effect on the incomes of the lone parents than of the two-parent families.

## LIVING STANDARDS

Having examined the level and sources of income of the FFS families in the previous section here we examine other indicators of the living standards of the families—expenditure and access to consumer assets. These give a more complete picture of the living standards of the families than simply considering income and show the extent to which low income translates into a restricted standard of living.

### Expenditure

Table 4.16 shows the mean level of cash expenditure on each of the eleven main commodity groups. In cash terms the total expenditure of the lone mothers was, of course, lower than that of the two-parent families reflecting their lower incomes. For cash expenditure the differences were particularly striking for transport (only £2.00 for the lone mothers compared with £7.74 for the two-parent families). As the ratios of the lone mothers' expenditure to that of the two-parent families shows, the degree to which expenditure differed varied for the main commodity groups. Thus, while overall the lone mothers' expenditure was equivalent to 0.61 of the two-parent families, their expenditure was closer to that of the two-parent families for housing (0.74), fuel (0.82) and clothing and footwear (0.73). The biggest differences between the two groups were for alcohol (0.14), transport (0.26) and to a lesser extent tobacco (0.50).

Looking at the proportion of total expenditure allocated to the main commodity groups then both the lone mothers and the two-parent families spend about a third of their income on food. This is very high compared with the average of all families with children, where the figure is nearer to one quarter. In terms of the type of food purchased (meat, vegetables, bread etc) both family types allocated their food expenditure in very similar ways. Meat and fish were the main items (accounting for about a quarter of all food expenditure) followed by bread and potatoes and dairy products. In this allocation of food expenditure the FFS families were very similar to all families with children.

Table 4.16

Expenditure on main commodity groups by family type: single-unit households

| Commodity | Mean Expenditure (£s) | | | As a proportion of total expenditure | |
| | Lone mothers £s | Two-parent families £s | Ratio | Lone mothers % | Two-parent families % |
| --- | --- | --- | --- | --- | --- |
| Food | 13.38 | 20.97 | 0.64 | 31.5 | 31.4 |
| Housing | 8.22 | 10.55 | 0.74 | 21.4 | 16.7 |
| Transport | 2.00 | 7.74 | 0.26 | 4.0 | 9.6 |
| Fuel | 4.58 | 5.60 | 0.82 | 11.5 | 9.2 |
| Clothing and footwear | 3.56 | 4.86 | 0.73 | 7.2 | 6.2 |
| Services | 2.83 | 4.46 | 0.63 | 6.6 | 6.2 |
| Durables | 1.97 | 4.04 | 0.49 | 4.5 | 5.0 |
| Other h/h goods | 3.27 | 4.96 | 0.66 | 7.4 | 6.9 |
| Tobacco | 1.69 | 3.35 | 0.50 | 4.1 | 5.0 |
| Alcohol | 0.32 | 2.20 | 0.14 | 0.7 | 2.7 |
| Miscellaneous | 0.58 | 0.66 | 0.88 | 1.2 | 0.9 |
| Total | 42.39 | 69.21 | 0.61 | 100 | 100 |
| Base (no. interviewed) | 754 (835) | 1307 (1688) | | 754 (835) | 1307 (1688) |

The lone mothers and the two-parent families also spend similar proportions on durable goods, services (ie items such as television licenses and rental, subscriptions, postage, telephone charges) and other household goods (ie items such as cleaning materials, toiletries, newspapers, pet food). This is perhaps not surprising—such items are more likely to be bought on a household basis than an individual basis and hence the lone mothers would not save by having only one adult in the family. The differences between the lone mothers and the two-parent families in cash spending are reflected in the proportions of expenditure devoted to particular groups of goods: the lone mothers spend a significantly higher proportion of their incomes on housing, fuel, clothing and footwear and a significantly lower proportion on transport, tobacco and alcohol.

## Assets

Table 4.17 compares the access to consumer assets. In comparison with all families with children the FFS families were less likely to have access to consumer assets. And among the FFS families the lone mothers were worse off in terms of access to assets than the two-parent families. Particularly striking are the low proportions of lone mothers with a car (9 per cent compared with 52 per cent of the two-parent families) and a telephone (39 per cent compared with 50 per cent of the two-parent families). The lack of these two items suggests that the lone mothers may be more socially isolated than the two-parent families. Only four per cent of the lone mothers had all six items listed compared with 22 per cent of the two-parent families. The lone fathers were more likely than the lone mothers to have access to a car but less likely to have household goods such as washing machines and fridges.

Table 4.17

Access to consumer assets by family type: single-unit households

| Proportion with: | FFS families | | All families[1] with children (FES) | |
| | Lone mothers % | Two-parent families % | Lone parents % | Two-parent families % |
| --- | --- | --- | --- | --- |
| Telephone | 39 | 50 | 62 | 74 |
| Television | 97 | 97 | 95 | 98 |
| Washing machine | 69 | 84 | 81 | 94 |
| Fridge/freezer | 88 | 92 | 95 | 98 |
| Car | 9 | 52 | 28 | 76 |
| Central heating | 45 | 47 | 55 | 65 |
| Base (no. interviewed) | 754 (835) | 1307 (1688) | 233 | 937 |

1.   *Family Expenditure Survey 1979*, Table 5.

## Patterns of expenditure

This section examines in more detail what the families did and, equally importantly, did not spend their money on. Expenditure consists of both current expenditure (eg housing, food) and items of irregular expenditure (eg durable goods, clothing). Families with constrained budgets might be expected to have less resources to devote to irregular expenditure or to non-essential items. For half of the main commodity groups at least 95 per cent of all families had some recorded expenditure. Table 4.18 shows the proportions spending on the remaining commodity groups and the average amount spent. Apart from clothing and footwear, in each case significantly lower proportions of lone mothers than of two-parent families had recorded any expenditure on these items. Only 26 per cent of the lone mothers had any recorded spending on alcohol compared with 63 per cent of the two-parent families, and the amount spent (even taking into account the difference in the number of adults) was substantially less. However, although lone mothers were less likely to be spending on tobacco, amongst those who did the amount spent was greater taking into account the number of adults in the family. The difference in transport expenditure is partly due to the fact that the two-parent families were more likely to incur travel to work costs than the lone mothers (38 per cent compared with 12 per cent).

Table 4.18

Expenditure on selected commodity groups: single-unit households

| Goods | Lone mothers | | Two-parent families | |
|---|---|---|---|---|
| | % spending | mean amount (£s) spenders only | % spending | mean amount (£s) spenders only |
| Alcohol | 26 | 1.22 | 63 | 3.22 |
| Tobacco | 61 | 2.77 | 71 | 4.70 |
| Clothing and footwear | 79 | 4.49 | 82 | 5.91 |
| Durable goods | 75 | 2.63 | 86 | 4.67 |
| Transport | 83 | 2.42 | 94 | 8.25 |

An alternative way of considering the question of whether expenditure was constrained is to examine the proportion of expenditure devoted to current necessities, and thus how much discretionary expenditure the families had. There is of course a problem in deciding which items should be regarded as necessities. Food, fuel and housing are usually regarded as essential items. However, if we consider items on which the vast majority (at least 95 per cent) of the families were spending this would suggest that we also include household goods and services as essential spending. As Table 4.19 shows expenditure on food, fuel and housing accounted for, on average, 64.4 per cent of the lone mothers' expenditure. This was significantly higher than the proportion which the two-parent families devoted to these items (57.3 per cent). Twice the proportion of lone mothers than of two-parent families (37 per cent compared with 18 per cent) were spending at least 70 per cent of their total expenditure on food, fuel and housing. Only one in six were spending less than half of the total on these items compared with one in three of the two-parent families. Using the wider definition of essentials there were also significant differences between the lone mothers and the two-parent families. About three-quarters of the lone mothers were devoting at least 70 per cent of their total expenditure to these items compared with just over half of the two-parent families.

Table 4.19

Proportion of total expenditure devoted to essentials by family type:
single-unit households

| Essentials | Lone mothers % | Two-parent families % |
|---|---|---|
| Food, fuel, housing as a proportion of total expenditure | | |
| Up to 50% | 17 | 29 |
| 50.1% to 70% | 47 | 53 |
| 70.1% plus | 37 | 18 |
| Total | 100 | 100 |
| Mean proportion | 64.4% | 57.3% |
| Food, fuel, housing, services, other household goods as a proportion of total expenditure | | |
| Up to 50% | 2 | 7 |
| 50.1% to 70% | 22 | 38 |
| 70.1% plus | 76 | 55 |
| Total | 100 | 100 |
| Mean proportion | 78.4% | 70.5% |
| Base (no. interviewed) | 754 (835) | 1307 (1688) |

Thus the overall comparison between lone mothers and two-parent families suggests that the former do have a larger proportion of their expenditure committed to current essential spending and hence have less to spend on other items. These other items may of course also be 'essentials', although spending on them may only be occasional.

If we look within the family type groups in order to examine why some families devote more to food, fuel and housing than other families then some interesting differences emerge. Taking the lone mothers first, as Table 4.20 shows, the mean levels of equivalent current net income varied very little whether expenditure on food, fuel and housing was low (up to 50 per cent of the total) medium (between 50 per cent and 70 per cent) or high (70 per cent plus). By contrast, the levels of total expenditure varied quite considerably: there was a difference of about £17 in the equivalent expenditure of the low and high groups but only a difference of about £2 in their equivalent net incomes. Only a small part of this difference was actually the result of differences in cash spending on the essential items of food, fuel and housing. Food expenditure hardly varied but those with a high proportion of their expenditure devoted to essentials were spending more than the others on fuel and housing. However a large part of the difference seems to have been the result of occasional (probably lump-sum) purchases—clothing and footwear and durable goods. Taking these items out of total expenditure then the difference in equivalent expenditure between the high and low groups fall from about £17 to about £8.

Thus it is appears that where a low proportion of total expenditure was devoted to essentials, rather than this being the result of substantially lower cash spending on essentials, it was more likely to be the result of spending on occasional items and this spending was not apparently financed through current income. This could suggest that, at these income levels, it is difficult to finance such expenditure out of current income. The additional expenditure could have been financed through saving or borrowing (from others or from future income) and it is interesting to note that the lone mothers with low expenditure on essentials (ie who were apparently more likely to have made large purchases) were more likely to be employed (38 per cent) and less likely to be receiving supplementary benefit (58 per cent) than the families with a high proportion devoted to essentials (13 per cent of whom were employed and 90 per cent were receiving supplementary benefit). This suggests that supplementary benefit recipients may be more constrained to live within their current incomes and hence less likely to be able to devote any expenditure to occasional items. It should be remembered that occasional does not necessarily mean inessential—replacements of clothing or indeed furniture will be essential at some time for everyone.

For the two-parent families a similar pattern was clear, and again the group with a low proportion devoted to essentials were more likely to have an employed head (71 per cent compared with 40 per cent of those with a high proportion devoted to current essentials) and were less likely to be receiving supplementary benefit (12 per cent compared with 44 per cent).

Table 4.20

Income and expenditure by expenditure on essentials: lone mothers in single-unit households

| | Spending on food, fuel and housing | | |
| Income/expenditure levels | Low (up to 50%) | Mid (50% to 70%) | High (70% plus) |
|---|---|---|---|
| Equivalent:[1] | | | |
| Mean current net income | 31.45 | 29.60 | 29.01 |
| Mean total expenditure | 43.62 | 31.76 | 26.16 |
| Mean difference income | −12.17 | −2.15 | +2.85 |
| Mean (equivalent) amounts spent on | | | |
| Food | 9.87 | 9.91 | 9.41 |
| Fuel | 3.30 | 3.30 | 3.75 |
| Housing | 5.04 | 6.03 | 7.17 |
| Total | 18.21 | 19.24 | 20.33 |
| Proportions spending on | % | % | % |
| Services | 100 | 98 | 92 |
| Other household goods | 97 | 97 | 91 |
| Clothing and footwear | 94 | 84 | 66 |
| Durable goods | 89 | 81 | 62 |
| Transport | 89 | 89 | 73 |
| Alcohol | 44 | 32 | 11 |
| Tobacco | 67 | 63 | 56 |
| Mean (equivalent) expenditure excluding durable goods, clothing and footwear | 32.98 | 27.74 | 24.76 |
| (Proportion of families) | (17%) | (47%) | (37%) |
| Base (no. interviewed) | 126 (129) | 254 (389) | 275 (317) |

1.   All income and expenditure figures are equivalent to control for differences in family size.

80

As described above the lone mothers are less likely to have access to a car and a telephone and were spending substantially less on transport than the two-parent families. This suggests that lone mothers might be more socially isolated, and this seems to be the case when we consider spending on 'social' items—holidays, hobbies, entertainment, newspapers, transport and a telephone. Only 29 per cent of the lone mothers had spent any money on entertainment compared with 40 per cent of the two-parent families. For both the groups the average amount spent (0.77p for the lone mothers, £1.03 for the two-parent families) would scarcely cover one visit to the cinema. The spending on meals out was similarly low. Altogether 29 per cent of the lone mothers had no expenditure at all on entertainment, meals out, alcohol, holidays or hobbies and 10 per cent had spent on three or more of the five considered. By contrast 28 per cent of the two-parent families had spent on three or more of the items and only 13 per cent had not spent on any. Nineteen per cent of the lone mothers had no daily newspaper, 17 per cent had spent nothing on travel during the survey period and 61 per cent had no telephone. (The respective figures for two-parent families were 9 per cent, 6 per cent and 50 per cent.)

On most of these indicators the lone parents therefore appear to have been worse-off than the two-parent families. However among the two-parent families there is the group who might be expected to be particularly badly-off—unemployed families in receipt of supplementary benefit. These families—unlike the lone parents—are never entitled to the long-term rate (which at the time of the FFS/FRS was payable after two years on benefit). A quarter (25 per cent) of the two-parent families were on supplementary benefit compared with over three-quarters (78 per cent) of the lone mothers, and Table 4.21 shows how these two groups compared in terms of the main indicators of living standards. The two-parent families on benefit were clearly worse off than the two-parent families not on benefit (as can be seen by comparison with earlier tables). However there was little difference among the supplementary benefit recipients—the lone mothers and the two-parent families seem to have been about equally hard-pressed. Among the families on benefit the lone mothers did tend to have slightly higher incomes than the two-parent families (a mean of 106.9 per cent compared with 97.0 per cent) and it might therefore be appropriate to control for this when comparing the living standards of those on benefit. However comparing families in the range of 90 to 110 per cent of supplementary benefit (49 per cent of the lone mothers, 70 per cent of the two-parent families) the results are almost exactly the same as those shown in Table 4.21. The two-parent families were still more likely than the lone mothers to have a washing machine and a car. Otherwise there were no significant differences.

Table 4.21

Expenditure and access to assets by family type for supplementary benefit
recipients: single-unit households

| Assets and expenditure | Lone mothers % | | Two-parent families % | |
|---|---|---|---|---|
| **Access to assets** | | | | |
| Telephone | 34 | | 29 | |
| Television | 96 | | 96 | |
| Washing machine | 67 | | 75 | |
| Fridge | 86 | | 83 | |
| Car | 5 | | 19 | |
| Central Heating | 45 | | 36 | |
| **Expenditure on essentials as a proportion of total expenditure** | | | | |
| Housing | 24.2 | ⎫ | 19.7 | ⎫ |
| Fuel | 11.7 | ⎬ 66.5 | 11.4 | ⎬ 63.9 |
| Food | 30.6 | ⎭ | 32.9 | ⎭ |
| **Proportion spending on 'single' items** | | | | |
| Entertainment | 27 | | 26 | |
| Meals out | 54 | | 54 | |
| Drinks | 24 | | 51 | |
| Holidays | 1 | | 1 | |
| Hobbies | 1 | | 1 | |
| Newspapers | 81 | | 88 | |
| Base (no. interviewed) | 588 (657) | | 311 (427) | |

## SUMMARY

The lone parents in the FFS were characterised by a very high degree of
dependence on supplementary benefit. For seven in ten of the lone mothers
supplementary benefit was the main source of income and three-quarters of
those receiving supplementary benefit had been in receipt for at least 12
months. The minority who were in employment had lower than average
earnings and most were also receiving some social security benefits (apart
from child benefit) in addition to their earnings. Maintenance was only
rarely a main source of income and two-thirds of those receiving maintenance
were also on supplementary benefit and hence had no financial gain from the
maintenance.

The two-parent families were less likely than the lone parents to be
supplementary benefit recipients, with unemployment, low earnings and

dependence on only one wage earner the main causes of low incomes for these families. Even within the limited range of income in the sample some groups were better off than others and the two-parent families tended to have slightly higher relative incomes than the lone parents. Among the lone mothers the worst off were young women with young children, living in rented accommodation and solely dependent on supplementary benefit. The better off were older women with older children who were more likely to have incomes from sources other than, or in addition to, supplementary benefit—earnings, widows benefits or maintenance. For all families the value of income in kind from state benefits would have meant that living standards were rather higher than was implied by considering only income levels.

Most of the current expenditure of these families was devoted to the basic essentials of food, fuel and housing. This was particularly likely to be the case for the lone mothers, who were spending almost two-thirds of their total expenditure on these items. Current income was apparently insufficient to cover the purchase of larger items. All the families (and especially the lone mothers) were less likely than families in general to have access to consumer assets. Many were not spending at all on leisure or social activities, indicating some degree of social isolation, especially for the lone mothers, as a consequence of their low incomes.

The main item of 'inessential' expenditure was on tobacco. Sixty-one per cent of the lone mothers and 71 per cent of the two-parent families recorded expenditure on tobacco. However the amounts involved were not particularly large (six or seven per cent of total expenditure for those who smoked). In addition 63 per cent of the two-parent families and 26 per cent of the lone mothers recorded some expenditure on alcohol. The two-parent families were also more likely to have a car than the lone mothers. These differences between the two family types can perhaps be attributed to the fact that the two-parent families included a man while the lone-mother families did not. This is likely to affect patterns of expenditure and consumption (Charles and Kerr, 1986; Dale, 1986; Graham, 1987) but unfortunately we do not have the data necessary to explore how expenditure was allocated within the family.

## Notes

1.  Maintenance payments were not coded separately in the FFS but altogether in one category were : allowances from friends or relatives; alimony; separation allowance; and allowances for foster children other than from a local authority. It seems very unlikely that payments other than alimony would have been very common and therefore this category has been taken to represent maintenance payments. It may however slightly overestimate the amount of maintenance received by the women.

2. Those paying both interest and principal mortgage repayments would however have only the interest part of the repayment met under the supplementary benefit scheme. In addition, for those renting levels of rent deemed to be excessive are not paid in full.

3. The estimate of the number in receipt of free school meals includes only those who were receiving free meals for all of their children, not those who were receiving free meals for some but not others. These figures do not represent an estimate of take-up. When the FFS was carried out a related survey (based on the original sample drawn from the Child Benefit register before the income sift was applied) was conducted in order to estimate take-up of free school meals. The take-up of free school meals for lone parents eligible through receipt of supplementary benefit or family income supplement was estimated to be 74 per cent, and for those eligible on low income grounds to be 31 per cent (Wilson, 1981).

# 5 Dependence on the state

State benefits were clearly a major source of income for these lone parents. As the previous chapter showed the majority were supplementary benefit recipients, but even among those who were not, state benefits were still an important component of their total incomes. This chapter looks at financial dependence on the state from two perspectives. The first section of the chapter concentrates on the 'working families'—the families not in receipt of supplementary benefit—and compares the support given by, on the one hand, the universal child benefit scheme and, on the other hand, the selective support through means-tested benefits. The aim of the analysis is to examine which of these two methods of support is of most value to these poor working families. The second section of the chapter concentrates on receipt of supplementary benefit and specifically at movements on and off benefit during the two years of the study in order to examine the extent of 'welfare dependency' the lone parents experienced.

## STATE SUPPORT FOR WORKING FAMILIES

The arguments about the relative merits of, on the one hand, selective support through means-tested benefits and, on the other, universal support through the child benefit scheme, are many and complex. At the centre of the pro-selective case is the argument that means-tested benefits are the most effective and efficient way to provide income support, that they ensure that resources go to those most in need and that they do not waste resources by paying benefits to those not in need of additional help. Implicit or explicit in this argument is the view that the primary or even the only function of social security is the relief of poverty. Thus, Dilnot, Kay and Morris (1985, p.43):

> The objectives of any social security system are many and complex . . .
> But it is for its effects on poverty that the system should, we believe, principally be judged.

The pro-universal arguments are, perhaps, less immediately striking. Those in favour of an enhanced role for child benefit stress the importance of horizontal as well as vertical re-distribution, the value of child benefit to mothers as it is of the few benefits paid directly to women,[1] the problems of the 'poverty-trap' caused by means-tested benefits, and the persistent problem of the non-take-up of means-tested benefits. As regards current government policy the selective approach is very much to the fore. Following the 1985 review of social security (fully implemented in 1988) means-tested benefits take a more important role, and while child benefit continues there is no guarantee that its real value will be maintained in the future. Indeed in 1985 the rate of child benefit was increased by about one third of the increase that would have been necessary to maintain its real value (Wicks, 1987, p. 85), and there was no increase in 1988, when the 'reformed' scheme of family support came into effect.

But does selectivity through the use of means-tested benefit really provide the most help to poor working families? This section considers the experience of the FFS families, first considering the contribution that child benefit makes to their incomes and secondly looking at the take-up of means-tested benefits and at the effects of non-take-up on family income.

### The contribution of child benefit to family income

Table 5.1 shows the average proportion of family income made up of child benefit for the FFS families who were not on supplementary benefit. For families in receipt of supplementary benefit any child benefit is fully taken into account in the assessment of benefit and therefore child benefit does not provide any additional financial income to such families. Lone parents are shown as a single group rather than separately as lone mothers and lone fathers. This is in order to provide a better sample size, the number of non-supplementary benefit receipts among the lone parents being fairly small. On average, child benefit contributed about 15 per cent of the gross weekly incomes of the lone parents and almost 20 per cent of their net disposable weekly incomes (which excludes net housing costs and any work expenses such as tax, national insurance contributions, travel and child-care costs). For two-parent families child benefit contributed, on average, about 12 per cent of gross weekly incomes and almost 18 per cent of net disposable weekly incomes. As child benefit is paid for each child, whereas other sources of income are not generally related to family size, the importance of child benefit to the family income rose as the number of children rose. Thus, for example, for a two-parent family with one dependent child, child benefit amounted to about a tenth of the net disposable weekly income but this rose to as much as a quarter for families with four or more children.

Table 5.1

The contribution of child benefit to income by family size and type: single-unit households not in receipt of supplementary benefit

| Family type | Average proportion of income made up of child benefit | |
| | Gross income % | Net disposable income % |
| --- | --- | --- |
| Lone parents: | | |
| One child | 10.4 | 13.8 |
| Two children | 15.4 | 20.6 |
| Three or more children | 20.0 | 26.0 |
| All | 15.0 | 19.8 |
| | | |
| Base (no. interviewed) | 179 | 179 |
| | (191) | (191) |
| | | |
| Two parent families: | | |
| One child | 6.0 | 10.3 |
| Two children | 10.7 | 16.6 |
| Three children | 14.6 | 21.2 |
| Four or more children | 18.9 | 25.6 |
| All | 11.8 | 17.6 |
| | | |
| Base (no. interviewed) | 996 | 996 |
| | (1261) | (1261) |

Child benefit is, of course, paid at the same rate for each child and therefore a lone parent with two children would receive the same amount as a two-parent family with two children. Thus, because the lone parents tended to have lower levels of income than the two-parent families, child benefit usually amounted to a higher proportion of their incomes. In addition some lone parents were receiving child benefit increase (now known as one-parent benefit) and for those in receipt this flat-rate supplement to child benefit added, on average, a further six per cent to net income (take-up of child benefit increase is discussed in the next section). In total therefore, the lone parents were receiving about 23 per cent of their net disposable incomes from child benefit and child benefit increase.

So far we have concentrated on non-recipients of supplementary benefit because these are families for which child benefit represents a direct financial gain. However, although families on supplementary benefit do not receive any such financial gain from child benefit there are nevertheless reasons why it is important to them. First child benefit is paid separately and often on a different day of the week from supplementary benefit. This may make budgeting across the week easier. Secondly child benefit is a regular and reliable payment, supplementary benefit may not be—for example, changes in circumstances might delay payment because of the need for re-assessment. Furthermore, in two-parent families the child benefit goes to the mother while the supplementary benefit usually goes to the father. Thus child benefit represents the proportion of family income which is directly available to the mother (see Walsh and Lister, 1985 for a discussion of the importance of child benefit to women). Table 5.2 therefore shows the contribution of child benefit to income for the FFS families on supplementary benefit. The lone parents were receiving a quarter (24 per cent) of their disposable incomes from child benefit and child benefit increase, rising to one third (34

Table 5.2

The contribution of child benefit to weekly net income by family size and type: single-unit households in receipt of supplementary benefit

| Family size | Average proportion of net income made up of child benefit | |
|---|---|---|
| | Lone-parent families % | Two-parent families % |
| One child | 14.9 | 21.1 |
| Two children | 21.4 | 19.0 |
| Three children | 29.0 | 24.1 |
| Four or more children | 33.6 | 29.7 |
| All | 21.4 | 20.7 |
| Including child benefit increase | 24.0 | n.a. |
| Base (no. interviewed) | 616 (687) | 311 (427) |

per cent) for families with four or more children. The two-parent families on supplementary benefit were receiving a fifth (21 per cent) of their incomes in the form of child benefit, and again this benefit was particularly important to large families.

For low-income families child benefit is therefore clearly an important source of income, making up about a fifth of their incomes. However it is not simply low-income families who receive child benefit, all families do and therefore it is interesting to consider how important child benefit is to families in general. Using data from the 1982 Family Expenditure Survey, Table 5.3 shows that for lone parents child benefit made up about 14 per cent of net disposable income rising to about 17 per cent if child benefit increase is included. Among the two-parent families child benefit contributed, on average, about 11 per cent of net disposable income and for families with four or more children as much as 21 per cent. Thus for families in general, and particularly large families, child benefit represents a significant component of income.

Table 5.3

The contribution of child benefit to income by family size and type: all families with children excluding supplementary benefit recipients (FES, 1982)[1]

| Family type | Average proportion of income made up of child benefit | |
| | Gross income % | Net disposable income % |
| --- | --- | --- |
| Lone parents: | | |
| One child | 5.7 | 8.2 |
| Two children | 11.3 | 15.9 |
| Three or more children[2] | 19.2 | 24.4 |
| All | 9.9 | 13.6 |
| Including child benefit increase | 11.1 | 16.9 |
| | (99) | (99) |
| Two parent families: | | |
| One child | 3.4 | 6.7 |
| Two children | 6.3 | 10.8 |
| Three children | 9.3 | 15.2 |
| Four or more children | 13.0 | 21.3 |
| All | 6.1 | 10.6 |
| Base (no. interviewed) | 1796 | 1796 |

1. Based on analysis of FES data supplied by the ESRC Data Archive.
2. Based on only 13 cases.

## Means-tested benefits

Turning to selective support the main national means-tested benefits available to the FFS families were family income supplement, rent rebates and allowances and rate rebates, and Table 5.4 shows the average contribution of each of these to the total incomes of non-supplementary benefit recipients. As can be seen these three main means-tested benefits contributed, on average, about seven per cent to the gross incomes of the lone parents and about nine per cent to the gross incomes of the two-parent families. For both family types this was substantially less than the contribution of child benefit (and child benefit increase in the case of the lone parents).

Table 5.4

The contribution of benefits to income by family type: single-unit households not in receipt of supplementary benefit

| Benefits | Lone parents | | Two-parent families | |
|---|---|---|---|---|
| | Proportion in receipt | Average % of total income | Proportion in receipt | Average % of total income |
| Child benefit[1] | 96 | 19.53 | 99 | 11.80 |
| Family income supplement | 1 | 1.02 | 11 | 8.01 |
| Rent rebate/ allowance | 36 | 4.15 | 17 | 0.89 |
| Rate rebate | 38 | 1.76 | 18 | 0.36 |
| Other benefits[2] | 35 | 19.15 | 17 | 7.34 |
| Total from benefits | | 45.61 | | 28.40 |
| Base (no. interviewed) | 179 (191) | | 996 (1261) | |

1. And child benefit increase for lone parents.
2. Widows benefit, unemployment benefit, sickness benefit.

Means-tested benefits were not therefore such an important source of income support for these poor families as child benefit. This could be either because the families were not eligible for means-tested benefits or because they were not receiving benefits to which they were entitled. The 'take-up rates' of the benefits—the proportion of those eligible who were in receipt—are therefore an important indicator of the effectiveness of the means-tested benefits. Low take-up means that the theoretical effectiveness of such benefits (that they concentrate resources on those most in need) is not in fact realised in practice. In addition, as Atkinson (1984, p.1) has pointed out low take-up is also a problem because it is a 'cause of low incomes' it means that 'people are living on incomes below the minimum which the maintenance provisions seek to guarantee'. This analysis pursues both of these questions: first by calculating take-up rates for the main means-tested benefits in order to show the extent to which these benefits were reaching those for which they are intended; and secondly by calculating the effect of non-take-up on the income of the families concerned.

The calculation of take-up rates from survey data is however far from being an exact procedure. Most surveys—including the FFS—do not have the exact information necessary to calculate income and entitlement in precisely the ways required and, of course, the data collected in surveys is self-reported income data and not necessarily always accurate. One of the initial aims of DHSS in carrying out the FFS was to provide information to calculate take-up rates, and indeed it was following the FFS calculations that the estimates for the take-up rate of family income supplement were revised downwards from previous estimates of 70-75 per cent to 50 per cent.[2] The FFS income data included, for example, questions on average earnings over the past five weeks rather than simply in the past week, as is collected in the Family Expenditure Survey. However, although the FFS was intended to be used for the calculation of take-up rates, it is a sample of low-income families and not all families eligible for means-tested benefits are included. In particular some families who were eligible and in receipt of benefits would have been excluded precisely because receipt of the benefits took their incomes above the cut-off income line for the sample. This would bias the estimate of non-take-up upwards because non-claimants would be more likely to be included in the sample than claimants. For the estimates of take-up this has therefore been dealt with by excluding those families who, had they claimed the benefit concerned, would have had incomes above the cut-off point for the sample.

The income cut-off used in the sample selection also means that non-claiming families with a large unclaimed entitlement would be more likely to be included than non-claiming families with a small unclaimed entitlement. Thus, the estimate of the income loss to the families arising from non-take-up relates specifically to the loss to low-income families and not to all eligible non-claimants. The calculation of income loss is also a maximum estimate: it assumes that the families claim the benefits in a way most financially advantageous, and that receipt of one benefit would not affect entitlement to other benefits. This latter assumption means that the estimate may be over-stated for a minority of families (eight per cent of those assessed) who were estimated to be entitled to housing benefits and either family income supplement, child benefit increase or both (receipt of which should be taken into account when determining entitlement to housing benefits).

Table 5.5 shows the take-up rates for family income supplement, rent rebates and allowances, rate rebates, supplementary benefit and child benefit increase. With the exception of family income supplement, the lone parents were significantly more likely that the two-parent families to be in receipt of the benefits to which they were entitled. There was however no consistent difference between the two family types in terms of the average amount of unclaimed entitlement—the lone parents were 'losing' more than the two-parent families through not claiming housing benefits but less through not claiming family income supplement and supplementary benefit. A more

Table 5.5

Take-up rates and mean amounts of unclaimed benefit by family type: single-unit households

| | Lone parents | | Two-parent families | |
|---|---|---|---|---|
| Benefits | Take-up rate % | Mean amount unclaimed per per family £s | Take-up rate % | Mean amount unclaimed per family £s |
| Family income supplement[1] | 53 | 3.80 | 50 | 4.66 |
| Rent rebate/ allowance | 78 | 7.29 | 43 | 3.29 |
| Rate rebate | 55 | 2.09 | 31 | 1.16 |
| Supplementary benefit | 95 | 10.21 | 87 | 15.60 |
| Child benefit increase[2] | 50 | 1.82 | na | na |
| Base (no. interviewed) | 795 (878) | | 1307 (1688) | |

1. *Source:* Knight (1981) Appendix D.
2. Calculated only for non-recipients of supplementary benefit. Child benefit increase rose from £1.00 to £2.00 in November 1978 (ie. about 2 months into the survey period).

detailed analysis of the FFS data on the take-up of the three housing benefits (Bradshaw and Beadham, 1984) showed that the higher take-up of these benefits by lone parents was not a function of higher entitlement—a comparison of the lone parent families and the two-parent families with similar levels of entitlement showed that the lone parents still had higher take-up rates. Thus it did not seem to be clearly the case that those who were claiming were those who had the most to gain.

The take-up rate of only 50 per cent for child benefit increase is particularly interesting. This benefit (known now as one-parent benefit) is not means-tested and therefore it is perhaps surprising to find such a low level of take-up.[3] The FFS does not contain the type of information necessary to consider *why* families failed to claim their benefit entitlements, which is best considered by means of small-scale, qualitative studies (eg Corden, 1983). However a small study of both claimants and non-claimants of one-parent benefit in Hackney, East London (Millar and Cooke, 1984) suggested that the principal reason for delayed take-up or non-take-up was lack of knowledge of the existence of this benefit (rather than, for example, failure to recognise eligibility or feelings of stigma).

### The effect of non-take-up on family incomes

These estimated take-up rates are not substantially different from the official estimates and confirm, once again, that means-tested benefits fail to reach a fairly significant proportion of those for whom they are intended. In order to examine the effect of this on family incomes we calculated how much money the families were losing by not receiving these benefits. Some of the families had unclaimed entitlement to more than one benefit and we therefore added all the unclaimed benefits together in order to estimate how much in total the families were forgoing. Families in receipt of supplementary benefit were excluded because such families would either not have been entitled to these benefits or, if entitled, would rarely have had any financial gain from receipt.

As Table 5.6 shows among non-recipients of supplementary benefit 64 per cent of the lone parents and 39 per cent of the two-parent families had some estimated unclaimed entitlement to one or more of these benefits. For a quarter (25 per cent) of the lone parents the loss accounted to less than £2.00 per week, but 14 per cent were losing more than £10.00 per week. Among the two-parent families the losses tended to be slightly lower—with 19 per cent losing less than £2.00 per week and five per cent more than £10.00 per week. Thus although take-up rates among the lone parents tended to be higher than those of the two-parent families, the lone parents were losing more money because of non-take-up. This was both because their generally lower incomes meant that they were more likely to be eligible for more than one benefit and because there was one more benefit—child benefit increase—potentially available to them.

Table 5.6

Unclaimed benefits by family type: single-unit households not in receipt of supplementary benefit

| Unclaimed benefits | Lone parents % | Two-parent families % |
|---|---|---|
| None | 36 | 61 |
| Up to £1.50 | 4 | 16 |
| £1.51 to £2.00 | 21 | 3 |
| £2.01 to £5.00 | 15 | 8 |
| £5.01 to £10.00 | 10 | 8 |
| £10.01 to £15.00 | 7 | 2 |
| £15.01 and above | 7 | 3 |
| Total | 100 | 100 |
| Base (no. interviewed) | 179 | 996 |
| | (191) | (1261) |

The potential contribution of these benefits to weekly income can best be seen by expressing the estimated amount unclaimed as a proportion of the current net weekly incomes of the families. This is shown in Table 5.7. Among all non-supplementary benefit recipients 13 per cent of the lone parents and 19 per cent of the two-parent families had unclaimed benefit which amounted to not more than five per cent of total income; but nine per cent of the lone parents and four per cent of the two-parent families had unclaimed entitlement to benefits which amounted to at least half as much again as their current incomes. Excluding those with no entitlement then this figure rose to one in seven (14 per cent) of the lone parents and one in ten (10 per cent) of the two-parent families.

Some families were therefore losing quite substantial potential additions to their incomes. However 17 per cent of the families with some unclaimed entitlement (and 51 per cent of those with unclaimed entitlement of at least £10 per week) were families apparently eligible for but not in receipt of supplementary benefit. About half of these families had been out of work for less than five weeks and therefore had probably only recently become entitled to benefit. Indeed it may have been delays in receiving supplementary benefit rather than non-take-up which was the problem for these families. The majority of families with some unclaimed entitlement were, however, working families and about one in ten of these families were estimated to have unclaimed entitlement of at least £10.00 per week.

Table 5.7

Unclaimed benefits on a proportion of income by family type: single-unit households not in receipt of supplementary benefit

| Unclaimed benefits as a % of net income | All | | Those with some unclaimed entitlement | |
|---|---|---|---|---|
| | Lone parents % | Two-parent families % | Lone parents % | Two-parent families % |
| None | 36 | 61 | – | – |
| Up to 5% | 13 | 19 | 20 | 49 |
| 5.1% to 10% | 19 | 5 | 30 | 12 |
| 10.1% to 20% | 10 | 6 | 15 | 15 |
| 20.1% to 50% | 13 | 5 | 20 | 14 |
| 50.1% and above | 9 | 4 | 14 | 10 |
| Total | 100 | 100 | 100 | 100 |
| Base (no. interviewed) | 179 (191) | 996 (1261) | 115 (120) | 391 (474) |

**The estimated effect of full take-up on incomes**
Non-take-up benefits was clearly a factor contributing to the low incomes of the families, which would imply that full take-up would reduce the number of poor families. In order to examine the extent to which this would be the case we compared actual net income (less housing costs) relative to supplementary benefit with an imputed net incomes which included the estimated value of the benefits. Excluding supplementary benefit recipients (who were not usually eligible for these other benefits and in any case would not have benefited from receipt) Table 5.8 shows how full take-up would have affected income. Of the lone parents with incomes below the level of supplementary benefit 86 per cent were estimated to have been entitled to one or more of the benefits. If these lone parents had been in receipt of all the benefits to which they were estimated to be entitled then as many as almost half (48 per cent) would have moved from below to above the level of supplementary benefit scale rates, leaving just 13 per cent of the lone

parents below the level of supplementary benefit. Taking a higher threshold—140 per cent of supplementary benefit—then 93 per cent of the lone parents already had incomes below that level and 84 per cent were still below that level when full take-up was simulated. A similar pattern is clear for the two-parent families. Of these families 23 per cent had incomes below supplementary benefit levels and 16 per cent remained below after simulating full take-up; 89 per cent had incomes below 140 per cent of supplementary benefit and 88 per cent would still have had incomes below 140 per cent with full take-up.

Table 5.8

Income relative to supplementary benefit assuming full take-up: single-unit households not in receipt of supplementary benefit

| Income relative to supplementary benefit | % of sample | % with unclaimed entitlement | % of sample with full take-up |
|---|---|---|---|
| Lone parents | | | |
| below 100% SB | 25 | 86 | 13 |
| below 120% SB | 57 | 75 | 40 |
| below 140% SB | 93 | 64 | 84 |
| | | | |
| Base (no. interviewed) = 179 (191) | | | |
| | | | |
| Two-parent families | | | |
| below 100% SB | 23 | 72 | 16 |
| below 120% SB | 48 | 60 | 42 |
| below 140% SB | 89 | 39 | 88 |

Base (no. interviewed) = 996 (1261)

For the purpose of comparison Table 5.9 shows the effect of simply doubling child benefit (leaving all other income as it stands). For those with very low incomes (below 100 per cent of supplementary benefit) the effect is almost exactly the same as the estimated effect of full-take-up of mean-tested benefits. For both family types almost half of the families with incomes below 100 per cent would move to above that level if child benefit were doubled. However the effect is much more dramatic for those with slightly higher incomes. For both family types as many as half of the families would have had incomes above 140 per cent of supplementary benefit if child benefit were doubled. Of course one of the main reasons why doubling child benefit is so much more effective at reducing low incomes than full take-up of means-tested benefits is because *all* the families benefit from this whereas relatively small proportions were eligible for means-tested benefits.

Table 5.9

Income relative to supplementary benefit with doubled child benefit: single-unit households not in receipt of supplementary benefit

| Income relative to supplementary benefit | % of sample | % of sample if child benefit doubled |
|---|---|---|
| Lone parents | | |
| below 100% SB | 25 | 13 |
| below 120% SB | 57 | 25 |
| below 140% SB | 93 | 51 |
| Base (no. interviewed) = 179 (191) | | |
| Two-parent families | | |
| below 100% SB | 23 | 10 |
| below 120% SB | 48 | 25 |
| below 140% SB | 89 | 51 |
| Base (no. interviewed) = 996 (1261) | | |

Thus it is clear that child benefit—although not primarily intended as an income support benefit—was a more important source of income for these poor families than were means-tested benefits. It represented a significant component of net income—particularly for the lone parents and for the large families. The take-up rates for means-tested benefits were low and this meant that many of the working families were losing money because they were apparently not receiving benefits to which they were entitled. The amounts lost were often fairly substantial in relation to their total weekly incomes and would have provided a valuable addition to their incomes. Nevertheless full take-up of these means-tested benefits would not appear to have been enough to 'solve' the problem of poverty for these families although it would have been likely to significantly reduce the numbers with very low incomes.

## SUPPLEMENTARY BENEFIT

At any one time more than half of all lone mothers are dependent on supplementary benefit, and among the FFS lone mothers as many as three-quarters were on supplementary benefit when they were first interviewed. However these cross-sectional figures cannot tell us anything about the dynamics of benefit dependency, and the extent to which families move on and off benefit. In this section therefore we follow the supplementary benefit experiences of the families over the two years.

### Supplementary benefit receipt at the FFS and FRS

Table 5.10 shows receipt of supplementary benefit at the two interviews by family type at the FFS. Of the original lone mothers 62 per cent were in receipt at both interviews—far higher than the proportion of FFS lone fathers (45 per cent) or two-parent families (15 per cent) in the same situation. Of

Table 5.10

Receipt of supplementary benefit at the FFS and FRS by family type at FFS

| | Family type at FFS | | |
| Receipt of Sup. Ben. | Lone mother % | Lone father % | Two-parent family % |
| --- | --- | --- | --- |
| FFS only | 16 | 14 | 10 |
| FRS only | 3 | 10 | 7 |
| FFS and FRS | 62 | 45 | 15 |
| No receipt at either | 19 | 31 | 68 |
| Total | 100 | 100 | 100 |
| % moving off benefit[1] | 20% | 23% | 40% |
| % moving onto benefit[2] | 12% | 24% | 10% |
| Base (no. interviewed) | 813 | 47 | 1346 |
| | (814) | (49) | (1713) |

1. Of all those in receipt at the FFS, proportion not in receipt at the FRS.
2. Of all those not in receipt at the FFS, proportion in receipt at the FRS.

98

the lone mothers on benefit at the FFS only 20 per cent had come off benefit compared with 40 per cent of the two-parent families.

Table 5.11 looks in more detail at the benefit receipt of the lone mothers at the two interviews. Included are all those women who were lone mothers sometime during the course of the study (this does not, however, include women who had a spell on benefit between the two interviews—this is discussed below). Between the two interviews the actual number on benefit fell from 634 to 567 (re-weighted numbers) but, because the lone mother group changed (as some women became lone mothers and others ceased to be lone mothers) the proportion of lone mothers on benefit at both interviews remained about the same (78 and 77 per cent). The overall fall was due to both women coming onto benefit (60 cases) and women leaving (127 cases). Of course not all those who could have come onto benefit were represented within the sample, nevertheless it is interesting to note that, of those lone mothers who did come onto benefit the majority (65 per cent) were 'new' lone mothers. Thus a change in marital status was an important factor bringing women onto benefit, and this was also true for those coming off benefit—again it is women who changed marital status who form the majority. Of the original lone mothers who came off benefit 57 per cent were no longer lone mothers, 35 per cent were in employment (including about 8 per cent who had already been in part-time jobs at the FFS). The remaining 8 per cent (ten cases) were not employed but were usually receiving

Table 5.11

Movements on and off supplementary benefit between the FFS and the FRS: lone mothers

| FFS | | | FRS |
|---|---|---|---|
| Lone mothers on supplementary benefit | Came on | Left | Lone mothers on supplementary benefit |
| 634 (reweighted) + cases | 60 cases | − 127 cases | = 567 cases |
| | 21 lone mothers 39 'ex two-parent families' | 73 into two-parent families 44 into employment 10 other | 528 lone mothers 39 'ex two-parent families' |
| 78% of FFS lone mothers | | | 77% of FRS lone mothers |

maintenance. Thus it seems that changes in marital status, rather than changes in employment status, account for a significant proportion of lone mothers leaving benefit.

Similar results were also found in an analysis of case-records of lone mothers on supplementary benefit carried out by the Economic Advisers Office (EAO) of DHSS, based on the 1976 Annual Statistical Enquiry (EAO, undated). The sample was very small (only 151 cases) and provided information on benefit receipt over the previous two years. Of the original 151 lone parents 50 (33 per cent) had ceased to be in receipt during the two years. About a third had married (or remarried or were cohabiting), another third were receiving other income, usually maintenance or part-time earnings and about 14 per cent were in full-time employment. The author(s) conclude

> This evidence, flimsy though it is because of the sample size, suggests that changes in the family are more likely to remove lone parents from supplementary benefit than are changes in work status but employment is nevertheless an important factor.

The FFS results would seem to bear out this conclusion.

The impact of changes in marital status on supplementary benefit receipt is shown even more clearly in Table 5.12—of the lone mothers who moved into two-parent families between the two interviews as many as 78 per cent of those who had been on benefit came off and none came on (although 19 per cent were in receipt at both interviews). Excluding those who changed marital status, of the women who remained lone mothers only 10 per cent came off supplementary benefit. Of the two-parent families who became lone mothers 17 per cent came off benefit but as many as 67 per cent of those who had not been in receipt of benefit at the FFS were in receipt at the FRS. This suggests that becoming a lone parent is very likely to mean a spell on supplementary benefit. This is also suggested by the fact that—as the social security statistics show—it is single and separated rather than divorced lone mothers who are most likely to be supplementary benefit recipients (approximately 80 per cent, 76 per cent and 37 per cent respectively in the early 1980s). Thus it seems likely that for many lone mothers their experience of lone parenthood will start with a spell on supplementary benefit.

Going back to the women who stayed lone mothers but who came off supplementary benefit then an obvious question is whether or not there was anything special about this group; whether lone mothers who came off benefit share particular characteristics that distinguish them from the women who stay on benefit. However, a comparison of the personal characteristics of the two groups (age, age and number of children, household composition, tenure) found no significant differences. The only difference between the two groups was that those who came off benefit were more likely to have been economically active at the FFS (33 per cent—19 per cent in part-time employment and 14 per cent unemployed and seeking work) than those who stayed on benefit (18 per cent—14 per cent in part-time employment and 4 per cent unemployed and seeking work). Those who came off benefit had also spent less time on benefit in the year prior to the FFS—a mean of 36 weeks compared with 47 weeks for those who stayed on benefit. This suggests that recent experience in the labour market might improve the chances of lone mothers coming off supplementary benefit and into employment.

### Table 5.12
#### Receipt of supplementary benefit at the FFS and FRS by changes in family type

| | Family type at FFS and FRS | | | |
| Receipt of SB | Lone mother at both | Lone mother to two-parent family | Two-parent family at both | Two-parent family to lone mother |
|---|---|---|---|---|
| FFS only | 8 | 68 | 10 | 7 |
| FRS only | 3 | 0 | 6 | 39 |
| FFS and FRS | 69 | 19 | 14 | 35 |
| No receipt at either | 20 | 14 | 70 | 19 |
| | | | | |
| Total | 100 | 100 | 100 | 100 |
| | | | | |
| % moving off benefits[1] | 10% | 78% | 42% | 17% |
| % moving onto benefits[2] | 14% | 0% | 7% | 67% |
| | | | | |
| Base (no. interviewed) | 685 | 107 | 1267 | 53 |
| | (749) | (118) | (1622) | (54) |

1. Of all those in receipt at the FFS, proportion not in receipt at the FRS.
2. Of all those not in receipt at the FFS, proportion in receipt at the FRS.

### Employment changes
An alternative way of considering the question of why some lone mothers are on benefit while others are not is to consider instead the question of why some lone mothers are in employment and others are not. This is a complex

question involving a number of different factors. These include the demand for female labour; the availability of suitable jobs; the financial incentives and disincentives of the benefit system; access to child-care facilities (and the level of charges for these) and also the characteristics of the women themselves (including personal characteristics such as age, age and number of children etc., as well as employment experience, educational levels, skills and so on). It is well known from both General Household Survey data and from the Women in Employment Survey (Martin and Roberts, 1984) that mothers of pre-school age children are much less likely to be employed than mothers of school-age children and that this is true for both married and lone mothers. But are there other characteristics that distinguish employed and non-employed lone mothers? The EAO paper cited above considered this question, taking into account a number of factors possibly affecting the propensity of lone mothers to take paid work. The analysis was somewhat hampered by the lack of adequate data but the results suggested that there was no clear line between those lone mothers in employment and those on supplementary benefit. A similar conclusion was reached following a multi-variate analysis of earning and non-earning lone mothers on supplementary benefit, which was carried out as part of the study of the effects of the introduction of the tapered earnings disregard (Weale et al., 1984, p. 152):

> The main conclusion that can be drawn from the analysis is that earners and non-earners are not clearly distinguished in their characteristics . . . Certain individuals, for example those with poor health or those with their youngest child under five, are less likely to participate in the labour market when we have controlled for other factors. But we cannot identify a set of individuals with a combination of characteristics which are highly likely to predict that they do paid work.

The FFS and the FRS are not the best data sources to consider employment changes, partly because such a small number of the lone mothers were in employment (particularly full-time employment) and partly because of the nature of the sample (being low-income families and not therefore representative of all employed lone mothers). However the FFS/FRS data does seem to confirm the results of those other studies. A comparison of the characteristics of the earning and non-earning lone mothers at the FFS showed that the former were more likely than the latter to have school-age children, to be older and to be owner-occupiers rather than council tenants (all factors which also showed up in the analysis by Weale et al. described above). However when changes in employment status and hours at work between the two interviews were examined no significant differences were found. Among those originally in employment there were no differences in the characteristics of those who left paid work and those who did not. Similarly for those originally in employment, there were no differences in the characteristics of those who took up paid work and those who did not. Nor were changes in the number of hours of paid work clearly associated with the characteristics of the lone mothers. Thus it was not possible to identify particular groups of lone mothers who were very likely to change employment status.

At the FRS the non-employed lone mothers were asked about their employment intentions which provides an opportunity to consider whether non-employed lone mothers were not in paid work because they preferred to stay at home. It is of course problematic to ask questions about employment intentions—perhaps particularly of women with children because their entry into the labour market may often be 'opportunistic', that is the result of a job 'coming up' rather than the result of active search or even the expressed wish for a job (Martin and Roberts, 1984). So answers to questions on employment intentions may not be a particularly accurate reflection of actual behaviour. The answers will also depend to some extent on the way the questions are asked.

Three questions about employment intentions were asked at the FRS. The first was the standard Family Expenditure Survey question used to classify employment status. Respondents were asked 'Are you doing any kind of paid work at the moment?' They were classified as unemployed if they satisfied one of three conditions:

(i)    they were in registered unemployment, or
(ii)   they were seeking work and had held a job within the past five years, or
(iii)  they were sick but intending to seek work.

On this definition 3 per cent of the lone mothers were unemployed.

The second relevant question was asked of those who were not in paid work, not defined as unemployed above and who had not done any paid work in the previous 12 months. These respondents were asked 'Are you looking for a job at the moment?' A further 12 per cent of lone mothers said that they were looking for a job.

Finally, mothers of school-children were asked 'Some mothers would like to go back to work if they could find someone to look after their children whilst others do not wish to take a job while the children are still young. Would you like to take a job now or not?' As many as half of the lone mothers said yes to this question—45 per cent without qualification and 4 per cent said yes but only if the hours were suitable and they could obtain help with child-care.

Thus, although the non-employed lone mothers were unlikely to be defined (or to define themselves) as unemployed, as many as half stated a preference for paid work. About one in seven said that they were looking for a job; and a further one in three, although not specifically looking for work, said that they would like to take a job.

In order to examine whether the preference for paid work was associated with particular characteristics Table 5.13 compares the characteristics of the women who said they were and those who said they were not interested in paid work. First, within the group who said that they would like to take a job, the table shows separately the women who were more actively seeking work (ie either unemployed or looking for a job) and those who said they would like a job but had not said they were looking for work. The only significant differences between these two groups were that the more active job-seekers tended to have smaller families and were more likely to have been economically active at the FFS. Secondly, comparing those who said they would like a job with those who said they would not, the only significant differences were that the latter group were less likely to have been economically active at the FFS and tended to be older women with older children. Thus, although the older women without recent experience of employment were the least likely to state a preference for paid work, otherwise this preference was not apparently related to family responsibilities or other characteristics of the women.

Other studies (eg Hunt et al., 1973; Evason, 1980; Letts, 1983) have also found that many lone mothers express a preference for paid work, tending to confirm the comment in the Finer report that 'many lone mothers who at present remain on supplementary benefit are anxious to work' (p. 412). Thus it does not seem to be the case that particular groups of lone mothers prefer full-time child care for their children over paid employment. For a significant group of lone mothers it may well be that limited opportunities rather than lack of interest in taking paid work is the much more important determinant of labour market participation.

### Total time on supplementary benefit

So far the analysis has concentrated on supplementary benefit receipt and employment status at two points in time (the FFS and at the FRS). However a better indicator of the extent of dependence on supplementary benefit is to examine the total number of weeks in receipt over the two years for which information is available. This measure is able to pick up the families who spent some time in receipt of benefit before the FFS and between the two interviews.

Table 5.14 shows the total time spent on benefit over the two years among the  families who did not change marital status. The lone mothers

## Table 5.13

### Characteristics by employment intentions: lone mothers at both interviews with at least one child under 16

| Characteristics at FRS | Would not like to take a job now % | Would like to take a job now | | |
| --- | --- | --- | --- | --- |
| | | Seeking Work[1] % | Other % | All who would like to take a job % |
| **Age of youngest child** | | | | |
| 0–4 | 34 | 34 | 32 | 33 |
| 5–10 | 24 | 46 | 51 | 50 |
| 11 plus | 32 | 19 | 17 | 18 |
| Total | 100 | 100 | 100 | 100 |
| **Number of dependent children** | | | | |
| 1 | 45 | 55 | 36 | 42 |
| 2 | 31 | 32 | 36 | 35 |
| 3 | 18 | 9 | 19 | 16 |
| 4 plus | 6 | 4 | 9 | 8 |
| Total | 100 | 100 | 100 | 100 |
| **Employment status at FFS** | | | | |
| In employment | 5 | 13 | 4 | 7 |
| Unemployed | 2 | 16 | 4 | 9 |
| Unoccupied | 93 | 71 | 92 | 85 |
| Total | 100 | 100 | 100 | 100 |
| **Tenure** | | | | |
| Rent:  local authority | 75 | 80 | 81 | 81 |
|           private | 10 | 11 | 10 | 11 |
| Owner-occupier: outright | 4 | 2 | 2 | 2 |
|                mortgage | 8 | 7 | 5 | 6 |
| Rent free | 3 | 0 | 1 | 1 |
| Total | 100 | 100 | 100 | 100 |
| **Age at leaving full-time education** | | | | |
| Up to 15 | 73 | 68 | 71 | 70 |
| 15–18 | 26 | 32 | 27 | 29 |
| 19 plus | 1 | 0 | 2 | 1 |
| Total | 100 | 100 | 100 | 100 |
| Proportion in receipt of SB | 83% | 90% | 91% | 90% |
| Income relative to sup. ben. | 110.1 | 105.1 | 107.8 | 107.0 |
| Median age (years) | 34.5 | 29.8 | 31.9 | 31.6 |
| Base (no. interviewed) | 232 | 69 | 158 | 226 |
| | (254) | (81) | (169) | (250) |

1. Those who were either defined as unemployed or said they were looking for a job.

105

were by far the most likely to be long-term recipients, with 54 per cent on benefit for at least two years compared with 32 per cent of the lone fathers and 8 per cent of the two-parent families. Only a very small minority—17 per cent—of the lone mothers were never in receipt of benefit during the two years. By contrast among the two-parent families 61 per cent had had no spells on supplementary benefit and a further 15 per cent had spent less than six months out of the two years on benefit. However, for the two-parent families, this measure is likely to underestimate the total time spent on benefit because this group also included some families who had spent some time unemployed and receiving unemployment, rather than supplementary, benefit. To give a more accurate comparison of the extent of dependence on benefit of the two-parent families compared with the lone parents, the final column of Table 5.14 shows the total time spent on either supplementary benefit or unemployment benefit for the two-parent families. The proportion of two-parent families with some experience of living on benefit rises to almost half (48 per cent). Nevertheless the difference between the lone mothers and the two-parent families, while less pronounced, remains very striking: over half the lone mothers were on benefit continuously while over half of the two-parent families were never on benefit during the two years.

Table 5.14

Receipt of supplementary benefit during the last two years prior to the FRS: families who did not change family status

| | Family type at FFS and FRS | | | |
| | Lone mother | Lone father | Two-parent family | |
| | | | SB | SB/UB[1] |
| Receipt of Sup. Ben. | % | % | % | % |
|---|---|---|---|---|
| None | 17 | 31 | 61 | 52 |
| Up to 6 months | 5 | 3 | 15 | 18 |
| 6 and less than 12 | 4 | 3 | 5 | 9 |
| 12 and less than 18 | 10 | 24 | 7 | 9 |
| 18 and less than 24 | 10 | 7 | 4 | 4 |
| 24 or more | 54 | 32 | 8 | 8 |
| | | | | |
| Total | 100 | 100 | 100 | 100 |
| | | | | |
| Base (no. interviewed) | 685 | 44 | 1267 | 1267 |
| | (749) | (45) | (1622) | (1622) |

1. Total length of time in receipt of either supplementary benefit or unemployment benefit.

In the EAO analysis of movement on and off benefit a comparison was made between the characteristics of short-term (under one year) and long-term (over five years) recipients. This showed a number of differences:

> Those who have been on supplementary benefit for less time are younger, with fewer and younger children, less likely to have housing costs and more likely to receive maintenance direct and thus receive less supplementary benefit than those who have been on longer. Those who have been on supplementary benefit longer are older, with older children, divorced rather than separated and have given up relying on directly paid maintenance. But do these differences reflect changes to people over time or are they different kinds of people? The only one way to answer this question is to follow through time a group of people coming onto supplementary benefit.

The FFS/FRS data does provide an opportunity to follow the supplementary benefit experience, not exactly of a group of people coming onto benefit, but of a group with different experiences of benefit receipt (including no receipt). Among the women who remained lone mothers it is possible to identify four main groups in terms of benefit receipt:

|       |                                                          |             |
|-------|----------------------------------------------------------|-------------|
| (i)   | those in receipt for at least two years continuously     | 54 per cent |
| (ii)  | those who receipt was long-term but less than two years  | 13 per cent |
| (iii) | those who moved on and off benefit during the two years  | 16 per cent |
| (iv)  | those never in receipt during the two years              | 17 per cent |

Among the first group there will be women with perhaps widely differing periods in receipt—all we know is that they had been on benefit for at least the two years of the study. The second group were women who had been on benefit for part of the year prior to the FFS, were on at the FFS and remained in continuous receipt up to the FRS. On average they had spent 79 weeks on benefit during the two years. They were thus different in terms of benefit receipt from the third group who moved on and off benefit, which included some with spells in receipt that spanned the two interviews and others who were in receipt only before the FFS or between the interviews. On average these women had spent 45 weeks on benefit during the two years.

Table 5.15 compares the personal and family characteristics of these four groups of women. Those with no receipt of supplementary benefit during the two years stand out as a particularly distinct group. They included very few young women (only 3 per cent under 24 compared with 18 per cent of all lone mothers) and thus their average age (of 40 years) was older than in the other groups. Very few had young children of under school age (12 per cent compared with 36 per cent of all lone mothers). Many of these women were widows (this is discussed in more detail below). The long-term recipients also stand out—here the women tended to be young (42 per cent under 24) with usually one pre-school age child. It seems very likely that many of this group were young, unmarried mothers. The two remaining groups—those in receipt continuously and those who moved on and off were very similar in their characteristics to each other and to the sample of lone mothers as a whole.

Table 5.15

Characteristics at FFS of women who remained lone mothers by experience of supplementary benefit over two years

| At FFS | Supplementary Benefit | | | | All lone mothers % |
|---|---|---|---|---|---|
| | Two years receipt % | Long-term receipt · % | On and off benefit % | No receipt % | |
| **Age of woman** | | | | | |
| Under 24 | 16 | 42 | 22 | 3 | 18 |
| 25–29 | 21 | 16 | 21 | 5 | 18 |
| 30–34 | 20 | 15 | 24 | 23 | 21 |
| 35–39 | 17 | 18 | 18 | 23 | 17 |
| 40 plus | 26 | 9 | 16 | 46 | 27 |
| Total | 100 | 100 | 100 | 100 | 100 |
| Mean age | 34 | 29 | 32 | 40 | 34 |
| **Number of children** | | | | | |
| 1 | 39 | 47 | 43 | 42 | 41 |
| 2 | 31 | 29 | 35 | 35 | 32 |
| 3 | 22 | 16 | 14 | 17 | 19 |
| 4 plus | 9 | 8 | 7 | 6 | 8 |
| Total | 100 | 100 | 100 | 100 | 100 |
| **Age of youngest child** | | | | | |
| Under 5 | 36 | 61 | 39 | 12 | 36 |
| 5–9 | 44 | 29 | 44 | 45 | 42 |
| 10 plus | 20 | 10 | 17 | 43 | 22 |
| Total | 100 | 100 | 100 | 100 | 100 |
| Proportion of lone mothers | 54% | 13% | 16% | 17% | 100% |
| Base (no. interviewed) | 367 (409) | 86 (93) | 115 (124) | 117 (123) | 685 (749) |

Thus in terms of their personal characteristics those on benefit continuously for at least two years were fairly hetereogenous. This was also true for those moving on and off and indeed it would be difficult to distinguish between these two groups—those who move on and off appear to be very similar to those who stay on. The women who seemed to be becoming long-term recipients were young and probably often single, unmarried mothers. Thus it seems likely that any differences in characteristics according to duration in receipt are the result of changes over time in the characteristics of recipients rather because there are than two distinct groups of lone mothers. Only those never on benefit stand out as representing a distinct group.

Table 5.16 shows receipt at the FRS of the three main sources of income which would be an alternative to supplementary benefit: widows benefit, earnings and maintenance. The main source of income which kept those never in receipt off supplementary benefit was a widows benefit. Forty per cent of these women were in receipt of a widows benefit compared with 9 per cent of the lone mothers as a whole; and indeed this group of non-recipients of supplementary benefit included 76 per cent of all the

### Table 5.16

Receipt of widows benefit, earnings and maintenance at the FRS by experience of supplementary benefit over two years

| | Supplementary Benefit | | | | |
| Sources of income | Two years receipt % | Long-term receipt % | On and off benefit % | No receipt % | All lone mothers % |
| --- | --- | --- | --- | --- | --- |
| Widows benefit[1] | 2 | 1 | 2 | 40 | 9 |
| Earnings | 14 | 19 | 56 | 53 | 24 |
| Maintenance | 15 | 27 | 49 | 43 | 27 |
| | | | | | |
| Proportion of lone mothers | 54% | 13% | 16% | 17% | 100% |
| | | | | | |
| Base (no. interviewed) | 367 | 86 | 115 | 117 | 685 |
| | (409) | (93) | (124) | (123) | (749) |

1.  Proportion does not total to 100% per cent because some lone mothers were receiving more than one of these sources of income.

109

widows in the sample. In addition over half (53 per cent) of the non-recipients of supplementary benefit were employed and two-thirds were in receipt of maintenance (43 per cent). Those who moved on and off benefit were rarely widows but receipt of maintenance and/or earnings were more common than among the other lone mothers. Very few of those in continuous receipt had sources of income other than supplementary benefit, but a substantial minority (27 per cent) of the long-term recipients were still receiving maintenance payments.

If the widows are excluded from the sample then both the degree of dependence on supplementary benefit and the sources of income which keep non-widowed lone mothers off benefit can be more clearly seen. As Table 5.17 shows when the widows are excluded, then the proportion never on

Table 5.17

Receipt of earnings and maintenance at the FRS by experience of supplementary benefit over two years: non-widowed lone mothers

| | Supplementary Benefit | | | | |
| Income at FRS | Two years receipt % | Long-term receipt % | On and off benefit % | No receipt % | All non-widows % |
| --- | --- | --- | --- | --- | --- |
| Earnings | 14 | 14 | 29 | 26 | 18 |
| Maintenance | 12 | 22 | 23 | 21 | 16 |
| Earnings and maintenance | 3 | 5 | 27 | 48 | 13 |
| Neither | 71 | 59 | 21 | 4 | 53 |
| Total | 100 | 100 | 100 | 100 | 100 |
| % of all non-widowed lone mothers | 57% | 14% | 18% | 11% | 100% |

| | Sources of income | | | | |
| Supplementary Benefit | Earnings % | Maintenance % | Earnings and maintenance % | Neither % | All non-widows % |
| --- | --- | --- | --- | --- | --- |
| Two years receipt | 45 | 42 | 15 | 77 | 57 |
| Long-term receipt | 11 | 18 | 5 | 15 | 14 |
| On and off benefit | 28 | 25 | 37 | 7 | 18 |
| No receipt | 16 | 15 | 43 | 1 | 11 |
| Total | 100 | 100 | 100 | 100 | 100 |

benefit during the two years falls to only 11 per cent and the proportion in receipt continuously for at least two years rises to 57 per cent. The main source of income which kept non-widowed lone mothers off benefit was in fact a combination of earnings and maintenance. About half (48 per cent) of the non-widowed lone mothers never on benefit had income from both these sources at the FRS, compared with 27 per cent of those who moved on and off benefit and only 3 per cent of those continuously in receipt. Earnings alone or maintenance alone were less successful at keeping the women off supplementary benefit. As the lower half of Table 5.7 shows 43 per cent of the women with a combination of earnings and maintenance at the FRS had never been on benefit during the two years compared with 16 per cent of those with earnings only and 15 per cent of those with maintenance only.

## SUMMARY

State benefits are clearly a very important source of income for low-income families, and especially for lone parents. For working families both child benefit and means-tested benefit provide valuable support—child benefit more so than means-tested benefit because of its almost full take-up.

Supplementary benefit is clearly of very great importance to lone mothers: for many it provides a continuing source of income on which they are dependent for several years, for others it provides a source of income to which they have recourse from time to time. Of non-widowed lone mothers the vast majority probably spend at least some time living on supplementary benefit.

Changes in marital status seems to be the main factor determining movements on and off benefit. Of the lone mothers in receipt of benefit at the FFS who had come off benefit at the FRS over half had changed marital status and were no longer lone mothers. Or to put it another way, of the lone mothers who (re)married (or who were cohabiting) the vast majority came off supplementary benefit. Conversely of the women who became lone mothers the vast majority came onto supplementary benefit.

Changes in employment status were less important than changes in marital status in taking lone mothers off benefit but that is not to say there is no scope for policy which would encourage more labour market participation among lone mothers. Mothers of very young children are less likely to be employed but in this sample neither those in paid work nor those who moved in and out of paid work were very different in their characteristics from those not employed. About half of the non-employed lone mothers said they would prefer to be in paid work. The likelihood of taking paid work is probably related less to the personal characteristics of the lone mothers than it is to external factors—availability of jobs, of child-care, and the level of earnings

111

that can be obtained. Here maintenance seems to play an important part—those lone mothers who can combine earnings and maintenance were particularly likely to be able to come off supplementary benefit.

Welfare 'dependency' and the extent to which those in receipt of benefits become long-term recipients in a 'dependency culture' has provided a backdrop for much recent policy discussion. The idea seems to have been largely based on what are in fact erroneous ideas about the American experience. The empirical evidence from the United States shows that there is a substantial degree of movement on and off welfare benefits, with only a minority of lone mothers forming a hard-core of long-term recipients (Ellwood and Summers, 1986; Rainwater et al., 1986; Duncan and Willard, 1987; Haveman, 1987; Moffit, 1988). The FFS/FRS study is only a relatively short longitudinal study but these results indicate that even over the period of one to two years there is a substantial degree of movement on and off benefit for many lone mothers.

## Notes

1.  Since 1983 couples claiming supplementary benefit or family income supplement have been able to nominate whether the man or the woman should be the claimant (provided certain conditions are met).

2.  See Knight (1981) for details. The new lower estimate of take-up was partly due to a change in the method of calculation of take-up of family income supplement. FIS is payable for a period of 12 months: at any one time therefore the number in receipt of benefit include both these currently eligible *and* those who may not be currently eligible but also were eligible at some point during the previous 12 months. Therefore the number eligible but not in receipt should be calculated on exactly the same basis (ie. all those who have been eligible over the previous 12 months, whether or not they are currently eligible). In practical terms, however, it would obviously be extremely difficult to identify this latter group. Prior to the FFS, take-up of family income supplement was estimated by relating 'the number receiving at a given date to the number entitled twenty-six weeks previously, on the assumption that, on average, this would be the number entitled at the given date' (Elton 1984, p.24-9). For the FFS calculations the estimate was made on the basis of relating the number currently eligible but not in receipt to the number currently eligible and in receipt (ie. excluding from those in receipt any families whose *current* income would make them ineligible).

3.  The name was changed in 1980, partly in an attempt to improve the visibility of the benefit and make it more apparent that it was a benefit for lone parent families. Official estimates suggest that this—and an administrative exercise whereby all those whose child benefit order books were in one name only were written to and told of the existence of the benefit—improved take-up from about 60 per cent in

1979 to 70 per cent in 1981/82. Nevertheless in 1981/82 unclaimed one-parent benefit amounted to £25 million, representing an annual loss to each non-claiming family of about £180 (House of Commons, 1983).

# 6 The persistence of poverty

The FFS and the FRS taken together are one of the few sources of data on changes in family income over time. Over roughly the same period as covered by the FFS/FRS, estimates from the Family Expenditure Survey (DHSS, 1983) show that the proportion of lone parents with net incomes below 140 per cent of supplementary benefit (including recipients) rose from 50 per cent in 1979 to 55 per cent in 1981 and for two-parent families the proportion rose from 11 per cent to 20 per cent. But the FES, being cross-sectional, cannot show the extent to which low incomes are persistent for the *same* families. Are those with low incomes likely to continue living in poverty for considerable periods or are they a continually changing group? This chapter focuses on changes in income between the FFS and the FRS in order specifically to discover how many families 'escaped' from poverty between the two interviews, and how this rise in income was achieved. Of particular interest is how changes in marital status for lone parents (ie marriage, re-marriage or cohabitation) affect income levels, and to what extent these 'new' or 'reconstituted' families have incomes above the poverty line.

In order to examine the extent to which the families were able to 'escape' from poverty it is necessary to decide how to define 'non-poverty' and this is discussed first, followed by an analysis of how many families 'escaped' poverty and how they did so. The second half of the chapter then moves onto consider the living standards of the lone mothers at the two interviews. Most of the lone mothers remained on supplementary benefit and it is therefore of interest to consider what this meant for their standards of living.

## DEFINING MOVEMENTS OUT OF POVERTY

The original criterion for a 'low income' in the FFS sample had been a net income of below 140 per cent of supplementary benefit and therefore it was decided that the first condition for defining 'non-poor' families should be that such families cross this threshold—that net income (after meeting housing costs) at the FRS should be *above* 140 per cent of supplementary benefit levels. However if this were the only condition applied then 'non-poor' families would include families whose rise in income was in actual fact fairly minimal (eg from 138 per cent of supplementary benefit to 142 per cent) It therefore seemed appropriate to include a second condition—that the rise in income should be fairly substantial, sufficient to reflect a real and noticeable increase. The second condition was therefore that the rise in income relative to supplementary benefit be of at least 20 percentage points.[1]

Thus 'non-poor' families at the FRS were defined by two conditions: crossing the 140 per cent threshold so that net income was below 140 per cent of supplementary benefit at the FFS and above at the FRS, *and* with a rise in income relative to supplementary benefit of at least 20 percentage points. It is important to remember that this analysis concentrates on *income* levels. An increase in income does not necessarily mean an improvement in standards of living. For example a two-parent family would have an increase in income if the mother took up paid employment, but at the same time there would be costs involved in this—particularly for the woman whose paid job would usually be undertaken in addition to her unpaid domestic labour. Similarly it is also important to note that the analysis is concerned with *family* income as a whole and is not able to examine how that income was shared within the family. This is especially relevant when considering the increases in family income for lone mothers who moved into two-parent families. Although many of these women did have a substantial increase in family income, at the same time they had become financially dependent on the men with whom they were living, insofar as the major component of the family income was now the man's earnings. Therefore we cannot draw the simple conclusion that the ex-lone mothers were themselves necessarily financially better-off.

## 'ESCAPING' FROM POVERTY

Table 6.1 shows that of all the FRS families 28 per cent had escaped from poverty, according to our definition (ie income crossed 140 per cent with a rise of at least 20 percentage points). The chances of moving out of poverty were significantly higher for the two-parent families than they were for the lone parents—34 per cent of the original two-parent families were in the 'non-poor' group at the FRS compared with only 17 per cent of the lone mothers and 14 per cent of the lone fathers.

Table 6.1

Escaping poverty: single-unit households at both interviews

| Family type at FFS | All FRS families | 'Non-poor' FRS families | 'Non-poor' families as a proportion of each family type |
|---|---|---|---|
| | % | % | |
| Two-parent family | 64 | 78 | 34% |
| Lone mother | 34 | 21 | 17% |
| Lone father | 2 | 1 | 14% |
| Total | 100 | 100 | 28% |
| Base (no. interviewed) | 1630 | 456 | |
| | (1944) | (502) | |

However the disadvantage of the lone parents relative to the two-parent families is even greater than the figures in Table 6.1 imply because of course some of these families had changed marital status by the time of the FRS.[2] Table 6.2 shows that only 11 per cent of the lone mothers who remained lone mothers had escaped poverty compared with 35 per cent of the two-parent families. Thus almost all the lone mothers who stayed as lone mothers remained in poverty, and two-parent families were about three times more likely to escape poverty than lone mothers. Of the original lone mothers who had escaped poverty about half were still lone mothers at the FRS while the other half had married or re-married. The women who married or re-married were the family type most likely to have escaped poverty—with 48 per cent of these 'new' two-parent families not in poverty.

Table 6.3 shows that, although the 'poor' and the 'non-poor' families at the FRS had had similar levels of income at the FFS, they were clearly differentiated at the FRS. Overall the 'non-poor' families had incomes at the FRS at about twice supplementary benefit levels. The increase in income relative to supplementary benefit level was smallest for the lone mothers who remained lone mothers. Thus not only were lone mothers most likely to

## Table 6.2

### Escaping poverty by changes in family type: single-unit households at both interviews

| Family type at FFS | All FRS families | 'Non-poor' FRS families | 'Non-poor' families as a proportion of each family type |
|---|---|---|---|
| | % | % | |
| Two-parent family at both | 61 | 76 | 35% |
| Lone mother at both | 29 | 12 | 11% |
| Lone father at both | 2 | 1 | 14% |
| Two parent to lone mother | 2 | 1 | 15% |
| Lone mother to two-parent | 5 | 9 | 48% |
| Other | 1 | 1 | Ø |
| Total | 100 | 100 | 28% |
| Base (no. interviewed) | 1630 (1944) | 456 (502) | |

Ø   Base too small for calculation

remain poor but even among those whose income did rise the increase was lower than for the other family types. The lone mothers who changed marital status had the largest average rise in income levels, as well as being the group most likely to have crossed the poverty line.

## Table 6.3

### Income relative to supplementary benefit for 'poor' and 'non-poor' families: single-unit households at both interviews

| | Income relative to supplementary benefit (mean) | | | |
|---|---|---|---|---|
| | 'Poor' families at FRS | | 'Non-poor' families at FRS | |
| Family type[1] | FFS mean | FRS mean | FFS mean | FRS mean |
| Two-parents at both | 111.8 | 116.6 | 108.8 | 203.6 |
| Lone mother at both | 108.7 | 108.4 | 108.5 | 172.3 |
| Lone mother to two-parent | 102.4 | 113.4 | 109.2 | 223.2 |
| All families | 110.1 | 113.1 | 108.9 | 203.7 |

1.   Only the main family types are shown separately because of small sample sizes in the other groups

117

## Lone mothers

Examining changes in the composition of income gives some indication of how the families managed to escape from poverty, and how this differed for the different types of family. Table 6.4 shows how the composition of income changed for the women who stayed lone mothers and who escaped from poverty. Between the FFS and the FRS the proportion in employment more than doubled from 33 per cent to 74 per cent and earnings increased as a proportion of total income from 17 per cent to 42 per cent. However, although earnings were clearly very important in taking these women out of poverty nevertheless social security benefits continued to be a very important component of income. A third (32 per cent) of these women were still receiving supplementary benefit and social security benefits contributed in total 43 per cent of gross income. In terms of income composition these 'non-poor' lone mothers had therefore become more like lone mothers in general—according to the 1979 Family Expenditure Survey earnings contributed on average 44 per cent of total income for all lone mothers and benefits 48 per cent.

Table 6.4

The composition of gross income at the FFS and FRS: 'non-poor' lone mothers in single-unit households

| | Proportion in receipt | | Average contribution to the total | |
| | at FFS % | at FRS % | at FFS % | at FRS % |
| Components of income | | | | |
|---|---|---|---|---|
| Earnings | 33 | 74 | 16.9 | 42.1 |
| Benefits : Child benefit | 100 | 100 | 15.6 | 11.6 |
| : Sup. Ben. | 60 | 32 | 41.4 | 19.9 |
| : Widows benefit | 6 | 6 | 4.5 | 3.4 |
| : Other benefits[1] | 47 | 58 | 5.2 | 7.9 |
| Maintenance | 38 | 54 | 15.2 | 11.5 |
| Other income[2] | 36 | 66 | 1.1 | 3.6 |
| Total | | | 100.0 | 100.0 |

Base (no. interviewed) = 53 (51)

1. Includes FIS, housing benefits and any other cash benefits.
2. Includes pensions, investment income, income from annuities.

Most of the 'non-poor' lone mothers were therefore in employment by the time of the FRS. Just under half (47 per cent) had taken up employment since the FFS (compared with 10 per cent of the 'poor' lone mothers) and 27 per cent had been in employment at the FFS but had had an increase in earnings (compared with 11 per cent of the 'poor' lone mothers). But taking a job did not necessarily guarantee 'non-poverty'—of all those who took jobs between the two interviews 39 per cent escaped from poverty, leaving as many as 61 per cent of those who had taken up employment still living in poverty. Full-time jobs (defined here as more than 24 hours per week in line with the family income supplement regulations) were obviously more likely to mean a move out of poverty than part-time jobs—63 per cent of those who took full-time jobs were 'non-poor' compared with 29 per cent of those who took part-time jobs. While employment was therefore an important factor in moving the lone mothers out of poverty nevertheless even full-time employment left a substantial proportion of the lone mothers in poverty.

A quarter (26 per cent) of the 'non-poor' lone mothers were not employed. Of these 13 women 11 were on supplementary benefit and had been for at least two years continuously. Therefore it is likely that it was the move onto the long-term rate (which at the time of the FFS/FRS was after two years in receipt) and receipt of additional requirements which put net income above the 140 per cent line.[3] Most of these women (eight out of the 13) were only just within our defined 'non-poor' group with a net income of less than 150 per cent of supplementary benefit.

It is not surprising to find that so few lone mothers moved out of poverty considering that—as described in the previous chapter—the majority remained dependent on supplementary benefit. Although the cash incomes of supplementary benefit recipients may change because of a change in requirements (eg the number and ages of the children, housing costs), this would not lead to a change in income relative to supplementary benefit because their supplementary benefit entitlement would also change. The only major ways in which income relative to supplementary benefit could change would be a change in disregarded income or a move on to the long-term rate. The main item of disregarded income for supplementary benefit purposes is earnings and, at that time, only the first £6.00 of net earnings were disregarded. Of those who stayed on benefit 15 per cent had had some rise in income (because of disregarded earnings or receipt of the long-term rate) and 10 per cent had had some fall (because of loss of earnings or loss of additional requirements). But for the vast majority of those who stayed on benefit there was little or no change in income relative to supplementary benefit—overall at the FFS their incomes were on average 108 per cent of supplementary benefit and at the FRS 110 per cent.

**Two-parent families**

As we have already seen the two-parent families were more successful than the lone mothers at moving out of poverty and the main factor contributing to this was earnings, in particular the earnings of both partners. As Table 6.5 shows in the 'non-poor' two-parent families 97 per cent of the men were employed and 44 per cent of the women were also employed. Whereas earnings had contributed 62 per cent of total income at the FFS this had risen to 88 per cent by the time of the FRS and dependency on benefits (apart from child benefit) was almost non-existent. Thus, unlike the 'non-poor' lone mothers, the 'non-poor' two-parent families had largely moved off benefit receipt.

Table 6.5

The composition of gross income at the FFS and FRS: 'non-poor' two-parent families in single-unit households

| Components of income | Proportion in receipt | | Average contribution to the total | |
| --- | --- | --- | --- | --- |
| | at FFS % | at FRS % | at FFS % | at FRS % |
| Earnings — man | 66 | 97 | 56.7 | 78.9 |
| Earnings — woman | 17 | 44 | 5.2 | 9.4 |
| Benefits : Child benefit | 99 | 100 | 11.7 | 6.9 |
| : Sup. Ben. | 14 | 1 | 7.2 | 0.1 |
| : Unemployment benefit | 11 | 1 | 10.3 | 0.3 |
| : Other benefits[1] | 30 | 1 | 7.5 | 3.6 |
| Other income[2] | 44 | 50 | 1.4 | 0.9 |
| Total | | | 100.0 | 100.0 |

Base (no. interviewed) = 346 (392)

1. Includes FIS, housing benefits and any other cash benefits.
2. Includes pensions, investment income, income from annuities.

Two-parent families, where there are two potential earners, clearly have the advantage over lone mothers and Table 6.6 shows that having two earners greatly increased the likelihood that the two-parent families would move out of poverty. In families where both the husband and the wife took up employment 79 per cent were 'non-poor' and had increased their incomes relative to supplementary benefit by, on average, about 135 percentage points. Similarly in families where the man was already employed and the woman took up employment 71 per cent were moved into the 'non-poor' group. However in families where the man returned to work from unemployment while the wife remained unoccupied only 47 per cent moved out of poverty. Thus the key factor was the presence of *two* earners, highlighting again the importance of women's earnings in reducing the risk of poverty for families (see also Layard et al., 1978).

Table 6.6

Escaping poverty by changes in employment: two-parent families in single-unit households

| | Two-parent families at both interviews | | | | |
|---|---|---|---|---|---|
| | 'Poor' | 'Non-poor' | All | % in non-poor' group | Mean rise in income relative to sup. ben. (percentage points) |
| Earners | % | % | % | | |
| Number of earners | | | | | |
| from 0 to 1 | 11 | 18 | 13 | 47% | + 50.9 |
| from 0 to 2 | 1 | 8 | 4 | 79% | +134.4 |
| 1 to 2 | 6 | 26 | 13 | 71% | + 83.7 |
| Increase in earnings | 42 | 45 | 43 | 36% | + 37.7 |
| No change in employment status or earnings | 41 | 3 | 27 | 3% | − 9.0 |
| Total | 100 | 100 | 100 | 35% | + 35.9 |
| Base (no. interviewed) | 653 (862) | 346 (392) | 999 (1254) | | |

Table 6.7 shows the employment status of the two-parent families at the FRS compared with those of two-parent families in general. At the FFS most of the two-parent families had either no earners (38 per cent) or only one earner (53 per cent) whereas at that time most (93 per cent) of all two-parent families had at least one earner and half (50 per cent) had two earners. At the FRS the 'poor' families were still largely dependent on one earner (48 per cent) or had no earners (40 per cent) while the 'non-poor' families had become much more like families in general—97 per cent had at least one earner and 44 per cent two earners.

## Table 6.7

### Employment status: FRS two-parent families and two-parent families in general

| | FRS two-parent families | | | All families |
| | 'Poor' | 'Non-poor' | All | GHS 1979[1] |
| Employment status | % | % | % | % |
|---|---|---|---|---|
| **At FFS** | | | | |
| Man employed and | | | | |
| – women employed full-time | 0 | 1 | 1 | 14 |
| – women employed part-time | 7 | 10 | 8 | 36 |
| – woman not employed | 52 | 55 | 53 | 43 |
| Total | 59 | 66 | 62 | 93 |
| **At FRS** | | | | GHS 1980 |
| Man employed and | | | | |
| – women employed full-time | 1 | 7 | 3 | 15 |
| – women employed part-time | 11 | 37 | 20 | 36 |
| – woman not employed | 48 | 53 | 50 | 41 |
| Total | 60 | 97 | 73 | 92 |

1. *Source: General Household Survey 1979,* Table 5.8; 1980, Table 5.11. Two-parent families with dependent children.

## 'New' two-parent families

The final family type we can consider are those women who were lone mothers at the FFS but living in two-parent families at the FRS. As already described this was the family type most likely to escape from poverty (in terms of family income) and where the increases in family income were most substantial. For these families the story was much like that for the continuing two-parent families described above. As Table 6.8 shows, of these ex-lone mothers 97 per cent of the 'non-poor' families had at least one earner and 38 per cent had two earners. Again it was these two-earner families who were the most likely to be in the 'non-poor' group. Among the 'non-poor' families earnings were contributing about 85 per cent of the total, most of this being the man's earnings. However it should be noted that almost a third (31 per cent) of these 'new' two-parent families had no earners, and these families had in fact suffered a slight fall in the level of income relative to supplementary benefit.

122

## Table 6.8

### Escaping poverty by employment status: ex-lone-mother in single-unit households

| Employment status | 'Poor' % | 'Non-poor' % | All % | % in non-poor group | Mean rise in income relative to sup. ben. (percentage points) |
|---|---|---|---|---|---|
| Man only employed | 31 | 57 | 43 | 63% | + 71.6 |
| Both employed | 10 | 38 | 34 | 78% | +128.9 |
| Woman only employed | 2 | 2 | 2 | Ø | Ø |
| Neither employed | 57 | 3 | 31 | 4% | − 5.4 |
| Total | 100 | 100 | 100 | 48% | + 60.5 |

Ø  Number too small for calculation.

The women who had married or re-married were therefore likely to have had an increase in family income—provided their partners, and preferably themselves as well, were employed. But, as noted above, we have no information on the distribution of income *within* the family. However, Table 6.9 looks at changes in tenure and in access to assets in relation to changes in marital status. These give some further indication of how living standards might have changed. Of the 'ex-lone mothers' the proportion in the owner-occupied housing sector had risen from eight to 18 per cent. Compared with the FFS, at the FRS these women were more likely to live in a family with access to a telephone, a washing machine and particularly a car. (The proportions in a family with access to a car having risen from 5 per cent to 50 per cent.) At the FRS almost half (45 per cent) had access to five or six of the consumer assets they were asked about compared with only 17 per cent at the FFS. Thus there seems to have been some improvement in material living standards for these women. Nevertheless they still remained below the average for all two-parent families with children.

## LIVING STANDARDS ON SUPPLEMENTARY BENEFIT

The disadvantage of the lone mothers who stayed lone mothers in comparison to other family types is clear. Most of these women stayed poor and most stayed on supplementary benefit. In this section we therefore consider how the living standards of the lone mothers on benefit changed during the course of the study.

Table 6.9
Tenure and access to assets at the FFS and FRS: ex-lone mothers

| Tenure and assets | | FFS % | FRS % | All families[1] with children % |
|---|---|---|---|---|
| **Tenure** | | | | |
| Rented | – local authority | 73 | 67 | 30 |
| | – private | 12 | 10 | 4 |
| Owner-occupier | – mortgage | 6 | 15 | 53 |
| | – outright | 2 | 3 | 9 |
| Rent free | | 7 | 4 | – |
| Total | | 100 | 100 | 100 |
| **Proportions with:** | | | | |
| Telephone | | 35 | 49 | 84 |
| Television | | 97 | 95 | 98 |
| Washing machine | | 77 | 93 | 95 |
| Fridge freezer | | 92 | 97 | 99 |
| Car | | 5 | 50 | 83 |
| Central heating | | 50 | 48 | 72 |

Base (no. interviewed) = 87 (94)

1. Tenure 1979/1980 combined *General Household Survey 1980:* couples with dependent children.
   Assets *Family Expenditure Survey 1980:* couples with two children.

The information available on living standards at the FRS falls into three main groups: information on access to assets (as at the FFS), information on savings and debts (the latter particularly in relation to fuel and housing costs), and a series of questions relating to subjective feelings of hardship. There are of course a number of problems in interpreting such data. Respondents were asked (for example): 'In the past 12 months have you (or your wife) had to cut down on anything you usually spend money on?'; 'Do your children need any essential clothes at the present time which you cannot afford?'; and 'Are there any other essentials which you find it difficult to afford?' Not only are respondents likely to vary from individual to individual in how they interpret essentials, but also different groups may have different expectations. Long-term supplementary benefit recipients, for example, may have limited their expectations to meet their income. Even the apparently 'harder' questions give rise to similar problems—thus, although respondents were asked about arrears for housing costs and fuel, no definition given for what constitutes arrears, leaving each person to use their own definition.

In order to examine living standards in relation to supplementary benefit we divided the lone mothers into three groups: those who were in continuous receipt of supplementary benefit for two years (53 per cent), those with some receipt but less than two years (33 per cent) and the remaining, much smaller group (14 per cent) with no receipt of supplementary benefit.[4] At the time of the study the long-term rate of benefit was payable to lone parents after two years in receipt. Therefore dividing the sample in this way allows comparisons to be made between those on the ordinary and those on the long-term rate of benefit.

Much of the FRS data has already been analysed for the two-parent families, therefore we have concentrated on the lone mothers only. However, although we have not made explicit comparisons between the lone mothers and the two-parent families, some of the tables include a 'standard' group of two-parent families. These are families who no longer had low incomes by the time of the FRS—that is their net incomes (minus housing costs) were above 140 per cent of supplementary benefit at the FRS. The reason for including this group is that for much of the FRS data there is no comparable information for families in general. We cannot therefore say whether these lone mothers were more or less likely than average to be (for example) unable to afford household equipment. Including the 'better-off' two-parent families provides a point of comparison, although of course these families are not representative of all two-parent families (in particular because they have all had a recent spell of living on a low-income).

For the first group of lone mothers—those on supplementary benefit for at least two years continuously—it might be expected that such a long period on benefit would lead to falling living standards (for example because families are unable to replace worn-out goods). However there are a number of reasons why this need not necessarily be the case. First, because these women should all have been in receipt of the long-term rate of benefit. Secondly, the fact that they have been living on a low income for some time may have led to reduced expectations. Finally, although their incomes had been low for some time, during that time their incomes would have been relatively stable. Not having to cope with fluctuations in income could make managing easier. As Table 6.10 shows, the incomes of this group tended to remain low, but the composition of income was apparently relatively stable.[5]

The second group (those with some receipt but not continuously on benefit) were the most likely to have had changes in both the level and the composition of their incomes. Thirty per cent had changed employment status, 6 per cent had started receiving some maintenance and 10 per cent

Table 6.10

Level and sources of income between FFS and FRS by receipt of
supplementary benefit over two years: lone mothers at both interviews

| Level and sources of income | Non-claimant (no SB) % | Irregular claimants (some SB) % | Stable claimant (two years SB) % |
|---|---|---|---|
| Income relative to SB | | | |
| at FFS: median | 119 | 102 | 109 |
| at FRS: median | 124 | 108 | 113 |
| Changes in income relative to SB | | | |
| Fall of more than 20 percentage points | 10 | 16 | 3 |
| Within 20 percentage points | 58 | 54 | 77 |
| Rise of more than 20 percentage points | 31 | 30 | 15 |
| Change in employment status | | | |
| Took up paid work | 10 | 23 | 7 |
| Left paid work | 3 | 7 | 4 |
| Changes in maintenance receipt | | | |
| Started receiving | 3 | 16 | 7 |
| Stopped receiving | 6 | 10 | 9 |
| Proportion below 140% SB at FRS | 75 | 84 | 91 |
| Base (no. interviewed) | 67 (70) | 152 (162) | 245 (276) |

had ceased to receive any. Twelve per cent had been receiving
supplementary benefit at the FFS but were not at the FRS, while the reverse
was true for 23 per cent. The majority still had low income at the FRS. So
this group appear to have been likely to have low, but fluctuating incomes,
and this variability may have had a significant impact on their living
standards.

The final group (those never on supplementary benefit) were mainly
older women, with older children and all but one of the widows were in this
group. The incomes of these women had been higher than those of the other
lone mothers at the FFS, and were more likely to have increased. The

composition of income remained relatively stable. Thus it seems likely that these women would have higher living standards than the women in the other two groups.

For convenience these three groups are termed the non-claimants (those not on supplementary benefit during the two years); the stable claimants (those on supplementary benefit continuously for two years); and the irregular claimants (those with some periods in receipt of supplementary benefit).

## Housing

Table 6.11 shows tenure at the FRS and changes of address. Those most likely to have moved were the irregular claimants (17 per cent) and those least likely to have moved were the non-claimants (4 per cent). This fits with the idea that these two groups of women would have the least and most stable circumstances. Not all moves involved a change across tenure type (and similarly not all changes of tenure type necessarily involve a move). As at the FFS, local authority housing was the most common form of tenure for the lone mothers. Of the irregular claimants 5 per cent had moved into local authority housing, and a similar proportion (4 per cent) had changed tenure

Table 6.11

Housing by receipt of supplementary benefit over two years: lone mothers at both interviews

|  | Lone mothers | | | 'Standard' two-parent families |
|---|---|---|---|---|
| Tenure at FRS | Non-claimant (no SB) % | Irregular (some SB) % | Stable claimants (2 years SB) % | % |
| Rent – local authority | 48 | 71 | 81 | 46 |
| – private | 10 | 12 | 10 | 6 |
| Owner – mortgage | 18 | 13 | 4 | 43 |
| – outright | 12 | 3 | 1 | 4 |
| Rent free | 12 | 1 | 2 | 2 |
| Total | 100 | 100 | 100 | 100 |
| % changed address | 4 | 17 | 9 | 12 |
| % staisfied with housing | 51 | 61 | 59 | 64 |
| Base (no. interviewed) | 67 (70) | 152 (162) | 245 (276) | 346 (392) |

from living rent free to mortgaged owner-occupied housing. This could represent changes in maintenance arrangements, as it is possible that help with housing costs could have been part of such agreements. Among all the families a substantial proportion were dissatisfied with their housing. This was particularly true for the non-claimants group, where only about half said that they were satisfied with their housing. Given that owner-occupiers were over-represented in this group this could suggest that it is not always the case that owner-occupation is a more desirable tenure than renting for lone mothers.

### Access to assets

Six consumer assets were specifically asked about. As Table 6.12 shows, among the lone mothers, the non-claimants were more likely to have access to these assets than the other two groups. Forty-four per cent of the non-claimants had access to five or six of these items compared with only 18 per cent of the stable claimants and 23 per cent of the irregular claimants.

Table 6.12

Access to assets at the FRS by receipt of supplementary benefit over two years: lone mother at both interviews

| | Lone mothers | | | |
| | Non-claimant (no SB) | Irregular (some SB) | Stable claimants (2 years SB) | 'Standard' two-parent families |
| Assets | % | % | % | % |
|---|---|---|---|---|
| Proportion with: | | | | |
| Telephone | 69 | 48 | 39 | 72 |
| Television | 99 | 99 | 98 | 99 |
| Washing machine | 85 | 73 | 78 | 94 |
| Fridge/freezer | 99 | 91 | 91 | 97 |
| Car | 28 | 9 | 7 | 65 |
| Central heating | 52 | 46 | 45 | 57 |
| Total no. of assets | | | | |
| One or two | 6 | 16 | 12 | 3 |
| Three or four | 50 | 61 | 70 | 30 |
| Five or six | 44 | 23 | 18 | 67 |
| Total | 100 | 100 | 100 | 100 |
| Base (no. interviewed) | 67 | 152 | 245 | 346 |
| | (70) | (162) | (276) | (392) |

It was in access to a telephone and a car where there was most difference, but those on supplementary benefit were also less likely than the non-claimants to have access to domestic labour-saving devices (washing machines and fridges). Despite the differences between them, all the three groups of lone mothers were worse off in terms of access to assets than the 'standard' group of two-parent families.

In general the families were more likely to have access to assets at the FRS than they had been at the FFS, and this was the case even for the lone mothers continuously on supplementary benefit. As Table 6.13 shows, 29 per cent of these women had gained assets. This is perhaps surprising, but on the other hand these women had had very little by way of assets at the FFS. The type of items most commonly gained were washing machines and fridges. Eleven per cent had lost some assets (again most commonly washing machine and fridges). The irregular claimants showed the most variation in their access to assets—27 per cent had fewer at the FRS and 15 per cent had more. Again this was probably associated with the fact that their incomes were more likely to have changed. The non-claimants had more assets than other lone mothers at the FFS and so were slightly less likely to have gained any by the FRS. This was also true for the 'standard' two-parent families, but the type of assets gained were different. The most common items for lone mothers were telephones (9 per cent) and washing machines (9 per cent) whereas for the two-parent families they were telephones (13 per cent), central heating (7 per cent) and cars (6 per cent).

Table 6.13

Changes in assets between the FFS and the FRS by receipt of supplementary benefit over two years: lone mothers at both interviews

| | Lone mothers | | | 'Standard' two-parent families |
| | Non-claimant (no SB) | Irregular (some SB) | Stable claimants (2 years SB) | |
| Changes in no. of assets | % | % | % | % |
| --- | --- | --- | --- | --- |
| Rise | 22 | 27 | 28 | 28 |
| Same | 75 | 58 | 61 | 67 |
| Fall | 3 | 15 | 11 | 5 |
| Total | 100 | 100 | 100 | 100 |
| Base (no. interviewed) | 67 | 152 | 245 | 346 |
| | (70) | (162) | (276) | (392) |

Table 6.14 shows the incidence of fuel and housing difficulties. Respondents were first asked if they had any difficulties paying for fuel or housing, and if they said yes, were then asked if they had been in arrears at any time in the previous 12 months. Those whose fuel was paid direct by supplementary benefit were not asked about difficulties or arrears; although the fact of having direct payments probably indicates that there had been some difficulties. Reported difficulties in paying for fuel were quite common for all the families, but it was the stable claimants who were the most likely to report difficulties and arrears. Only a third of these women said they did not find paying for fuel a problem, 16 per cent were having

Table 6.14

Housing and fuel problems at the FRS by receipt of supplementary benefit over two years: lone mothers at both interviews

| | Lone mothers | | | |
| | Non-claimant (no SB) | Irregular (some SB) | Stable claimants (2 years SB) | 'Standard' two-parent families |
| Fuel and housing | % | % | % | % |
|---|---|---|---|---|
| **Fuel** | | | | |
| Paid directly by DHSS | 0 | 6 | 16 | 0 |
| No difficulties | 44 | 43 | 34 | 56 |
| Difficulties | 46 | 34 | 30 | 32 |
| Arrears | 9 | 17 | 21 | 12 |
| Total | 100 | 100 | 100 | 100 |
| **Housing** | | | | |
| No difficulties | 39 | 59 | 66 | 71 |
| Difficulites | 7 | 14 | 10 | 11 |
| Arrears | 10 | 27 | 24 | 19 |
| Total | 100 | 100 | 100 | 100 |
| **Housing and fuel** | | | | |
| No difficulties | 39 | 28 | 24 | 43 |
| Arrears for both | 0 | 6 | 7 | 4 |
| **Insufficient heating** | | | | |
| To save money | 38 | 31 | 37 | 17 |
| Other reasons | 11 | 21 | 20 | 17 |
| Base (no. interviewed) | 67 | 152 | 245 | 346 |
| | (70) | (162) | (276) | (392) |

deductions from their benefit for fuel and a fifth reported they had been in arrears for fuel in the previous 12 months. The irregular claimants were also very likely to report difficulties in paying for fuel (51 per cent) and 17 per cent had had some arrears. Reported difficulties in paying for housing were less common, but amongst those reporting difficulties arrears were more common. In the case of housing those most likely to report problems were the irregular claimants, of whom 27 per cent reported arrears during the previous 12 months. In terms of budgeting housing and fuel are likely to present different problems—most of these families were local authority tenants for whom housing would be a weekly or fortnightly expense. Fuel bills on the other hand are larger but more infrequent. Thus it is probably not surprising to find more difficulties in meeting fuel bills but more arrears for housing (as missing only one week means some arrears have accrued). That the irregular claimants had the most problems with housing seems again to be likely to follow from irregular levels of income. The non-claimants were the least likely to report difficulties paying for housing (less likely than the standard two-parent families) which is probably because quite a substantial proportion of these women lived in rent free accommodation (12 per cent) or in fully-owned houses (12 per cent). Their housing costs would therefore consist of rates only. In each of the three groups of the mothers half or more said that they did not always have sufficient heating—37 per cent of the lone mothers continuously on benefit said that this was because they could not afford it.

**Feelings of hardship**
Survey data is not the best source of information to probe feelings of hardship and therefore we can only make a very limited attempt to measure these. Table 6.15 shows how the women answered three questions relating to perceived need for household equipment, whether they had cut back on spending, whether they felt there were any essential terms they could not afford. The picture which emerges seems to tally with our other findings. Although many of the 'standard' two-parent families reported unmet needs the lone mothers were significantly more likely to do so. Within the group of lone mothers again the non-claimants seem to have been better-off than the other two groups.

Amongst the stable claimants, only one in ten said they had no unmet needs—61 per cent said they were short of household equipment, 63 per cent said they had cut back on spending and 49 per cent said there were essential items they could not afford. The results were very similar for the irregular claimants—57 per cent said they were short of household equipment, 65 per cent that they had cut back on spending and 39 per cent that there were essential items they could not afford.

## Table 6.15

## Measures of hardship at the FRS by receipt of supplementary benefit over two years: lone mothers at both interviews

| | Lone mothers | | | |
| Measure of hardship | Non-claimant (no SB) % | Irregular (some SB) % | Stable claimants (2 years SB) % | 'Standard' two-parent families % |
|---|---|---|---|---|
| **Items of h/h equipment needed** | | | | |
| None | 60 | 43 | 39 | 58 |
| One or two | 32 | 48 | 52 | 38 |
| Three ot more | 8 | 9 | 9 | 4 |
| Total | 100 | 100 | 100 | 100 |
| **Cut back on spending (no. of items)** | | | | |
| None | 41 | 36 | 37 | 50 |
| One or two | 28 | 30 | 31 | 25 |
| Three or more | 32 | 35 | 32 | 25 |
| Total | 100 | 100 | 100 | 100 |
| **Essential items cannot afford (no. of items)** | | | | |
| None | 70 | 61 | 51 | 76 |
| One or two | 24 | 29 | 36 | 20 |
| Three ormore | 7 | 10 | 13 | 4 |
| Total | 100 | 100 | 100 | 100 |
| **Proportion with at least one item in any of the above three** | 79 | 84 | 89 | 70 |
| Base (no. interviewed) | 67 (70) | 152 (162) | 245 (276) | 246 (392) |

Table 6.16 shows the main type of items mentioned in response to each question. Particularly striking are the proportions who said they found it difficult to afford children's clothing and shoes—nine in ten said this—and the fact that food was the item most likely to be mentioned as having been cut down. This may well reflect the fact that lone mothers devote most of their expenditure to essential items. The potential for cutting back must therefore be limited. This would also account for the fact that the lone mothers were less likely than the 'standard' two-parent families to say they had cut back on luxuries.

132

## Table 6.16

Missing items and cut backs at the FRS by receipt of supplementary benefit over two years: lone mothers at both interviews

| Missing items | Lone mothers | | | 'Standard' two-parent families |
|---|---|---|---|---|
| | Non-claimant (no SB) % | Irregular (some SB) % | Stable claimants (2 years SB) % | % |
| H/H equipment[1] | | | | |
| Furniture | 21 | 27 | 33 | 22 |
| Carpets | 15 | 11 | 18 | 12 |
| Bedding | 7 | 10 | 11 | 1 |
| Electrical goods | 20 | 25 | 25 | 16 |
| Cut back on | | | | |
| Food | 46 | 46 | 45 | 26 |
| Adult clothing/ shoes | 26 | 23 | 16 | 13 |
| Children's clothing/shoes | 15 | 16 | 12 | 5 |
| Luxuries[2] | 18 | 21 | 18 | 29 |
| Going out[3] | 36 | 42 | 42 | 35 |
| Travel | 2 | 2 | 3 | 9 |
| Fuel | 2 | 10 | 7 | 4 |
| Items cannot afford | | | | |
| Food | 3 | 5 | 7 | 4 |
| Adult clothing/ shoes | 6 | 18 | 17 | 8 |
| Children's clothing/shoes | 90 | 94 | 91 | 72 |
| H/H equipment | 13 | 9 | 16 | 5 |
| Fuel | 2 | 4 | 2 | 3 |
| Housing | 2 | 6 | 2 | 3 |
| Base (no. interviewed) | 67 (70) | 152 (162) | 245 (276) | 346 (392) |

1. Respondents could mention more than one item in each case.
2. This includes alcohol, tobacco, sweets and entertainment.
3. This includes those who say they never went out.

Finally, respondents were asked whether they had taken a holiday in the previous 12 months. Of the 'standard' two-parent families half (51 per cent) had compared with 45 per cent of the lone mothers who were non-claimants, 32 per cent of the stable claimants and 30 per cent of the irregular claimants.

# SUMMARY

Most of the FFS families—whatever their marital status—remained poor at the FRS. Perhaps the most striking conclusion is that, without two earners, working-class families in manual jobs are very likely to be financially hard-pressed, living close to the poverty line. It took two jobs (or perhaps more accurately one and a half) to be reasonably certain of a substantial increase in income. Lone mothers have no possibility for two earners—unless, of course, they cease to be lone mothers. Roughly speaking the lone mothers who did escape poverty were about equally divided between those who found a husband and those who found a job. The 'ex-lone mothers' were the most likely of all family types to escape poverty (remembering, however, that the analysis is in terms of *family* income) and often their family income rose quite substantially but again the significant factor in this was the employment status of the new couple. Some of 'ex-mothers' were living with an unemployed man, others were living with a man in low-paid employment and these families stayed poor—sometimes even experiencing a fall in income. Thus it is *employment* that is the key to escaping poverty for *all* family types.

Looking at the various indicators of the living standards of the lone mothers on benefit the main impression was of a life of some financial hardship and of a very restricted life-style. Those never on benefit (mainly widows) were better-off on all the indicators than those continuously on benefit or with some experience of benefit receipt. Those continuously on benefit for two years would have been receiving the higher long-term rate of benefit but this did not appear to significantly improve their standard of living, leaving many with unmet needs, debts and difficulties. However those who moved on and off benefit also appeared to be hard-pressed financially—and perhaps the financial advantage that might be gained by leaving supplementary benefit for employment is largely off-set by the consequent instability (and possible irregularity) of income. Thus if the choice is between long-term dependence on the low income of supplementary benefit or short-term dependence interspersed with spells in probably low-paid employment then neither seems to provide an adequate standard of living.

# Notes

1. This was set on the basis of a comparison of changes in the real levels of cash incomes and changes in the level of income relative to supplementary benefit. A number of different measures of changes in income and movements out of poverty were calculated and compared, but there was little variation in the overall results. For details see Millar (1987).

2. Changes in marital status—from one to two adults in the family or vice versa—mean that 'needs' as measured by supplementary levels would have changed as well as income. 'Needs' could also change for families without a change in marital status—for example because of the birth of a child or if a child had left home. Overall of the group defined as having had a rise in income 14 per cent had had a change in family composition which meant that their 'needs' had risen by at least 10 per cent. This group included all the 'new' two-parent families and 7 per cent of the two-parent families at both the FFS and the FRS. Five per cent had had a change which meant that their 'needs' had fallen. This included all the 'new' lone parents, 2 per cent of the two-parent families and 4 per cent of the lone mothers. But if family composition had not changed 97 per cent of the group defined as having had a rise would still have been included in that category. The 3 per cent who would not have been included all but one of the 'new' lone mothers, 2 per cent of the two-parent families and 2 per cent of the lone mothers.

3. For example in 1979 the short-term rate for a single householder was £15.55 and the long-term rate was £18.30. A lone mother on benefit for two years and with two children aged six and 11 would therefore have received £32.25 (approximately 110 per cent of the ordinary rate). Maximum disregarded earnings of £6.00 would take her up to about 130 per cent, receipt of additional requirements of about £2.50 would take her up to 140 per cent. An analysis of the 1982 FES showed that about 12 per cent of lone mothers on supplementary benefit had net incomes above 140 per cent of the ordinary scale rates (Millar, 1985).

4. Only single-unit households are included here which explains the slight difference between these figures and those given in the previous chapter.

5. It is therefore, perhaps, surprising that the incomes of these women were not slightly higher. In theory, all should have been receiving the long-term rate, which is about 25 per cent higher than the ordinary scale rate. In fact only about a quarter had incomes above that level. There are a number of possible reasons for this. First, the ordinary and long-term scale rates for children are exactly the same. Thus the larger the family or the older the children, the greater the proportion of supplementary benefit income is accounted for by the children's component, and therefore the smaller the gap between the long-term and ordinary scale rate. (For example, in 1979 the ordinary single households rate was £18.30 and the long-term rate was £23.70: equivalent to 129.5 per cent. If the claimant had two children, one

aged 5-10 and the other aged 13-15 the ordinary rate would become £33.99 and the long-term rate £39.39: equivalent to 115.9 per cent). Secondly, about a quarter of the women were having deductions made from their benefit for fuel direct. These were not counted as part of income (although housing direct deductions were) and hence the cash incomes of those with fuel direct payments would be correspondingly lower. Finally, it could be the result of differences in definitions: the calculation of income and housing costs from survey data need not necessarily be the same as the calculation for supplementary benefit purposes; and it may also be that some of the women over-stated the length of time they had been on benefit.

# 7 Income support in comparative perspective

As described in Chapter One Great Britain has not been alone in experiencing the changes in family structure that have lead to an increase in the proportion of families headed by a lone parent. Other industrialised countries have faced and are facing similar situations and this chapter therefore looks at the policy responses of other countries, concentrating mainly on Western Europe but also including material from Australia, Canada and the United States. It is divided into five main sections. The first three examine in turn each of the principal sources of income support for lone parents—employment, maintenance and social security. The final two sections examine the outcomes for lone parents in terms of income levels and the risk of poverty, and consider the relationship between benefit provisions and employment.

## EMPLOYMENT

We start with employment because it provides not only the context for income support policy but is also the outcome of particular mixes of benefits, fiscal policy and services. Table 7.1 shows the employment rates among women by marital status in the EEC countries in 1984. It includes only women aged 25 to 49, that is the age group most likely to have care of dependent children (published information is not separately available for women with dependent children only). Three points stand out from the table. First, widowed and divorced women are usually more likely to be employed than married women. The two exceptions to this are Denmark and the UK.

137

Secondly, there seems to be some association between the employment rates for married women and those of widowed and divorced women. Thus, for example, Denmark has high employment rates for both groups and Ireland has low rates for both groups. The main exception to this is Luxembourg where the employment rate of married women is 35 per cent while that of widowed and divorced women is 73 per cent. Thirdly, the UK stands out in the very high proportion of employed married women who are in part-time jobs—56 per cent compared with, for example, 42 per cent in West Germany which has the second highest rate of part-time employment.

Table 7.1

Female employment rates[1] in the EEC 1984 by marital status: women aged 25–49

| Country | Single | Marital status | | All | Proportion of employed married women aged 25–49 in part-time jobs |
| | | Married | Widowed or divorced | | |
| --- | --- | --- | --- | --- | --- |
| Begium | 71.5 | 49.4 | 53.7 | 51.3 | 22.0 |
| Denmark | 76.6 | 77.8 | 74.4 | 77.2 | 40.3 |
| FR Germany | 78.9 | 49.8 | 69.4 | 54.8 | 42.2 |
| France | 80.9 | 59.8 | 75.1 | 63.8 | 24.4 |
| Greece | 65.3 | 39.2 | 57.3 | 42.5 | 9.2 |
| Ireland | 76.8 | 22.5 | 39.1 | 31.2 | 24.2 |
| Italy | 65.0 | 40.5 | 63.9 | 44.2 | 10.6 |
| Luxembourg | 86.8 | 34.8 | 72.5 | 44.0 | 23.5 |
| UK | 75.9 | 58.5 | 57.7 | 59.9 | 56.1 |
| Europe[2] | 75.0 | 51.3 | 67.1 | 55.0 | na |

1.  Persons in employment as a percentage of the population of working age (14 and above) living in private households.
2.  Excluding the Netherlands, not included in 1984 LFS.

*Source:*  Statistical Office of the European Communities, *Labour Force Survey 1984*, Tables T07 and T41.

Focusing specifically on mothers, Table 7.2 shows the employment rates among lone and married mothers in four of the EEC countries (Denmark, France, Germany and the UK) and four other countries (Australia, Canada, Sweden and the United States). In general the patterns identified above seem to apply again: high employment rates for married and lone mothers seem to go together but lone mothers are usually more likely to be employed than married mothers. The UK is still an exception with married mothers more likely to be employed than lone mothers, and this is also true for Australia. In part this may be because the figures for the UK and Australia are more recent than those for the other countries, and in both these countries employment rates for lone mothers have fallen quite substantially in recent years. However going back to the late 1970s in the UK at that time 49 per cent of lone mothers were employed compared with 50 per cent of married mothers and in Australia the figures were 43 per cent and 45 per cent respectively. Thus the relatively low employment rates of the lone mothers compared with married mothers in these countries is not just a recent phenomenon. The table also shows that, of those in employment, full-time jobs are much more common for lone mothers than for married mothers.

Table 7.2

Proportions in employment, lone mothers and married mothers: various countries

| Country | Proportions in employment | | Of those employed, proportion in full-time jobs[1] | |
| | Lone mothers | Married mothers | Lone mothers | Married mothers |
| --- | --- | --- | --- | --- |
| Australia (1985) | 35 | 47 | 59 | 43 |
| Canada (1979) | 63 | 58 | – | – |
| Denmark (1978)[2] | 89 | 79 | 64 | 40 |
| France (1979) | 69 | 41 | – | – |
| FR Germany (1982) | 60 | 42 | 63 | 42 |
| Sweden (1979) | 86 | 64 | – | – |
| UK (1982/84) | 39 | 49 | 44 | 29 |
| US (1980) | 71 | 60 | 80 | 64 |

1. Definitions of full-time vary, but at least over 30 hours in all cases.
2. Those with two children only, includes employed and registered unemployed.

Sources: Australia: Dept. of Social Security (1986a) Table 8.
Canada: Kamerman and Kahn (1983) Table 5.
Denmark: Derived from EEC (1982) Table Denmark 3.
France: Kamerman and Kahn (1983) Table 5.
FR Germany: Derived from Schwarz (1986) p.152 and Table 5.
Sweden: Kamerman and Kahn (1983) Table 5.
UK: OPCS (1985b) Table 14.
US: Derived from Nichols-Casebolt (1986) Table 6.

How employment rates for lone mothers might be associated with income support policy is discussed in more detail later in the chapter, but it is useful to consider briefly here some of the factors that might account for the variations in employment rates among women with children across the different countries. Table 7.3 shows women's earnings relative to those of men in the EEC countries in 1972 and 1982. Over those ten years there was generally an increase in the earnings of women compared with men but nevertheless in most countries a significant gap remains. There is some suggestion of an association between employment rates for women and their level of earnings relative to men. Denmark and France both have relatively high proportions of women in employment and relatively high earnings for women compared with those of men. Ireland, Greece and Luxembourg have relatively low proportions of women in employment and relatively low earnings for women compared with men.[1]

Table 7.3

Women's average gross hourly earnings as a percentage of men's, manufacturing industry, EEC 1972 and 1982

| Country | 1972 | 1982 |
|---|---|---|
| Belgium | 68.1 | 72.4 |
| Denmark | na | 89.3[1] |
| FR Germany | 70.6 | 72.6 |
| France | 77.1 | 79.9 |
| Greece | na | 66.6[1] |
| Ireland | na | 68.4 |
| Italy | 76.4 | 88.7 |
| Luxembourg | 58.3 | 62.8 |
| Netherlands | 65.8 | 73.1 |
| UK | 58.8 | 69.4 |

1.   1981

*Source:*   Rimmer (1986b) Table 6.

The employment of women with children is likely to be determined to some extent by the availability of day care. It is very difficult to get accurate and comparable figures on day care, especially as most women rely not on officially provided day care but on making their own arrangements with relatives, friends, childminders and so on. This is the case even in France and Denmark which have the most extensive provision of day care in the

EEC countries (Cohen and Clarke, 1986). Table 7.4 gives some figures for the proportion of children aged three to five in education or day-care in various countries in 1982. The relatively high level of provision in France is apparent and indeed two-thirds of all day care places for children under three in the EEC are in France (House of Lords, 1984, p. 54). Belgium also has very high provision for this age group. Denmark has the highest level of provision of day care among these countries.

Table 7.4

Participation in education and day care among children aged three to five: various countries, 1982

| Country | Percentage of 3–5 year-olds in | |
|---|---|---|
| | Education | Day care |
| Belgium | 97 | – |
| Canada | 34 | 9 |
| Denmark (1984) | 11 | 65 |
| Finland | na | 33 |
| France | 97 | – |
| FR Germany | 60 | – |
| Ireland (1981) | 50 | 14 |
| Italy | 76 | – |
| Luxembourg | 62 | – |
| Netherlands | 66 | – |
| Norway (1981) | na | 27 (3 and 4 year old) |
| Sweden | 18 | 27 (3 and 4 year old) |
| UK | 61 | 27 |
| USA | 52 | – |

*Source:* DES (1986) Table 1.

Labour market participation rates among mothers are also likely to be affected to some extent by the employment protection given in the form of maternity rights and the arrangements for parental leave to care for children. In these respects the UK has tended to lag behind the other EEC countries (House of Lords, 1984) and indeed the UK is still blocking the EEC proposals for the introduction of a minimum right to parental leave. As regards maternity leave then in the UK paid leave is only available to women who have had at least two years continuous employment with the same employer, working at least 16 hours a week (or five years and eight to 16 hours). Daniel (1980) found that fewer than one-fifth of employed, pregnant women were able to fulfil these requirements. Maternity pay and maternity allowance (the contributory benefit) have recently been replaced by 'statutory maternity pay' which is administered by employers, with a lower rate of maternity allowance for women who do not qualify for statutory maternity pay. Re-instatement is now no longer guaranteed for women working in small establishments (less than five employees). In other EEC countries there are no conditions regarding length of employment and maternity benefit is usually earnings-related. No parental leave arrangements are available in the UK (except insofar as individuals or trade unions can make arrangements with employers) whereas most of the other EEC countries do have some statutory entitlements to parental leave (Ireland and the Netherlands being the other two countries with no parental leave).

As Cohen and Clarke (1986) point out most of the increase in labour market participation among mothers has taken place in the absence or relative shortage of state provided or subsidised child-care provision and most employed mothers make private arrangements for care. Nevertheless, factors such as day care provision, maternity rights and parental leave make it much easier for mothers to stay in, or take up, paid employment. The provision in these areas is less well-developed in the UK than in many other countries nor does the UK provide any subsidies in the form of tax relief. Thus it perhaps is not surprising to find part-time employment much more common among women with children in the UK than in other countries.

## MAINTENANCE

In order to compare different countries' policies towards maintenance there are four main areas that need to be considered: the liability to maintain, how decisions about the level of maintenance are reached, how payments are enforced and the value of these payments to the custodial parent. These are each considered in turn here.

### Setting and enforcing maintenance payments

A general trend across a number of countries has been towards limiting the extent of the liability to maintain. In general both parents are liable to maintain the children but the extent to which the man is liable to maintain the woman does vary from country to country. In England and Wales[2] the man's liability towards his ex-wife is limited, with the intention that both parties should become financially 'self-sufficient' after divorce. This is also broadly the situation in West Germany and Sweden. In Australia, Denmark and the United States spouses may be liable to maintain each other, depending on the economic circumstances of each. In France there is generally no liability for the spouse, unless this is specifically negotiated at the time of the divorce. In practice, in all these countries, maintenance for

142

the ex-partner is rare and in effect maintenance has largely become an obligation for child support.

Maintenance payments are generally set by the courts, and the two main factors usually taken into account in setting the level of awards are the needs of the children and the financial circumstances of the parents. In most countries conduct is no longer directly taken into account when determining maintenance awards although this is not the case in some Canadian provinces and American states and since 1984 in England and Wales conduct has been re-introduced as one of the factors that can be taken into consideration. The courts often have fairly wide discretionary powers in determining the amount of maintenance to be awarded. In the Nordic countries this discretion is limited by detailed guidelines and many other countries are also moving in this direction (see below).

The courts are also usually responsible for enforcement and most countries give the courts power to enforce awards through a variety of procedures such as the attachment of earnings, seizure of property, fines and ultimately imprisonment. These normally come into effect after default has occurred, although 'automatic enforcement' (that is, making the arrangements for deductions from earnings at the time the maintenance award is made) is operated in some Canadian provinces and American states.

As Griffiths et al. (1984, p. 3) point out:

> When discussing social developments it is rare that a general statement will hold true for all Western countries, but widespread non-compliance with maintenance orders seems to be a universal phenomenon.

Usually it is the custodial parent who is responsible for seeking to enforce the awards through the courts. However social security departments may become involved in this. Griffiths et al. (1984) distinguish between two broad approaches to state involvement. First, in the Nordic countries and more recently in European countries such as France and West Germany, there are 'advanced maintenance payments' schemes. Under these the state pays the child support maintenance (usually at a fixed amount) and seeks to recover the costs from the non-custodial parent. Although linked to private maintenance in their operation such schemes are better characterised as part of the social security system and are discussed in more detail below when we examine social security provisions for the lone parents.

The involvement of the state in enforcing maintenance in the UK, the US, Canada and Australia mainly comes into effect for lone parents who are receiving social assistance. In the UK supplementary benefit scheme the parent can assign her maintenance award to the DHSS. She then receives her supplementary benefit (assessed in the usual way) and DHSS seeks to enforce the award through the courts in order to try and recoup some of the costs. In 1984 there were 357,000 separated, divorced and single women on supplementary benefit where a third party had some liability to maintain (of whom 322,000 had dependent children). Approximately 8 per cent of the cost of benefit to these families was recouped from the liable relative (DHSS, 1986b, Table 34.94). In America the states are obliged (since 1974) to operate 'Child Support Enforcement Programs' with the aim of reducing the cost of the AFDC programme. For families claiming AFDC the Child Support Enforcement Programs seeks to obtain and enforce child support maintenance orders. Families not on AFDC may also make use of the service, usually for a fee. Quite wide powers are available to enforce payments including the attachment of earnings, collection through the tax system, and imprisonment. Any money received is off-set against AFDC payments and in 1982 it was estimated that approximately 7 per cent of total AFDC benefits paid were recouped in this way (Robins and Dickinson, 1984).

**The value of maintenance to the custodial parent**
Leaving aside the Nordic countries (which make extensive use of 'advanced maintenance schemes'—see below) then it seems to be generally true that maintenance is only of fairly limited financial value to divorced lone mothers. There are three main reasons for this: the low level of awards, the irregularity of payments and the fact that many of the awards made are never actually paid by the absent parent. In France, Charlesworth (1988) reports that 25 per cent of awards are not paid at all and 33 per cent are paid irregularly. A West German study (Napp-Peters, 1986) of 400 lone-parent families found that only 42 per cent of the divorced women received regular maintenance payments. For Great Britain estimates from the General Household Survey for 1982/83 show that about 50 per cent of divorced women with dependent children receive some maintenance but this is usually only a fairly small component of their income. Mitton et al. (1983) in their comparative study of poverty in France, West Germany and Britain found that, of non-widowed lone mothers (ie including unmarried mothers) 29 per cent were receiving maintenance in Rheims, 45 per cent in Saarbrucken and 22 per cent in Bristol.

A similar picture applies in the non-European countries. Estimates from Canada (Alberta Province) suggest that, only about a third of maintenance orders were paid in full and 30 per cent were not paid at all. Another Canadian study showed that the awards made were usually low, on average equivalent to only three-quarters of basic social assistance levels (all quoted in Griffiths et al., 1986). Australian estimates suggest that between 24 per cent and 29 per cent of lone mothers receive regular maintenance

(Charlesworth, 1988 and Griffiths et al., 1986). In 1981/82 71 per cent of those receiving maintenance were receiving less than 40 Australian dollars a week. In America, estimates from 1978 suggest that only 59 per cent of women potentially eligible to receive support actually have awards made to them. Of all children awarded support 49 per cent receive the full amount and 28 per cent receive nothing at all (Garfinkel, 1984).

Thus maintenance seems to be rarely a significant source of income for divorced lone mothers. Furthermore, even where awards are made and complied with there may still be no direct financial gain to the custodial parent. If she is receiving social assistance then usually any maintenance received will reduce, or even eliminate, the benefit entitlement. In all the countries considered here maintenance is taken into account in the means-test for social assistance and often claimants are required to make a claim for maintenance as a condition of receiving social assistance. The extent to which social assistance is a major part of social security for lone parents varies from country to country, depending on the availability of other benefits (see below). In the UK where supplementary benefit is the main source of income support for lone parents then in effect maintenance is of no financial value to non-employed lone mothers.

Not only does maintenance usually count as income for social assistance but the reverse may also be true—that, in setting the level of maintenance awards, the courts may take into account receipt or potential receipt of social assistance. This happens in many Canadian provinces and until the recent changes, in Australia where it was incorporated among the criteria used to determine the need for maintenance laid down in family law (Bartlett and Finlay, 1988).

## The future of maintenance

Maintenance has largely become a question of child support with few countries making provision for continuing support of ex-spouses. But despite this limitation on the obligation to maintain, it seems that maintenance raises the same problems almost everywhere. There is little agreement as to how the level of awards should be determined and judicial discretion means that there may be a great deal of variability and inconsistency. Awards made are often low and paid irregularly if at all. Enforcement procedures are weak. However in a number of countries there have been moves towards reform of family law as regards maintenance, probably mainly in response to the increasing costs of marital breakdown to social security. These reforms take three main forms: increased interest in 'advanced maintenance payments' (see below); moves to tighten up enforcement usually by making provision for automatic deduction of maintenance payments from wages; and moves to making decisions about the level of maintenance and the procedures for enforcement an administrative rather than a judicial function.

Australia has introduced major changes to child support following a report from the Cabinet Sub-Committee on Maintenance (1986). A Child Support Agency is to be established to assess child support obligations according to a set formula and to enforce collection and distribution through the Department of Social Security (Brennan, 1987; Saunders and Whiteford, 1987). In America the 'Wisconsin experiment' is one of the most developed schemes reflecting this 'new' approach to maintenance (Garfinkel, 1984). This scheme, which first ran as a pilot experiment, has now been introduced more generally in Wisconsin, and incorporates both a standard formula for determining child support and provisions for automatic deductions through the tax system. Other states in America are also moving in a similar direction 'away from judicial discretion towards the routinisation associated with taxation and social insurance' (Garfinkel and Wong, 1987, p. 8).

The aim of such reforms is to make maintenance work more efficiently and effectively. But alongside this there has been some pressure to make more radical changes to the way financial settlements are decided following divorce. Particularly influential in this has been the work of Weitzman (1981) evaluating the impact of 'no fault' divorce in California. Under this Californian law there are provisions for an equal division of property following divorce, but what Weitzman's research indicated is that this 'equal' division is in fact very unequal and very unfair to women. She argues that the current way of defining property fails to take into account the real economic contribution of women to marriage. This means that the supposed equal division of property is in fact unequal because it ignores the 'new property', that is the career assets that pertain to men but are lost to women because their employment is interrupted by domestic responsibilities.

Funder (1988), using empirical data from a large scale study of the employment histories during marriage of divorced men and women, puts forward a similar argument for Australia. The aim of these proposals is to re-value the contribution of women to marriage through their domestic work and thus to ensure that divorce settlements give some recognition to the unpaid labour of women as wives and mothers.

SOCIAL SECURITY

Aside from doing nothing, there are broadly three possible approaches to providing income support for lone parents:

(i)   include such families in the existing provisions for widows;
(ii)  modify or supplement the existing provisions that are available to

146

families with dependent children in general and/or those for low
income families;

(iii)   introduce 'new' benefits, specifically designed to meet the needs of
lone parents.

## Treat as widows

No country has entirely adopted the first option although Australia and
Ireland have both introduced benefits for certain categories of lone parents
which parallel the existing provisions for widows. In Australia the 'widows
pension' is payable to widows and to women who are divorced, 'deserted'
(for at least six months) or whose husbands are in prison. As with all main
social security benefits in Australia the benefit is both asset-tested and
means-tested (but with quite high levels of disregarded income, which vary
according to family size). In addition there is the 'supporting parents benefit'
which is payable to separated and unmarried mothers, widowers, and male
divorcees. The income and assets tests are the same as for the widows
pension. In total approximately 83 per cent of all lone parents in Australia
were receiving some form of state income support in 1985. The proportion
in receipt of benefits has grown steadily over recent years, up from about 57
per cent in 1974. Lone mothers are much more likely than lone fathers to be
in receipt of benefits (89 per cent compared with 29 per cent) and the majority
of lone mothers are receiving the supporting parents benefit rather than the
widows pension (Raymond, 1987).

The situation in Ireland is rather different. Here there is essentially a
three-tier system of social security consisting of social insurance benefits,
categorical social assistance benefits which are means-tested, and local
social assistance schemes which are means-tested and discretionary. In the
early 1970s the 'deserted wives benefit' was introduced. This is a social
insurance benefit for separated women (divorce is not allowed under Irish
civil law) payable at the same rate as the widows benefit and probably the
only example of marital breakdown being covered within a national
insurance scheme. For those who cannot meet the contribution conditions
there is a parallel categorical social assistance benefit (the 'deserted wives'
allowance') and a similar benefit for single mothers (the 'unmarried mothers
allowance').

The deserted wives benefit and allowance have fairly strict qualifying
conditions. They cannot be claimed for the first three months of 'desertion'.
The woman must prove desertion—if the couple have agreed to part (or are
deemed to have done so) this will disqualify her. She may be able to receive
the benefit if she left her husband, but only if she can prove she was 'forced'
to do so (for example, because he was physically violent). If he left her, but
she was judged to be at fault, then she can also be disqualified. She must

also show that she had made 'reasonable efforts' to trace her husband and obtain maintenance from him. If he does pay an 'adequate' amount of maintenance she will be disqualified. Not surprisingly many of the claims made fail, with as many as half of all applications for these two benefits being refused (Commission on Social Welfare, 1986) and even for those granted benefit there are often considerable delays (O'Connor et al., 1986).

## Amend existing provisions

Amending or adding to existing benefits in order to provide additional assistance for lone parents is a much more common approach. Additions to family allowances are perhaps the most obvious way to do this and both Britain and France have such additions, as do Denmark, Norway and Iceland. In Britain the 'one-parent benefit' is a small weekly addition to child benefit, available to all lone parents except widows. In France there are a number of means-tested supplements to the basic family allowance scheme (which does not cover one child families). There are two of particular relevance to lone parents—the 'complément familiale' (for those with at least one child under three or at least three children) and the 'allocation de parent isolé' (available for a maximum of 12 months or until the youngest child is aged three). This benefit provides a guaranteed minimum income for lone parents but is reduced for other income at an implicit tax rate of 100 per cent. It therefore provides little incentive to take paid employment and tends to be a short-term alternative to social assistance rather than a benefit paid alongside earnings. In 1984 only about 7 per cent of French lone parents were receiving the allocation de parent isolé (Charlesworth, 1988). Outside Europe, in Canada the national family allowance scheme contains no additions but local provinces may vary the scheme within certain limits and some provide additional assistance for lone parents in this way.

The tax system is also often used to provide additional help to employed lone parents. Additional tax allowances or rebates are available in, for example, Sweden, West Germany, Australia the US and the UK. In France tax liability is related to family size and marital status. In Canada lone parents can receive a tax allowance on child-care costs.

Lone parents also receive help through various means-tested provisions which are intended for all low-income families with children (rather than specifically for lone parents). Help with housing costs is commonly provided (in for example Sweden, West Germany, France and the UK). Supplements to low earnings through 'family income supplement' schemes are available in the UK, Ireland and Australia.

For non-employed lone parents, however, the absence of specific benefits in most countries means that such families will be dependent on the lowest rung of the social security system—the social assistance schemes.

148

They may however receive social assistance on slightly more generous terms than two-parent families. For example, in the UK lone parents on supplementary benefit are eligible for the higher long-term rate of benefit after one year while two-parent families where the man is unemployed never receive this higher rate. Lone parents are also allowed to retain more of their earnings from part-time employment than other claimants of supplementary benefits.

### 'New' benefits

The main benefit that would be included in this category are the 'advanced maintenance payments'. These are not strictly speaking 'new'—the Nordic countries have used such benefits for some years (Svenne-Schmidt, 1988)—but in recent years the idea has been taken up much more explicitly as a way of trying to improve the incomes of lone parents. Under these schemes the state guarantees to pay child maintenance usually when the non-custodial parent has defaulted on payments. The state then seeks to recoup the costs from the absent parent. In Sweden the advance maintenance payment is a non-means-tested, tax-free cash payment equivalent to 40 per cent of the 'base amount' used in Sweden as the basis for setting benefit levels. Thus the amount received in advance maintenance payment is standard and may be above or below the level of maintenance set by the courts. The allowance is also paid to unmarried mothers and is not dependent on the custodial parent having a court order for maintenance. In 1984 about 15 per cent of all children aged under 18 in Sweden were receiving advance

Table 7.5

Advance maintenance payments in the Nordic countries, 1984

| Children | Denmark | Finland | Iceland | Norway | Sweden |
|---|---|---|---|---|---|
| Number of children receiving (000) | 173 | 83 | 10 | 90[1] | 256 |
| As a percentage of all children under 17/18 | 13.7 | 7.1 | 13.6 | 9.0 | 14.7 |
| Amounts repaid as a pro-portion of amounts paid | 85 | 42 | 58 | 55 | 32[2] |

1. Estimated.
2. Of the total amount of which repayment may be claimed, approximately 78 per cent is repaid.

*Source:* Statistical Report of the Nordic Countries (1987) Table 4.3.3.1

maintenance payments. Approximately 32 per cent of the total costs were recovered. However this includes cases where there was no obligation for re-payment, excluding these then as much as 78 per cent of the costs were recovered (Statistical Report of the Nordic Countries, 1987). Denmark, Norway, Finland and Iceland all have similar schemes, and as Table 7.5 shows significant proportions of children receive such payments and recovery levels are quite high, particularly in Denmark where 85 per cent of the total is repaid.

Of the European countries both West Germany and France have recently introduced similar, although more restricted, schemes. The German scheme was introduced in 1980 and is available only where the custodial parent has obtained a court order regarding maintenance and the absent parent has defaulted. The amount—which is non-means tested, tax-free and a standard amount—is available for a maximum of three years or until the child reaches the age of six. Similarly in France the scheme (introduced on a trial basis in 1981 and fully enacted in 1984) is restricted to families where a court order for maintenance has been made and the absent parent has missed at least two months consecutive payments. The level is set according to the maintenance award, up to a maximum which is equivalent to the guardians allowance for one child (this latter is a benefit for orphans or children abandoned by one or both parents). The payment is not means-tested. Neither the French nor German schemes are very extensive as yet. Only 2,000 children were receiving some support through the French scheme in 1981. In West Germany unmarried mothers seem to be more likely to benefit from the scheme than divorced or separated women, with 38 per cent of the former but only 9 per cent of the latter receiving payments (Department of Social Security, Australia, 1986b).

The advance maintenance payments schemes seem to offer a number of advantages as a method of providing financial assistance to lone parents. They provide something of a bridge between the private and the public system of income support, providing the custodial parent with guaranteed support without entirely undermining the obligation of the absent parent to provide support. In addition, as Kamerman and Kahn (1983, p. 461) point out, the focus is on the support of the child and not on support for the parent,

> Increasingly, the issue of child support is no longer viewed as the need to compensate a single-parent family for the loss of the income of the absent parent. Instead, the need is for compensation for the absence of that parent's contribution toward the support of the child.

Thus unlike widows' benefit, these payments are not based on the assumption of dependency but rather assume that parents are self-supporting while recognising the need for extra help in the costs of raising children.

Different countries can be categorised according to these different broad approaches to income support for lone parents. Australia and Ireland come the closest to treating all lone parents in the same way, regardless of marital status. The Nordic countries use 'advanced maintenance payments' in order to provide direct and non-means-tested support, intended for the children and not the custodial parent. Western European countries, including the UK, are more likely to have amended or added to existing programmes for families with children rather than making any radical changes, although some are now experimenting with advanced maintenance payments.

However one country which does not fit very happily into this schema is the United States. In the United States widows may be eligible for a national insurance benefit (a 'survivors pension'). Other lone parents may be eligible for the Aid to Families with Dependent Children (AFDC) programme, which (within Federal guidelines) varies from state to state. However in many states *only* lone-parent families are eligible for AFDC assistance, two-parent families are not. Thus the American approach has been effectively to provide very limited social assistance support for lone parents, but to provide better support for lone parents than for other families with children. Alongside this the United States has also concentrated on improving and enforcing maintenance payments for divorced and separated lone mothers—that is policy has concentrated on seeking to make private support operate more effectively rather than increase public support.

## OUTCOMES

Having examined the sources of income of lone parents in various countries this section examines how successful the different form of provision are in maintaining the incomes of lone parents. In order to compare income support for lone mothers in different countries it is necessary to have a common standard for comparison. The usual method adopted for such comparisons is to make, within each country, comparisons between the incomes of a given family type (in this case a lone mother) and average earnings or average incomes for another standard family type (for example a two-parent family). This does not of course provide a comparison of the relative living standards between different countries: lone mothers in country A may have higher incomes relative to the standard than those in country B, but incomes in general may be substantially lower in country A than in country B. For the purposes of comparing the success of different types of income support policies for lone parents it makes sense to compare each country relative to its own standard, rather than relative to a fixed standard for all countries, which would make it difficult to disentangle differences in general living standards from differences in income support provisions.

These comparisons—of 'model' types of families of a specified size and with specified incomes—cannot be used as a straightforward guide to the actual situation in different countries. The 'model' family types may be representative of all lone-parent families to a greater or lesser degree in different countries, and the benefits that exist in theory for different groups may not in practice be received by those groups. In the UK for example the take-up rates of means-tested benefits are often not complete. Family income supplement, intended as a wage supplement for families with low earnings (and hence a potentially important benefit for lone parents), is estimated to be received by only about half of those entitled. The French 'allocation de parent isolé' also has a fairly low take-up rate. Thus the rank ordering of the countries in terms of the benefits they provide in theory could be completely altered by differences in the efficiency with which they deliver the benefits to those for whom they are intended. We therefore begin by looking at the 'model family' comparisons and then go on to examine the outcome in practice by describing the results of national and cross-national poverty studies. Finally we look at the relationship between employment rates and social security provision.

### 'Model' families

Kahn and Kamerman's (1983) study of income support provision in eight countries provides the most recent (referring to 1979) and extensive information. Three types of lone-mother family were considered in their study. In each of the three the family structure is the same—a separated lone mother with two children aged two and seven. In the first type the lone mother is not employed, having last worked before her second child was born. In the second type the situation is the same except that the lone mother has a court order for child support maintenance which the absent parent does not in fact pay. In the third type she is employed part-time (for 25 hours a week) earning half of the average manual worker's wage in each country. The countries included are Australia, Canada, France, West Germany, Israel, Sweden, the UK and the US.

In terms of income levels the first and second type of lone-mother family come out almost exactly the same in all the countries. At that time only Sweden among these countries had an 'advance maintenance payment' scheme and in the Swedish system the scheme operates regardless of whether or not the custodial parent has a court order for maintenance.[3] The most interesting comparisons are therefore between the employed and the non-employed lone mothers. Table 7.6 shows the results for these two types of lone-mother families, comparing their incomes with average earnings of male manual workers. The countries are shown in rank order according to their relative 'generosity' to employed lone mothers. As the table shows

152

Sweden comes at the top of the ranking in terms of support to both employed and non-employed lone mothers. The state of Pennsylvania comes out at the bottom in both cases. The UK is in the middle ranks for both. The non-employed lone mother 'lives on a very tight income level in most countries' (Kahn and Kamerman, 1983, p. 18)—with incomes at the level of only around half of average male manual earnings in five of the countries. Employment generally provides quite a substantial boost to income. The two exceptions to this are France and West Germany where the income levels of employed and non-employed lone mothers seem to be very similar.

Table 7.6

The incomes of lone mothers by employment status in relation to average wages in eight countries, 1979

| | Net income as a proportion of APWW[1] | |
| | Lone mother with two children, aged 2 and 7 | |
| Country | Employed[2] (rank) | Not employed (rank) |
| --- | --- | --- |
| Sweden | 123.1 (1) | 93.8 (1) |
| US New York | 100.8 (2) | 54.9 (4) |
| France | 87.8 (3) | 78.6 (2) |
| UK | 83.0 (4) | 51.7 (6) |
| Australia | 78.8 (5) | 50.0 (7) |
| Canada | 75.9 (6) | 52.5 (5) |
| Israel | 71.5 (7) | 50.0 (7) |
| FR Germany | 70.9 (8) | 67.3 (3) |
| US Pennsylvania | 69.2 (9) | 44.0 (9) |

1.  Average Production Workers Wage
2.  At 25 hours per week, earning half the average production workers wage.

*Source:*  Kahn and Kamerman (1983) Table 5.0.

In order to see how these income levels are obtained Tables 7.7 and 7.8 show the sources of income for first the employed and then the non-employed lone mothers. From Table 7.7 it can be clearly seen that the most 'generous' countries to employed lone mothers are those which provide substantial supplements to earnings. In Sweden the earnings of the lone mother are almost doubled by the other sources of income, with 'advance maintenance payments' providing about a fifth of the total income. The importance of family allowances in France can also be seen.

153

## Table 7.7

### Sources of income, part-time employed lone mothers with two children, eight countries, 1979

| Country | Family allowance | Housing benefit | Social assistance | Advance maintenance payments | Other | Earnings |
|---|---|---|---|---|---|---|
| Sweden | 10.1 | 16.7 | – | 21.8 | – | 51.3 |
| US New York | – | – | 28.5 | – | 11.8[1] | 59.7 |
| France | 23.7[2] | 13.9 | – | – | – | 62.4 |
| UK | 16.9 | – | – | – | – | 88.0 |
| Australia | 5.8 | – | 23.5 | – | – | 70.7 |
| Canada | 5.4 | – | 4.1 | – | 8.4[3] | 82.1 |
| Israel | 12.0 | – | – | – | – | 88.0 |
| FR Germany | 13.1 | 8.2 | – | – | – | 78.7 |
| US Pennsylvania | – | – | 6.9 | – | 9.9[4] | 83.2 |

1. Refundable tax credits 3.6%; Food stamps 8.2%.
2. Family allowance (8.4%) plus Family Allowance Supplement (15.5%).
3. Refundable tax credits.
4. Refundable tax credits 5.2%; Food stamps 4.7%.

*Source:* Kahn and Kamerman (1983) Table AB–2.

Table 7.8 shows the sources of income for non-employed lone mothers, here in rank order of 'generosity' towards these families. The most 'generous' countries are those which rely least on social assistance as such, although the top three countries do use means-tested benefits. All three use housing benefits, in France the 'allocation de parent isolé' is means-tested as is unemployment assistance in West Germany. However it is the countries which rely almost entirely on social assistance where incomes tend to be very low.

Thus the results from this study suggest that if lone mothers are not employed this usually means dependence on social assistance and social assistance usually means a fairly low income. Employment will therefore usually mean a rise in income, especially where other sources of income are available to supplement earnings. Family allowance schemes are particularly important in this respect and the extensive family allowance schemes in France are reflected in the high ranking of France in terms of income support to lone mothers. In Sweden the 'advance maintenance payments' are a major source of income for both employed and non-employed lone mothers.[4]

154

## Table 7.8

### Sources of income, non-employed lone mothers with two children, eight countries, 1979

| Country | Family allowance | Housing benefit | Social assistance | Advance maintenance payments | Other |
|---|---|---|---|---|---|
| Sweden | 13.3 | 22.0 | 36.1 | 28.6 | – |
| France | 26.5[1] | 21.1 | – | – | 52.4[2] |
| FR Germany | 13.9 | 11.2 | – | – | 75.0[3] |
| US New York | – | – | 79.5 | – | 20.5[4] |
| Canada | 7.8 | – | 80.1 | – | 12.1[5] |
| UK | 27.1 | – | 72.9 | – | – |
| Australia | 9.2 | – | 90.8 | – | – |
| Israel | 17.1 | – | 82.9 | – | – |
| US Pennsylvania | – | – | 77.6 | – | 22.4[4] |

1. Family allowance (9.4%) plus Family Allowance Supplement (17.1%).
2. Allocation de parent isolé.
3. Unemployment assistance.
4. Food stamps.
5. Refundable tax credit.

*Source:* Kahn and Kamerman (1983) Table AB–1.

The Kahn and Kamerman study also included comparisons of a whole range of different types of family, not just lone mothers. Without going into details two points of interest emerge from these. First, the countries that are most 'generous' to lone-mother families also tend to be most 'generous' to families with children in general. Thus it is not simply that lone mothers receive special treatment in these countries, indeed it would perhaps be more accurate to say that the level of income support available to lone parents depends to a large extent on the generosity or otherwise of existing income support schemes for all families with children. Secondly, although non-employed lone mothers are usually dependent on social assistance, on a per capita basis in most countries they tend to be at least marginally better-off than the other group who are also likely to be dependent on state benefits for all or most of their incomes—the long-term unemployed. Nor are 'large' two-parent families treated very generously in any of the countries, although such families would generally be slightly better-off than a non-employed lone mother. In terms of what might be considered particularly vulnerable families (lone parents, large families, families experiencing unemployment) the lone mothers appear to be relatively well-protected—provided they can obtain some employment.

## The risk of poverty
The 'model families' approach looks at how different systems work in theory but empirical research is needed to see what actually happens in practice. There are in fact very few studies which compare income levels and poverty in more than one country on a standard basis. One study which does allow comparisons to be made between different countries was carried out by Mitton et al. (1983) as part of the first EEC anti-poverty programme. This comparative study was based on interviews carried out in three towns in Britain (Bristol), France (Rheims) and Germany (Saarbrucken). The main focus of the study was unemployment and poverty, but some interesting comparisons emerge with regard to lone mothers. The poverty line was defined in this study in relation to a 'standard income' which was set in each town at the level of the median income of the households in the sample where the head was in full-time work. Taking into account household size, 'poor' households were those with incomes below 60 per cent of this standard. In Bristol 33 per cent of the lone mothers were found to be in poverty, compared with 26 per cent in Rheims and 40 per cent in Saarbrucken. For two-parent families the proportions in poverty were 12 per cent, 21 per cent and 18 per cent respectively.

The risk of poverty was substantially lower if the lone mother was employed and employment rates were significantly higher in both Rheims and Saarbrucken than they were in Bristol. However of those not employed the lone mothers in Bristol had the lowest risk of poverty. The authors of the report suggest that the existence and structure of the supplementary benefit scheme is the major difference between Bristol and the other two towns. The vast majority of the non-employed lone mothers in Bristol were receiving supplementary benefit and this kept them at a 'middling-to-poor but not very poor level', whereas the non-employed lone mothers in Rheims and Saarbrucken would receive only very low social assistance payments.

This study suggests some caution in interpreting the 'model family' comparisons reported in the previous section. The first is that, despite their advantages in theory, in practice the French and German systems do not appear to be significantly better than the British system in preventing poverty amongst lone parents, and indeed 'extreme poverty' is apparently less likely under the British system. This suggests that the importance of supplementary benefit as a 'safety-net' should not be underestimated, a point also stressed by Walker et al. (1984) in their survey of anti-poverty policy in Europe. The survey results also probably reflect the extent to which the benefits available in theory are actually received in practice. Thus for example, while the French system appears reasonably comprehensive in theory, in practice

> Several of these benefits and grants, however, depend on a very active effort on the part of the applicant, and it is well known in France that there are often problems in obtaining social rights and in receiving the benefits to which one is formally entitled. (EEC, 1982, p. 38)

In the UK take-up is also well known to be a problem—however the take-up of supplementary benefit is generally higher than the take-up of other means-tested benefits, and it may also be the case that take-up of supplementary benefit is higher than that of the more discretionary and locally administered French and German social assistance schemes. The wider means-tests operated for social assistance in France and Germany (where parents of a lone parent have an obligation to provide support) may also deter some potential claimants in those countries.

In addition the calculations made by Kahn and Kamerman were based on particular assumptions, not only with regard to full take-up of all benefits, but also with reference to the family types chosen. In Germany the non-employed lone mothers were assumed to be eligible for unemployment rather than assistance benefits. In practice it would appear that the discretionary assistance benefits are both more commonly received and less generous. In France the assumption that the lone mother had a child aged two meant that the calculations for the non-employed lone mother included the 'allocation de parent isolé'. This is a means-tested benefit available for up to one year or until the child is aged three, and in Kahn and Kamerman's calculations provided over half of the income of the non-employed lone mother. But in practice very few families receive this benefit. Thus, the gap between incomes in and out of work for lone mothers, although in theory not very high in France and Germany, is in practice probably rather more substantial.

That lone-parent families have a much higher risk than average of poverty in most countries is also confirmed by a recent study based on an analysis of the Luxembourg Income Data—a collection of national data sets relating to household income and expenditure which can be analysed on a comparable basis (Smeeding et al., 1988). As Table 7.9 shows, using a poverty line set by the US poverty line converted into national currencies, in all eight countries included (with the exception of Sweden and to a lesser extent Switzerland) children in lone-parent families run a very high risk of poverty. Over half were estimated to be living in poverty in Australia and in the USA and about two-fifths in the UK, Canada and West Germany. In all countries children in two-parent families had a much lower risk of poverty—although it should be remembered that most poor children will be living with two parents not one, simply because two-parent families are the majority.

Table 7.9

Poverty rates of children by family type for selected countries, 1979–1982

| | Poverty rates[1] of children | |
| | Lone-parent families | Two-parent families |
| Country | % | % |
| --- | --- | --- |
| Australia | 65.0 | 12.4 |
| Canada | 38.7 | 6.8 |
| FR Germany | 35.1 | 4.9 |
| Norway | 21.6 | 4.4 |
| Sweden | 8.6 | 4.5 |
| Switzerland | 12.9 | 4.1 |
| UK | 38.6 | 9.5 |
| USA | 51.0 | 9.4 |

1.   Proportion who have adjusted disposable income below the US poverty line converted into national currencies using the OECD purchasing power paritites.

*Source:*   Smeeding, Torrey and Rein (1988) Table 6.

## SOCIAL SECURITY AND EMPLOYMENT

In the first section of this chapter it was noted that the employment rates of lone mothers varied quite substantially across different countries, and that they were particularly low in the UK and Australia.  France and West Germany provide an interesting contrast with the UK and Australia in this respect.  In all four countries the employment rates for married mothers are similar (at around 40 to 50 per cent) but in France about 70 per cent of lone mothers are employed, in West Germany about 60 per cent, in the UK only about 40 per cent and in Australia only about 35 per cent (see Table 7.2). Having described the income support arrangements in these countries, can any conclusions be reached as to whether these differences in employment rates are the result of differences in the structure and level of social security provisions?

It does indeed seem to be the case that the UK and Australia on the one hand, and France and West Germany on the other, start from different assumptions about employment. In the UK provision for lone parents is largely based on the premise that lone mothers should not have to work, that they should be allowed to stay at home to care for their children. This was one of main principles of the Finer report, and remains implicit in many of the rules governing entitlement to benefit for lone mothers. Thus lone parents on supplementary benefit are not required to register for employment and are effectively guaranteed long-term (albeit subsistence level) support for as long as the children are dependant. Unlike the unemployed (where one of the chief concerns influencing policy is the perceived need to maintain work incentives) lone parents receive the higher long-term rate of benefit after one year. Furthermore there is little by way of positive policies to encourage employment. Child-care services are minimal and there is no financial assistance with child-care costs. As women, the earnings that lone mothers can achieve are usually low, but (apart from child benefit and the rather low one-parent benefit) the only additional assistance that employed lone mothers receive is means-tested help through the family income supplement and housing benefit schemes. There are problems with the take-up of both of these benefits and, perhaps more importantly, they also mean that lone parents are likely to be caught in a 'poverty trap' which extends across a wide range of earnings. Thus the financial incentives for lone parents to take employment are weak. (According to Joshi, 1987a the change to the new schemes of income support and family credit in 1988 does not significantly alter this.)

The situation in Australia is similar where the assumption is also that lone parents should not have to take paid work. The discussion paper on lone parents produced as part as the current Australian review of social security (Raymond, 1987, p. 9) states that

> lone parents should be provided with the opportunity to stay at home to care for their children, although at the same time financial or other barriers to workforce participation or family reformation should be minimised.

As in the UK, lone parents on benefit in Australia do not have to pass a 'work-test' (ie they are not required to be seeking employment) and the means-tested structure of provision creates in effect high marginal tax rates and a financial disincentive to employment. Child-care provision is very limited, and a background study to the review (Frey, 1986) found that about 60 per cent of the non-employed lone mothers said that difficulty with child-care was the major barrier to their taking employment. However (and as in the UK) many of the non-employed lone mothers said that they would prefer to be employed (about half saying they would like part-time work and about a third full-time work).

In France and West Germany the situation is different in three main respects. First there is an assumption that lone mothers should be employed and thus the same 'work tests' apply to lone parents on benefits as to other claimants. In West Germany social assistance is administered locally and Kahn and Kamerman (1983, p. 93) note that 'in most places the policy expressed is that if the youngest child is under three ... at least part-time work is expected; a full day's work is expected in many places as children reach older ages'. Secondly subsidised child-care provision is much more widely available in these countries (as Table 7.4 showed). Thirdly the approach to social assistance in these countries is very different from that of the UK (although not of other European countries). Social assistance in France and West Germany is much more discretionary and administered at a local rather than a national level. The rates of benefit also tend to be much lower in relation to the cost of living. Thus the high employment rates of lone mothers in France and West Germany may be, at least in part, because these countries offer no adequate alternative to even low-paid jobs. As Mitton et al. (1983, p. 109) conclude:

> The idea implicit in the British system is that benefits for this group can be, if necessary, an alternative to earnings. In France and Germany, by contrast, benefits for one-parent families seem to be seen as a supplement to earnings rather than an alternative; a one-parent family living without earnings and without income of some other kind, such as maintenance payments, would have to get by on a very low income from benefits alone.

In most other countries also it seems to be the case that income support provision for lone parents starts from the assumption that lone parents should be employed. This is certainly true in the Nordic countries and in these countries advance maintenance payments, being non-means-tested and tax-free, act as an effective supplement to earnings. In the United States lone parents receiving AFDC are not only required to register for employment as a condition of receiving assistance but increasingly in many states they are required to accept employment or training under the various schemes that make up 'workforce'. Burghes (1987) provides a description of these schemes which cover a whole range of different types of programme, including those which require employment at the minimum wage rate to 'work off' the AFDC benefit.

The UK and Australia therefore seem to be rather out-of-step with many other countries in assuming that employment should be a choice rather than a necessity for lone parents. The disadvantages of this approach are that the financial incentives to employment tend to be weak and long-term dependence on benefit likely to be the result—in effect the 'choice' is limited by the failure to develop positive policies to encourage employment. On the other hand this may be better than encouraging employment 'negatively' by providing only very limited support for those who are not employed. Furthermore in a situation of high unemployment many lone parents will be unable to obtain jobs and there will obviously be a need for continued income support for such families.

## SUMMARY

Looked at in comparative perspective there have been quite wide variations in policy response to the increased numbers of lone-parent families. As regards private maintenance many countries have been seeking ways to make this operate more efficiently. Maintenance for ex-spouses is now uncommon and the issue is generally how to make child support obligations both equitable and effective. As part of moves towards more standardised provisions in a number of countries there has been a shift away from judicial to administrative responsibility for decisions about maintenance. Stricter enforcement measures have also been developed including provisions for the automatic collection of maintenance through the tax system.

As regards social security policy one of the most crucial differences between countries relates to whether or not it is considered appropriate for lone parents to be in paid employment. In the UK, and also in Australia, the assumption is that ideally lone mothers (in particular) should not be forced to take paid employment. This is very different from the approach of most other European countries, of the Nordic countries and of the United States; and the outcome of this can be seen in the different labour market participation rates of lone mothers across the various countries. Thus in most countries income maintenance policy for lone parents is based on the premise that social security benefits should act as a supplement to, rather than as a replacement for, earnings.

Within this basic difference the most common approach to meeting the needs of lone parents has been to amend or add to existing provisions for families to provide additional help to lone-parent families. However some European countries have recently begun to borrow the traditional Scandinavian approach and introduced 'advance maintenance payments' schemes. These schemes involve the state paying a cash benefit to the custodial parent and where possible, recovering this from the absent parent. The benefit is intended to offer child support and not as an income-maintenance benefit for the parent. Thus the principle could be defined as the need for additional financial support for children who are in

161

the sole care of one parent rather than as compensation to the family for loss of the 'breadwinner'. Such a shift in focus seems to offer a number of advantages: it could bring more closely into line the systems of private maintenance and public support for lone-parent families, it fits better with individual entitlement to benefits rather than entitlement derived through others, and it can be seen as a benefit which can run in conjunction with, rather than as a replacement for, earnings.

In most of the countries for which information is available it is clear that lone mothers and their children have an above average risk of being in poverty. For non-employed lone mothers the risk is particularly high because, in the absence of other sources of income, social assistance generally only provides a basic subsistence income. For employed lone mothers the risk of poverty is lower, but nevertheless low earnings mean that many employed lone mothers will also be poor, particularly as they are likely to have relatively higher costs (for example, for housing and child-care) than two-parent families. Furthermore in some countries lack of adequate provision for non-employed lone mothers may mean that the women are being 'pushed' into low-paying jobs. While the risk of poverty may be higher or lower in different countries (and indeed for different types of lone parents within countries),[5] in general the income maintenance policies do not prevent significant proportions of lone mothers from being in poverty. The main exception to this seem to be Sweden (and perhaps also the other Nordic countries) where high employment rates, with earnings supplemented by advance maintenance payments appear to be sufficient to lift the families from poverty and achieve a fairly equitable distribution of income between different family types.

## Notes

1. See Ermisch (1983) for a discussion of the possible factors which have led to the increase in labour market participation among women. He concludes that a significant factor in this has been the changing industrial distribution of employment towards those services and industries where there is a high demand for female labour. However increases in female real wages are also an important factor.

2. The situation is slightly different in Scotland and Northern Ireland. Here we describe the position in England and Wales only.

3. Kahn and Kamerman do not discuss the outcome if the absent parent had been paying the child support. But, given that maintenance is usually taken into account in assessing eligibility to social assistance and given that the non-employed mothers were usually receiving social assistance, then the outcome if maintenance was being paid would presumably have been more or less the same.

4. It is interesting to compare these results with the study by Cockburn and Heclo

(1974) carried out as part of the Finer report. The Cockburn and Hecklo study referred to the early 1970s and included Norway, Sweden, Denmark, the Netherlands, West Germany and the UK. The three Nordic countries were the most generous and again advance maintenance payments were an important factor in this. In the three Nordic countries employed lone mothers had incomes significantly higher than those of non-employed lone mothers and their incomes were close to (or even above) those of one-earner two-parent families.

5.   There are, for example, differences according to race.  In the United States black lone mothers are significantly more likely to be poor and/or to be welfare recipients than white lone mothers (Robins and Dickinson, 1984; Ellwood, 1986).

# 8 Current and future policy

This final chapter has three main aims. First to summarise the main results from the FFS/FRS analysis, secondly to set these in the context of recent economic and policy changes, and thirdly to consider the future of income support policy for lone parents in the UK.

## THE FFS/FRS: SUMMARY AND DISCUSSION

Lone parents are not an homogenous group, they include a wide variety of different types of family—young, single women caring for babies, divorced and separated women caring for both pre-school and school age children, widows and widowers whose children are in their final years of education, battered wives who have fled violent husbands, professional women 'choosing' lone motherhood, divorced couples who are 'part-time' parents sharing their children with their ex-spouse, fathers who have had little experience of child care, mothers who have had little experience of paid employment—and so on. Nor, on the evidence of this analysis, are poor lone parents an homogenous group. Certainly some families are much more at risk of poverty than others—lone mothers more so than lone fathers, non-widowed lone mothers more so than widowed lone mothers, those who are not employed more so than those in employment, large families more so than small families, and those with young children more so than those with older children. But even within a low-income sample such as in the FFS

164

there were some quite substantial variations in income. The worst-off were the young women with young children, living in rented accommodation and entirely dependent on supplementary benefit. The better-off were older women with older children. These women usually had sources of income other than, or in addition to, supplementary benefit—widows benefits, earnings or maintenance—or, better still a combination of earnings with either of the other two. (It should be remembered, of course, that these women were only 'better-off' relative to the other lone parents in the sample—they still had low incomes.)

However in stressing the differences between the lone parents it is important to note also the similarities in the circumstances of these families. Chief among these is the very high degree of dependence on supplementary benefit. At each of the interviews eight out of ten lone mothers were on benefit. Only 17 per cent of the lone mothers in the sample were never on benefit during the period of the study, and those who had no experience of benefit were most commonly widows or the women who were able to supplement income from earnings with maintenance payments. More than the other types of family (lone fathers and two-parent families) the lone mothers were likely to be continuously on benefit—over half of the non-widowed lone mothers were on benefit for the full two years of the study. Another third had recourse to supplementary benefit on one or more occasions during the two years. Most of the women who separated from their partners came onto benefit. Supplementary benefit is clearly a very important source of income for lone mothers—even more so than is suggested by the cross-sectional statistics on the number in receipt at any one time.

Furthermore social security benefits are an important source of income to those lone mothers who are in employment. Almost half of the employed lone mothers at the FFS were combining part-time employment with receipt of supplementary benefit and a further 9 per cent were receiving family income supplement. Of the non-supplementary benefit recipients six in ten were receiving help with housing costs. However it was child benefit rather than means-tested benefits that provided the most substantial contribution to the incomes of the lone mothers not on supplementary benefit. Child benefit contributed, on average, about 20 per cent of the net incomes of the lone parents. Poor take-up of means-tested benefits meant that some families were losing quite substantial amounts of income. The number of lone parents on very low incomes (below ordinary supplementary benefit rates) would have fallen by about half had the families received all the means-tested benefits to which they were entitled. Benefits in kind, such as free school meals, also made a significant contribution to the living standards of the families.

Another circumstance that the lone parents were very likely to experience in common was the very high risk that they would stay poor. The two-parent families most likely to escape poverty between the two interviews were those who became two-earner families. Indeed for the two-parent families if the only change was the man returning to paid work from unemployment while the woman remain out of employment, then the risk of poverty stayed high. Given that male earnings alone were often insufficient to prevent poverty then it is not too surprising to find that even among the lone mothers who took full-time jobs a substantial proportion (about 40 per cent) did so with little or no improvement on their supplementary benefit income.

Among the lone mothers who escaped poverty about half had done so effectively because they were no longer lone parents. Living with an employed man, and being employed herself, seems to have been the best strategy for a lone mother to achieve a substantial increase in family income. Much of this income did, however, come from the man's earnings and thus while 'family' income was substantially higher the 'direct' or 'personal' income of the lone mother may have been lower. However this change in marital status did also seem to bring an improvement in general living standards—in housing, access to assets and so on. Marriage (or re-marriage or cohabitation) was also very likely to mean that the lone mothers came off supplementary benefit—and indeed was the most common reason for lone mothers ceasing to receive benefit.

Crudely speaking, in the current situation there are two options open to lone mothers in order for them to escape poverty and dependence on supplementary benefit. They can either form a 'new' two-parent family or seek full-time employment. Both carry risks of course. The 'new' two-parent family will only be out of poverty if the man, and preferably both the man and the woman, are in full-time work and keep out of unemployment. The lone mother will lose some degree of control over income and this financial control is often very important to lone mothers (Graham, 1987). Full-time employment for the lone mother will certainly reduce her risk of poverty but low wages and the costs of employment (such as child-care, travel and so on) mean that the risk is still relatively high.

One of the main aims of the study was to examine the living standards of low-income lone parents in order to try and assess the adequacy of their incomes to meet their needs. In particular, given the high degree of dependence on supplementary benefit and the increasing numbers of lone parents dependent on benefit for very lengthy periods (representing several years of childhood for their children) then the adequacy of supplementary benefit is a central concern. However it is very difficult to draw any firm conclusions about this question. As Baldwin and Cooke (1984) point out

166

there are no agreed criteria by which to judge the adequacy of supplementary benefit. Baldwin and Cooke identify five different approaches to measuring adequacy: how benefit levels were originally set and changes in their real value; equity between different types of claimant; the extent to which benefit rates meet basic needs; differences in living standards between those on and those not on benefit; and normative standards, that is views about the standard of living which the benefit levels *ought* to provide.

This study used a mixture of these approaches and focused in particular on the long-term rate of benefit. In terms of equity between lone mothers and two-parent families on benefit then the long-term rate did seem to give the lone mothers a slight advantage over the two-parent families, but this was very minimal, and when families within the same income range were compared then both groups seem to have been about equally hard-pressed. This does not exactly tally with the results obtained by Berthoud (1984) in his study of the impact of the 1980 Social Security Act. His results suggest that unemployed two-parent families were rather worse-off than lone parents, being more likely to report financial hardship, debts and difficulties in making ends meet. In fact this may be because Berthoud was essentially comparing lone parents on the long-term rate with two-parent families on the ordinary rate. In addition Berthoud's analysis was of the reformed scheme (ie after the 1980 Act) and (as discussed below) these changes probably did benefit lone parents more than unemployed two-parent families.

In terms of meeting basic needs then these can, of course, be defined fairly narrowly to include only such things as housing, food and fuel or more widely to include, as the Supplementary Benefit Commission put it, 'normal expenditure on day to day living'. What basic needs the scale rates are supposed to cover are no longer defined in any detail, but the 1977 Supplementary Benefit Handbook gives these as follows (p. 26):

> The scale rates are regarded by the Commission as covering all normal needs that can be foreseen, including food, fuel and light, the normal repair and replacement of clothing, household sundries (but not major items of bedding and furnishing) and provision for amenities such as newspapers, entertainments and television licences. It is not possible to say how much of the scale rates is appropriate to any one item since this will depend both on the circumstances of the person, eg a younger person may need to spend more on food and an older person more on fuel, and on his personal preferences, eg a person may prefer to spend less on entertainments in order to enjoy a higher standard of household amenities. What the scale rates provide is an amount for people to meet all ordinary living expenses in the way that suits them best.

In many respects the FFS families seemed to be falling below these criteria. The bulk of expenditure was going on the essentials of food, fuel

167

and housing leaving very little with which to express 'personal preference' in expenditure. Current income was apparently insufficient to cover the purchase of larger items. Very few of the lone mothers were spending on leisure or social activities. At the FRS most of the lone mothers said that there were items which they needed but could not afford—clothing and particularly clothing for children often being mentioned. Difficulties in paying for the basic items of housing and fuel were commonly reported and substantial minorities had fallen into arrears for these items. The lone mothers who had been on benefit for at least two years seemed to have the lowest living standards although those lone mothers who moved on and off benefit did not seem to be substantially better-off. As Bradshaw and Morgan (1987) conclude in their study of consumption patterns among families on supplementary benefit 'the evidence reveals that families on supplementary benefit can only afford an extremely restricted and drab lifestyle' (p. 13).

The FFS/FRS data, of course, refer to the late 1970s. Since then there have been a number of changes—demographic, social, economic and in policy —which might be expected to have affected the standards of living of lone-parent families. In the next section therefore we look at the current situation in order to try and assess how things might have changed for lone-parent families.

## LONE-PARENT FAMILIES IN THE 1980S: ECONOMIC POSITION

Recent years have seen a sharp decline in the proportion of lone mothers in full-time employment (unfortunately the most recent figures refer only to 1984). As Table 8.1 shows the proportion in full-time employment fell from 24 per cent in 1976-78 to 17 per cent in 1982-84. Thus, of all lone mothers the proportion employed has fallen from about half throughout the 1970s to about two-fifths in the early 1980s. Those with pre-school children are particularly likely to have been affected by this, with the proportion in employment falling from 28 per cent in 1976-78 to only 17 per cent in 1982-84. Among lone fathers, however, the proportion in employment seems to have remained fairly stable. In 1978 about 70 per cent of lone fathers were estimated to have some income from earnings (Popay et al., 1983) and Haskey (1986a) makes the same estimate for 1984 (based on Labour Force Survey data). This is rather surprising given that the figures for the receipt of supplementary benefit among lone fathers (Table 8.2) show that this has risen quite substantially. This could however represent a shift from unemployment benefit to supplementary benefit.

The total number of lone-parent families in receipt of supplementary benefit rose from 339,000 in 1978 (about 40 per cent of all lone parents) to 518,000 in 1984 (more than 50 per cent of all lone parents). Among lone mothers the proportion on supplementary benefit has risen from about 43 per cent to about 53 per cent. Single (unmarried) mothers and separated women are the most likely to be in receipt of supplementary benefit (Table 8.2).

Table 8.1

Employment status of lone mothers by age of youngest child 1976–1984

| Age of youngest child | 1976–78 % | 1978–80 % | 1980–82 % | 1982–84 % |
|---|---|---|---|---|
| Youngest child under 5 | | | | |
| Working full-time[1] | 15 | 14 | 11 | 6 |
| Working part-time[2] | 13 | 12 | 13 | 11 |
| All working[3] | 28 | 26 | 24 | 17 |
| Base = 100% | (366) | (381) | (386) | (416) |
| Youngest child 5 and over | | | | |
| Working full-time[1] | 27 | 26 | 27 | 23 |
| Working part-time[2] | 28 | 30 | 30 | 27 |
| All working[3] | 55 | 56 | 58 | 50 |
| Base = 100% | (910) | (932) | (932) | (837) |
| All | | | | |
| Working full-time[1] | 24 | 22 | 22 | 17 |
| Working part-time[2] | 23 | 25 | 25 | 22 |
| All working[3] | 47 | 48 | 48 | 39 |
| Base = 100% | (1276) | (1313) | (1318) | (1253) |

1. 30 or more hours per week.
2. Up to 30 hours per week.
3. Includes a few women whose hours of work were not known.

*Source:* OPCS (1985b) *General Household Survey Monitor*, Table 14.

The fall in the proportion of lone mothers in employment and the increase in the numbers dependent on supplementary benefit are reflected in the income composition of the families. As Table 8.3 shows, in 1979 48 per cent of lone mothers had benefits as their main source of income, by 1981 this had risen to 55 per cent. The proportion with earnings as the main source fell from 44 per cent to 34 per cent. Increased levels of unemployment meant that the proportion of two-parent families with benefits as their main source doubled (from 4 to 8 per cent).

## Table 8.2
### Receipt of supplementary benefit, lone parents by marital status
### 1978–1984

| Lone parents | 1978 | 1980 | 1982 | Thousands 1984 |
|---|---|---|---|---|
| Lone fathers | 15 | 16 | 24 | 27 |
| Lone mothers | 325 | 320 | 417 | 491 |
| – single | 87 | 100 | 135 | 169 |
| – widowed | 11 | 7 | 10 | 10 |
| – divorced | 109 | 109 | 132 | 147 |
| – prisoner's wife | 4 | 4 | 4 | 4 |
| – separated | 113 | 100 | 136 | 161 |
| Total lone parents | 339 | 336 | 441 | 518 |

*Source:* DHSS (1986b) *Social Security Statistics 1986,* Table 34.32.

This shift from earnings to benefit is also reflected in the estimates for the number of low-income families (Table 8.4). According to these estimates the proportion of lone parents on supplementary benefit rose from about 38 per cent in 1979 to about 59 per cent in 1985. However the proportion not

## Table 8.3
### Main source of income by family type, 1979 and 1981

| Main source of income | Lone mothers 1979 % | 1981 % | Lone fathers 1979 % | 1981 % | Two-parent families 1979 % | 1981 % |
|---|---|---|---|---|---|---|
| State benefits | 48 | 55 | 30 | 27 | 4 | 8 |
| Earnings | 44 | 34 | 70 | 82 | 95 | 92 |
| Maintenance | 7 | 10 | – | – | – | – |
| Other | 1 | 1 | – | – | ∅ | ∅ |
| Total | 100 | 100 | 100 | 100 | 100 | 100 |

∅   Less than 1 per cent.

Sources:   1979 figures from Popay et al. (1983) Table 2.
1981 figures from Rimmer (1986b) Table 3.

on benefit but with incomes below the 140 per cent level stayed about the same (at about 11-13 per cent). Thus while the proportion of lone parents with 'low incomes' rose from about 50 per cent to about 70 per cent, this increase was entirely accounted for by an increase in dependence on supplementary benefit.

Among two-parent families the proportion with 'low incomes' rose very dramatically between 1979 and 1983 from 11 per cent to almost 22 per cent, and fell back slightly in 1985. There was a more than three-fold increase in the numbers dependent on supplementary benefit but there was also a significant increase in the number of working families with low incomes. According to the government approximately one-third of the increase in the number of low-income families between 1981 and 1983 was due to improved rates of supplementary benefit (quoted in CPAG/Low Pay Unit, 1986). Nevertheless this still leaves a substantial increase in the number of families living at or close to supplementary benefit levels.

Table 8.4

Low-income families, 1979, 1983 and 1985

| Family type | 1979 N(000s) | % | 1983 N(000s) | % | 1985 N(000s) | % |
|---|---|---|---|---|---|---|
| Lone parents | | | | | | |
| In receipt of Sup. Ben. | 320 | 37.6 | 460 | 48.4 | 540 | 59.3 |
| Below 100% Sup. Ben. | 40 | 4.7 | 30 | 3.0 | 30 | 3.3 |
| 100–140% Sup. Ben. | 70 | 8.2 | 80 | 8.4 | 70 | 7.7 |
| Total below 140% | 430 | 50.6 | 570 | 60.0 | 640 | 70.3 |
| Two-parent families | | | | | | |
| In receipt of Sup. Ben. | 130 | 2.1 | 390 | 6.4 | 440 | 7.4 |
| Below 100% Sup. Ben. | 110 | 1.8 | 170 | 2.8 | 160 | 2.7 |
| 100–140% Sup. Ben. | 450 | 7.2 | 770 | 12.7 | 530 | 8.9 |
| Total below 140% | 690 | 11.1 | 1330 | 21.9 | 1130 | 19.0 |

*Source:* DHSS (1986a) *Low-Income Families 1983;* DHSS (1988) *Low-Income Families 1985.*

The main reason for this increasing dependence on supplementary benefit is, of course, the huge increase in unemployment levels and in the extent of long-term (over one year) unemployment. A number of changes in the way unemployment is counted have been introduced since 1979—the most important being the shift in 1982 to counting only those claiming benefits in respect of unemployment rather than all those registered as unemployed (DE, October 1986b). These changes make it difficult to compare unemployment levels over this period—the Unemployment Unit estimate that if the way of counting the unemployed had not changed the total for June 1987 would stand at 3,597.3 rather than 2,905.4 as estimated by the Department of Employment and shown in Table 8.5 (Unemployment Unit, 1987). Whatever way the count is made it is however very clear that unemployment has risen very steeply for both men and women, and currently about two-fifths of the registered unemployed have been out of work for at least one year.

Table 8.5

Unemployment in Great Britain: 1978, 1979, 1980 and 1987

| Unemployment | 1978 | 1979 | 1980 | 1987[2] |
|---|---|---|---|---|
| Number registered unemployed[1] (thousands) | | | | |
| Men | 995.2 | 919.6 | 1180.0 | 2023.0 |
| Women | 414.4 | 405.9 | 535.8 | 882.4 |
| All | 1409.7 | 1325.5 | 1715.9 | 2905.3 |
| Unemployment rate | | | | |
| Men | 7.1% | 6.6% | 8.5% | 12.3% |
| Women | 4.4% | 4.2% | 5.5% | 7.8% |
| All | 6.0% | 5.6% | 7.3% | 10.5% |
| Proportion unemployed for over 52 weeks[3] | | | | |
| Men | 27.0% | 30.2% | 26.0% | 47.1% |
| Women | 16.0% | 19.2% | 16.0% | 32.4% |
| All | 23.9% | 27.1% | 23.0% | 42.6% |

1. Unadjusted annual averages including school leavers.
2. June, figures for 1987 on a basis of claimant count (see text).
3. April of each year

*Sources:* 1979–1980 *Employment Gazette*, January 1981, Tables 2.2 and 2.8.
1986 *Employment Gazette*, September 1987, Tables 2.1 and 2.8.

Another factor which is likely to have affected the extent of low-incomes among two-parent families, and hence the relativities between lone parent and two-parent families, has been the slight decline in the proportion of two-earner families. In 1979 58 per cent of married couples were two-earner families, by 1982 this had fallen to 53 per cent. However it was among the childless couples rather than those with children for whom this fall was greatest (from 68 per cent to 62 per cent for the former and from 51 per cent to 48 per cent for the latter).

Although the number of two-earner families has declined slightly nevertheless about half of all families do have two earners and it has been argued (Pahl, 1984; Rimmer, 1986a) that an increasing polarisation is taking place between 'employed' and 'unemployed' households. Unemployed men rarely have wives who are in employment (Moylan et al., 1984) and therefore such families tend to be entirely dependent on state benefits. Nevertheless, despite increasing unemployment and poverty for two-parent families such families have had (on average) higher increases in incomes over the past five to six years than have lone parents. According to FES data between 1978 and 1985 the average gross weekly incomes of couples with two dependent children more than doubled, rising from £127.26 to £270.95. Over the same period the average gross incomes of lone parents rose from £62.68 to £112.81 which is an increase of 80 per cent. In terms of expenditure (which is probably a better indicator of living standards than income) the average weekly expenditure of lone parents fell from about 66 per cent of that of two-parent families with two children in 1978 to only about 53 per cent in 1985. This difference remains—although it is less pronounced—if family size is controlled for by calculating 'equivalent' expenditure. If expenditure had risen at the same rate as inflation between 1978 and 1985 then the average expenditure of the two-parent families with two children would have been £179.95—the actual figure was £199.11. For the lone parents, however, the 1985 figure would have been £119.09 whereas the actual figure was only £105.89 (Millar, 1988). Roll (1988) has also calculated (on the basis of FES data) that lone-parent households have had a significant fall in real income between 1979 and 1985.

For families on supplementary benefit, benefit levels have risen faster than the rate of inflation. Between 1979 and January 1987 the RPI rose by 171.1 points or about 77 per cent. For a lone mother with two dependent children aged four and seven and living as a householder the ordinary rate of benefit rose by about 98 per cent and the long-term rate by about 96 per cent. However the RPI is not necessarily a good indicator of changes in the cost of living as experienced by poor families, whose patterns of expenditure are not reflected in the calculation of the RPI (Godfrey and Bradshaw, 1983). Furthermore in relation to average gross male manual wages the levels of benefit remained fairly constant, in 1978/79 the lone mother described above would have received benefit equivalent to about 26 per cent of average gross male manual wages on the ordinary rate and equivalent to about 30 per cent on the long-term rate. In 1986 the figures were 27 per cent and 32 per cent respectively. Thus while in real terms benefit levels have improved slightly, in relative terms there has been little change.

For lone parents the main difference between the late 1970s and the mid 1980s is the increased dependence on supplementary benefit and the fall in the proportion in full-time employment. Since the FFS/FRS lone parents have probably become more homogenous in their incomes and standards of living, and the FFS/FRS results—particularly in relation to the duration of low incomes—would be now likely to apply to more lone parents than in the late 1970s. For two-parent families the situation seems to be more complex. Many more two-parent families are now living on supplementary benefit or on incomes not much above supplementary benefit levels and those on supplementary benefit have the lowest levels of income of any group of recipients (taking family size into account). However, for those in employment, average incomes have risen faster than prices and thus there seems to have been an increasing polarisation in the standard of living of those in and out of employment.

## SOCIAL SECURITY POLICY

The social security system has recently been reviewed (DHSS, 1985a and 1985b) and a number of quite extensive changes have been introduced during 1987 and in April 1988. These are discussed below, first we briefly examine the main changes introduced in 1980, following the 1978 *Social Assistance* review. A number of these changes would have had quite substantial effects on the living standards of lone parents. First, eligibility to the long-term rate was extended to those not required to register for employment after one instead of two years. The long-term rate for adults is about 27 per cent higher than the ordinary rate. However there is no long-term rate for children so the actual increase in family income afforded by the long-term rate is rather less than this. In 1986/87 a lone mother with two children aged under 11 would receive about 16 per cent more on the long-term rate as on the ordinary rate. Secondly, the rates for children were collapsed into two instead of four age-bands which meant that the rates for children aged under five and those aged 11 to 12 were substantially increased. Thirdly, a tapered earnings disregard was introduced for lone parents. Prior to 1980 only the first £6.00 of any net earnings (after meeting work expenses) were disregarded. Under the tapered earnings disregard, the first £4.00 were disregarded as were half of all earnings between £4.00 and £20.00—giving a maximum disregard of

£12.00 per week. Weale et al. (1984) found that while the introduction of the tapered earnings disregard seemed to have little effect on the proportions in employment it did increase the incomes of those who were employed.

The 1980 Act also abolished discretionary payments (the 'exceptional needs payments' and the 'exceptional circumstances additions') in favour of entitlement to 'additional requirements' and 'special needs payments' under conditions as laid down in regulations. This led to an initial reduction in the number of such payments followed by a very substantial increase (Walker, 1984). Research examining the impact of the 1980 reforms (Berthoud, 1984; Walker, 1984, 1986) shows that many claimants remained unaware of their entitlements, and also showed the extent to which supplementary benefit recipients continued to experience hardship and very low living standards.

Help with housing costs has also been 'reformed' with the abolition of the separate rent rebates, rate rebates and rent allowances and the incorporation of these into the housing benefit scheme (introduced 1982/83). Housing benefit also covers the housing costs of supplementary benefit recipients. Responsibility for the administration of housing benefit lies with the local authorities and the implementation of the new scheme was much criticised (Raynsford, 1985). Since then the housing benefit scheme has been cut quite substantially and has been reduced still further as a result of the 1985 review.

Lone parents probably did relatively well out of the changes introduced in 1980 particularly in comparison with unemployed families. What will happen as a consequence of the 1986 Social Security Act is not yet very clear. Supplementary benefit has been re-named 'income support'. The separate rates for householders and non-householders, the different ordinary and long-term rates and the 'additional requirements' and 'single payments' have been abolished. Instead there are basic rates of benefit, with lower rates for those aged under 25 (18 for lone parents), and 'client group' premiums. Lone parents will receive two of these premiums: the 'family premium' (for all families with dependent children) and the 'lone-parent family premium'. The simulation of the effect of the changes reported in the Technical Annexe to the White Paper (Table 11B) suggests that 42 per cent of lone parents would gain (31 per cent gaining over £5.00 a week), 25 per cent would have little change in their income, and 33 per cent would lose (2 per cent losing over £5.00 a week), presumably because they would be paying 20 per cent of their rates. However this is the only one of the other proposed changes that is taken into account in these figures and they may therefore be rather misleading. No account is taken of the likely effect of the abolition of additional requirements or single payments. In 1984 72 per cent of lone parents on benefit were receiving additional requirements and the average amount was £2.95 per week (DHSS, 1987). Calculations made by Berthoud

(1986) estimate that, when all the changes are taken into account, then 39 per cent of lone parents would gain (14 per cent by more than £5.00 a week), 5 per cent would have little change, and 56 per cent would lose (21 per cent losing over £5.00 a week). Thus when all the changes are taken into account the gains to lone parents are likely to be relatively small and probably mainly confined to those currently on the ordinary rate of benefit. Lone parents, however, do come out better than two-parent families. Berthoud estimates that only 32 per cent of these families gain (one per cent by more than £5.00 a week) while 40 per cent lose (10 per cent by more than £5.00 a week).

Changes have also been made to the rules regarding disregarded earnings. The tapered earnings disregard is to be replaced by a flat-rate disregard of £15.00 for lone parents and work expenses (eg fares, child-care costs) are not to be taken into account. The change to a flat-rate disregard will probably make the rules clearer to lone parents—the present system is complex and most claimants are unaware of how it works (Weale et al., 1984). However the £15.00 level is in fact below the amount that would be necessary to maintain the real value of the 1975 flat-rate disregard for lone parents (ie the value before the tapered disregard was introduced). In addition the removal of work expenses from the disregard will mean that some lone mothers will lose out. As described in Chapter Four a significant proportion of lone mothers in part-time jobs and on supplementary benefit do incur work expenses (in the FFS sample 41 per cent had some travel costs and 17 per cent were paying for child-care). The change does not therefore necessarily mean a gain for all lone mothers and for some it may even mean a loss. A re-analysis of the data from the tapered earnings disregards study suggested that the majority of lone mothers would gain by the change, with an average gain of £2.37. However, a substantial minority—11 per cent—would lose, with an average loss of £3.90. Those who lose tend to be women working for longer hours and with higher work-related expenses. The effect of a flat-rate disregard based on net earnings without taking into account work expenses may therefore be to discourage lone mothers from taking jobs with longer hours (or increasing their hours) because such jobs are more likely to involve work-related and child-care expenses.

Turning to families not on supplementary benefit the two major changes are the replacement of family income supplement with family credit and the changes to the housing benefit scheme. Again the likely impact of these changes is difficult to assess. Family credit will be extended higher up the income scale and therefore more families will be eligible. However whether take-up will improve above the 50 per cent for family income supplement remains to be seen, and the gains under the family credit scheme (with its higher rates of benefit) will to some extent be offset by the losses from cuts to housing benefit and the loss of automatic entitlement to free school meals (which, as described in Chapter Four, can be a very valuable benefit in kind to low-income families). Under the new Housing Benefit rules lone parents will no longer be assessed on the same basis as couples (although one-parent benefit will be disregarded). The Technical Annexe suggests only very limited gains to current lone-parent recipients from these changes—an average gain of only 40p, with 39 per cent gaining (28 per cent over £5.00 a week) and 56 per cent losing (22 per cent over £5.00 a week). In addition Parker (1985) has calculated that the problem of the 'poverty plateau' for lone parents will not be substantially alleviated under the new scheme. She calculates that a lone mother with two children on gross earnings of £60.00 a week will have a disposable income of £85.00. On gross earnings at more than double that level—£140 a week—disposable income will be £100.00, an increase of only £15.00. Joshi (1987b) suggests that the employment disincentive effects of the old structure of support are very largely carried on into the new scheme.

These changes to social security will certainly have some impact on the incomes and living standards of lone parents but they do not reflect any new approach to the needs of such families. It is therefore unlikely that the financial position of lone parents will improve, low incomes and benefit dependency will still be a dominant feature of their lives.

## DIVORCE LAW

In 1984 the Matrimonial and Family Proceedings Act made a number of changes in the law relating to divorce and these might be expected to have an impact in the future on the living standards of women coming into lone parenthood through marital breakdown. The first part of the Act allowed divorce after a minimum of one (rather than three years of marriage). The second part altered the basis for the financial provisions following divorce. Instead of attempting 'to place the parties in the financial position they would have been in had the marriage not broken down' the courts are required to give priority to the needs of the children and secondly to promote the principle of 'self-sufficiency' by either 'clean-break' divorce (ie a once and for all financial settlement) or by maintenance orders which are of limited duration. In addition, when making financial arrangements, the courts may take into account the conduct of the parties, where it would be 'appropriate' to do so.

Some of the effects of the first change—divorce after a minimum of one year of marriage—are already apparent. In an analysis of the divorce statistics in 1984 and 1985 Haskey (1986b) found that there was an immediate increase in the number of divorces and a fall in the average duration of marriage at divorce. Many of these 'new' divorces involved younger couples without dependent children. However his analysis suggests two points which might be particularly important as regards lone parents. First the increase in the number of divorces was more likely to involve couples with younger rather than older children. The number of divorcing couples with a child aged under five increased by about 4 per cent between 1984 and 1985, accounting for almost all of the increase in the number of divorcing couples with dependent children at that time. Thus one of the effects of allowing divorce earlier in the marriage may be to bring more mothers with very young children into lone parenthood. Lone mothers with pre-school children are, of course, one of the most financially vulnerable groups because of their difficulties in taking paid employment. Secondly there was an increase in the proportion of divorces granted on the grounds of adultery or unreasonable behaviour. This would follow in part from the provisions of the Act which allows divorce on these grounds after one year of marriage but requires two years for separation or desertion. But it may also reflect the fact that conduct can be taken into account in the financial settlement and these grounds may be useful in attempting to show unreasonable conduct by one of the partners.

The changes to the law regarding the financial arrangements following divorce were very controversial, and as several commentators pointed out (eg the Law Commission, 1981; Rimmer, 1983), were largely based on assumptions about how the current arrangements work rather than on any detailed empirical information on the financial costs and consequences of divorce and how these are distributed between the two divorcing people. The changes were primarily directed towards limiting the right of ex-wives to life-long maintenance from their ex-husbands. The arguments for this were basically two-fold. First that the life-long obligation to maintenance is inappropriate and does not reflect modern reality where the majority of married women are in paid employment and able to support themselves. Secondly it was argued (particularly by pressure groups such as the Campaign for Justice in Divorce) that such an obligation to maintain places an unfair burden upon men while providing women with a 'meal ticket' for life.

However all the evidence that is available (eg Gibson, 1982; Davis et al., 1983; Smart, 1984; Eekelaar and Maclean, 1986a and 1986b) shows that divorced women are very rarely awarded maintenance from their husbands if there are no dependent children, that even where there are dependent children the amounts awarded tend to be very low, and furthermore that there is a very high degree of non-compliance with these orders. As Gibson (1982, p. 139) notes:

> Past surveys had recorded the small amounts normally contained within magistrates' courts maintenance orders . . . Yet even this knowledge did not forestall the amazement upon finding that among orders for the benefit of the wife alone only one of 12 such orders had maintenance of £5 or more payable for her at midsummer 1981 . . . Among orders containing maintenance for the wife and two or more children there was only one order out of five with maintenance totalling £20 or more.

Figures from the General Household Survey 1982/83 show that of divorced women aged 18 to 49 only 13 per cent of those were receiving any maintenance compared with 49 per cent of those with dependent children (32 per cent for the children only, 16 per cent for both the mother and the children).

Furthermore there is little evidence to suggest that the receipt of maintenance encourages women to remain dependent on their former husbands and discourages them from self-sufficiency through their own employment. Indeed rather the reverse seems to be the case, both Davis et al. (1983) and Eekelaar and Maclean (1986b) found that women who received maintenance payments were more likely to be employed than those not receiving maintenance. (This is also suggested by the FFS/FRS data, as reported in Chapter Four.) Eekelaar and Maclean (1986b, p. 52) point out

> it appears that the mothers best able to work and survive were those who were receiving small but regular maintenance payments . . . Far from maintenance encouraging women to stay at home and fail to seek economic self-sufficiency, this private transfer payment actually enabled some mothers to afford to go to work.

On the question of whether the obligation to pay maintenance places an unfair burden upon men the evidence is rather limited. Eekelaar and Maclean (1986a) found that of the 29 divorced men in their sample nine were not paying maintenance, in five cases because the man was unemployed. Of those who were paying two-thirds were paying only a very small proportion (less than 20 per cent) of their current incomes and this varied very little according to the level of their incomes. Thus Eekelaar and Maclean concluded that while unemployment, low incomes or the needs of second families mean that some men do find it difficult to pay maintenance, nevertheless for others (eight of their sample of 29) it would be possible to pay more without a serious reduction in their living standards. Research from the USA has been more detailed on this question: Weitzman (1981), in a study of 228 divorced people, found that while divorce meant a rapid move downwards in living standards for women (on average a decline of 72 per cent in income relative to needs) divorced men actually improved their living standards (on average an increase of 42 per cent in income relative to needs).

This led her to conclude that 'most fathers have the ability to comply with support orders while still maintaining a comfortable standard of living' (Wietzman, 1981, p. 1265).

Given that even before the 1984 Act maintenance rarely made a substantial contribution to the incomes of divorced lone mothers and their children it seems likely that the provisions of the Act will have only a limited impact in practice. For lone mothers on supplementary benefit maintenance is, in any case, fully taken into account in assessing the amount of benefit to be paid. However it is possible that a long-term effect may be to further reduce the proportions of divorced lone mothers in employment since there may be less possibility of using maintenance to supplement earnings. Indeed the stress on 'self-sufficiency' seems particularly unrealistic, ignoring both the limited earnings opportunities to lone mothers with dependent children and the likelihood that these opportunities will have been reduced precisely because of the mothers' child-rearing responsibilities within marriage.

## THE FUTURE OF INCOME SUPPORT POLICY FOR LONE PARENTS

From the FFS/FRS analysis and from the comparative material a number of possible directions for income support policy for lone parents in the UK can be outlined in broad terms. The comparative review suggests that income support policy can vary across a number of different dimensions. These different dimensions and their relationship to each other can be summarised in terms of the question: 'where is the primary financial obligation to support lone parents assumed to lie?'. Table 8.6 attempts to set out potential answers to this question and the policy implications that would follow. Four potential locations for financial support are identified. The first would be self-support, primarily through employment. This could be encouraged through 'positive' policies to promote employment opportunities, or through 'negative' policies which offer no alternative to employment (or, of course, through a combination of both). Secondly, the primary location for support could be assumed to lie with the 'absent partner'. This would mean the adoption of policies to encourage this financial obligation—through the courts, the social security system or the tax system. Thirdly, support could be assumed to be the responsibility of any 'current partner'. This could be encouraged through cohabitation rules, or perhaps less punitively, through more general policies which confer financial advantages on married couples. Finally, the state could be assumed to have the primary responsibility, and could discharge this obligation in a number of different ways, for example by adding to existing provision or by introducing new benefits.

Of course it is not necessary that the question of where the financial obligation to support lone parents is to be located should be answered in the

## Table 8.6

### The location of the financial obligation to support lone parents

| Where is the finacial obligation? | What state policy follows? |
|---|---|
| (1)  Self-support | encourage positively through, eg<br>(1)  employment protection<br>(2)  day-care provision<br>(3)  equal pay |
| | encourage negatively through eg,<br>weak social assistance |
| (2)  'Ex-partner' | enforce maintenance obligations<br>through, eg<br>(1)  the courts<br>(2)  liable relative rules<br>(3)  child support taxes |
| (3)  'Current partner' | enforce through, eg<br>(1)  cohabitation rules<br>(2)  tax advantages to marriage<br>(3)  marriage grants |
| (4)  The state | add to existing provisions, eg<br>(1)  child benefits/family<br>      allowances<br>(2)  means-tested support |
| | introduce new benefits, eg<br>(1)  'advanced maintenance<br>      payments'<br>(2)  one-parent family benefits |

same way for all lone parents. For example many countries including the UK treat widows differently from other lone parents. This is saying in effect that the primary responsibility to support widows lies with the state, but that this is not the case for other lone parents. Similarly the primary obligation for lone fathers is assumed to be self-support through employment, but there is much more ambiguity about this in relation to lone mothers. In practice, also, these policies are not mutually exclusive and in general policy would be based on the assumption that some combination of these four sources of support should be encouraged. For example, in the United States, the expectation seems to be that support lies in a combination of self-support through employment and private support through the 'ex-partner' and that state support should take a minimal role (Garfinkel and Wong, 1987). In Sweden there is also a strong commitment to self-support through employment, but there it is the state rather than private support which provides the main back-up. Previous partners and current partners both represent 'private' support and in practice 'current partners' are more likely to be obliged to provide support than 'ex-partners'. As Maclean (1987) points out in the UK maintenance obligations are not strenuously enforced and therefore effectively support for a second (or current) family is given priority over support for a first (or previous) family.

Putting the two private sources of support together then support for lone parents can essentially vary across three dimensions—public support through the state, private support through past or present partners and self-support through employment. Table 8.7 attempts to locate some of the countries discussed in the comparative review across this three-dimensional typology (even though representing three dimensions in such a way is not very easy). As regards state support the key feature seems to be child or family support—as the comparative analysis showed it is those countries who are most 'generous' to families in general who are also most generous to lone-parent families. Thus the table begins with public child support on a continuum from 'strong' to 'weak'. Private support is represented in terms of the extent to which it is seen as an alternative to public support or as an

Table 8.7

A typology of different approaches to income support for lone parents

Public Child Support

Strong ———————————————————————— Weak

Private support - - - - - -Integrated - - - - - - - - - -Alongside - - - - - - - Alternative
with public

| | Integrated with public | Alongside | Alternative |
|---|---|---|---|
| Self support: Employment expected and positively encouraged | Sweden Denmark | | |
| Employment expected | France W. Germany | | USA |
| Employment not necessarily expected | | UK Australia Ireland | |

adjunct. Employment is considered in terms of the extent to which it is expected and encouraged, although of course within one country it is possible to have both positive and negative inducements to employment (eg France has both extensive public child-care provision but provides only limited social assistance to those not employed). The table does not do justice to the complexity of the different situations in different countries and it would be extremely useful to have further comparative research to fill out more details. However some indication of where the different countries are in relation to each other can be seen. The countries which provide the most extensive support for lone parents tend to be those with positive employment policies, a strong state commitment to child support and a more subsidiary role given to private support.

Kamerman and Kahn (1987) in their review of provisions for lone mothers in West European countries also suggest that a strong 'family policy' is an important feature in ensuring adequate support for lone parents, and that a key factor is the extent to which (and at what age of children) lone mothers should be expected to take paid employment. They distinguish between four strategies of support in European countries:

(i)  anti-poverty strategy: supporting lone mothers at home (UK);
(ii)  categorical strategy: also supporting lone mothers at home but with specific benefits (Norway);
(iii)  universal young child strategy: supporting mothers at home in the early years of childhood (France, Hungary, Austria, West Germany, Finland);
(iv)  combining labour market and family policy to permit parenting and gender equity (Sweden).

The obvious question is whether and how the UK could change its policies along the three dimensions identified in Table 8.6 in order to improve the situation of lone parents. Here we can look back on the FFS/FRS analysis, and at evidence from other studies, in order to cast light on what might be feasible policy options. First, therefore, what would be the situation as regards encouraging employment? Certainly there would seem to be a good deal of scope to do this—about half of the non-employed lone mothers in the FFS expressed a preference for paid work, and there were few differences in the characteristics of the employed and non-employed women. However these policies would probably have to include both financial and non-financial incentives to employment. As the evaluation of the tapered earnings disregard showed (Weale et al., 1984) limited financial incentives alone are unlikely to increase labour supply. Even if the financial return from employment is sufficient to cover the real costs of working, other practical support—especially child care provision—is also likely to be essential.

Secondly, what of the option of encouraging private support? As regards the extent of support from the 'absent partner' then this was very limited among the FFS lone mothers and many of those who did receive such support simply saw their supplementary benefit reduced accordingly. More research is clearly needed on the financial consequences of divorce for the absent parent because as yet there is little clear evidence as to whether or not this parent cannot pay or will not pay. In addition it is necessary to look at the way maintenance is treated under supplementary benefit regulations in order to allow such payments to give some financial benefit to the lone-parent family. In contrast to the limited support from ex-partners, private support from a current partner through re-marriage or cohabitation can be, as the FFS/FRS analysis showed, one of the most successful routes off supplementary benefit and into a substantially increased family income. There could be policies to encourage re-marriage (for example, marriage grants) or at least policies to remove barriers to re-marriage (perhaps paradoxically, here a relaxation of cohabitation rules might be beneficial so that financial considerations are not an immediate barrier to new relationships—see Donnison, 1982). However policies to encourage re-marriage must be treated with a great deal of caution—not all lone parents want or are able to re-marry; many second marriages end in divorce; re-marriage does not always automatically mean the end of poverty (about a third of the 'ex-lone mothers' in FFS were living with men who were 'poorer' than they were); re-marriage reinforces rather than tackles the problem of the financial dependency of women on men which it can be argued is the root cause of poverty for lone mothers (this is discussed in more detail below); and finally, many re-marriages are between divorced partners and could therefore mean simply a 'displacement' of the poverty—as one family escapes poverty through re-marriage another comes into existence as a lone-parent family. Thus re-marriage hides rather than solves the problem of poverty among lone parents.

Thirdly, what of the option of increased state child support, which in the UK could be most simply done through the child benefit scheme. As regards improving the incomes of lone-parent families this option would certainly seem to have an immediate impact—as Chapter Five showed doubling child benefit would substantially increase the incomes of poor lone parents. However, as with maintenance, this would not improve the incomes of supplementary benefit recipients unless child support and adult support were separated (as, for example, in the Finer proposals for the GMA).

On all three dimensions of income support changes could therefore be made which would improve the circumstances of lone parents. However, in Chapter Two it was pointed out that there are a number of unresolved questions regarding the principles for income support policy for lone parents.

184

These are concerned with first, the basis or justification for state support for lone parents, second the relative roles of public support and private maintenance and third the role of self-support through employment. These three can be seen as effectively parallelling the three dimensions of support shown in Table 8.6. One of the problems involved in trying to 'solve' these 'unresolved' questions is that the desired outcomes may be incompatible, especially as regards current policy objectives. For example there is a general push towards encouraging more self-support through employment in order to reduce benefit 'dependency'. However encouraging more lone mothers to take employment means that their role as mothers would have to take second place—which is not in keeping with the value attached to the 'family'. As Ellwood and Summers (1986, p. 73) put it (in the context of the USA but the point is well taken here too):

> The peculiar nature of the welfare problem for single mothers is the fact that society generally recognises and encourages mothers to stay at home and care for children, but it also sees self-sufficiency as a virtue and it is increasingly unwilling to accept welfare dependence among single mothers.

Thus one important set of questions concern the *balance* between state and other form of support. However there is also a lack of clarity about the nature of state support itself. Essentially three perspectives on the needs of lone parents can be identified:

(i)   the needs of lone parents as a specific group;
(ii)  the needs of poor families, of whom lone parents are one sub-group;
(iii) the needs of women, especially mothers, in combining motherhood and paid employment.

These different perspectives have different policy implications. However in relation to the first two these are differences of emphasis rather than substantive differences. This is clear when a dynamic rather than a static view is taken. Looking at family structure over time shows clearly the variety of different family situations in which individuals—both adults and children—live and highlights the fact that two-parent families become lone-parents families and vice versa, and thus needs in common can be identified. The similarities and needs in common of lone parent and two-parent families were highlighted in a recent Australian study (Jordan, 1987). This study used statistical techniques to 'sort' a large sample of households into coherent groups. However

> at no point has the method of analysis resulted in the segregation of sole-parent families from other kinds of income unit . . . sole parents are not a coherent population but about as diverse as other parents and in

much the same ways . . . The only generalisation to be made about sole as opposed to married parents is that their incomes, specifically of sole mothers, tend to be very low. (pp. 96-7)

The third approach—focusing on lone mothers primarily as women—raises rather more fundamental challenges to the structure of current policy and specifically the way the 'family' is treated. The 'family' is assumed to consist of two adults and their own dependent children, and within the family a sexual division of labour is assumed to operate whereby the father primarily acts as the financial provider while the mother primarily acts as the emotional provider. The current policy approach towards lone-parent families (and indeed for 'step-families') has been treat such families as far as possible in the same way as two-parent families. Thus there are no separate special provisions but only additions to existing provisions. Furthermore the prescribed roles for men and women within the family are assumed to continue even when the 'family' no longer exists—thus it is assumed that men should continue to be the financial providers (through maintenance) or that the state should take on this role of financial provider in place of the father, and women should continue to be the carers (and not therefore in full-time employment).

The structure of the family (real and assumed) and the sexual division of labour which assigns men the role of financial provider and women the role of carer are also much more fundamentally the primary cause of the high risk of poverty among lone mothers. For lone mothers their sex rather than their marital status is the real key to understanding why they are poor. The final section of the chapter therefore looks at the links between gender and poverty, and how these work out in practice for lone mothers.

## WOMEN, CHILDREN AND POVERTY

It has long been obvious that it is lone mothers rather than lone fathers who have a very high risk of poverty, but the explanations put forward for this have not usually gone beyond noting that men tend to have higher earnings than women. This is illustrated by the discussion of this issue in the Finer report (1974, p. 261):

> It has consistently been shown that, with only a few individual exceptions, fatherless families are considerable worse off financially than two-parent families. They are distinguished particularly by their dependence on one adult alone to provide the family's income, and handicapped by the relatively low level of earnings which mothers with children, particularly young children, can achieve, mainly because of low rates of pay for women's work, but also, to a much lesser extent, because of the restriction they may have to place on the hours for which

186

they can work . . . In financial terms the lone fathers, too, will normally be better off than the lone mother. In comparison with the two-parent family his income is likely to be somewhat less as he may have to take a lower paid job or refuse overtime because of the demands which caring for the family make upon him, and there is no wife to supplement the family's income through her own earnings. His earnings are, however, likely to be sufficient to keep his family some way above supplementary benefit levels and, unless he has a large or very young family, he will be unlikely to spend long periods out of work and claiming supplementary benefit.

Layard et al. (1977, p. 98) make similar points:

> . . . it is important to understand the causes of income poverty in these families. The explanation is relatively simple. All but 15 per cent of single parents are women. If they do not go out to work, their income consists mainly of social security benefits apart from allowances from the absent father, which only about half of them get. Due to the structure of the social security system, there is little financial incentive for a single-parent mother to go out to work unless she is going to work full-time at a reasonable hourly rate. But, as we have seen, women's hourly earnings are much lower than men's. Thus the direct influence of low pay on poverty is probably greatest in the case of single-parent families.

It is difficult to argue with either of these statements as a description of the circumstances of lone-parent families but as an explanation they leave a number of questions unanswered. In order to understand the causes of poverty for lone mothers it is necessary to recognise first that their poverty does not start only with the onset of lone parenthood but has its roots much further back.

This is true first of all at a quite simple level—many lone mothers come from poor families. Those most likely to have (and keep) 'illegitimate' children are very young women (Moss and Lav, 1985) who are likely to have very few resources of their own. Furthermore, as Burgoyne et al. (1987, p. 156) point out 'there is a long established link between poverty and marriage breakdown'. This is perhaps less true today than in the past, but nevertheless couples in social class V have divorce rates about twice the average (Murphy, 1985), those who marry young, mainly working class couples, have a particularly high risk of divorce (Kiernan, 1986); unemployed couples are particularly at risk (Daniel, 1981 and Chapter Three here). Ermisch et al. (1987) in a re-analysis of the Women in Employment Survey data also suggest that women in poor economic circumstances have a greater than average 'risk' of divorce (and also that those lone mothers most likely to re-marry are those who are better-off).

Houghton (1972, p. 222) in her study of separated women on supplementary benefit noted that many of these women 'had always been hard up . . . Many had been families with stringencies and shortages ever since their children were born'. Thus living in poverty is itself likely to be a contributory factor in marital breakdown, and some lone mothers start off with very limited resources and with little or no likelihood that maintenance will be forthcoming from the absent parent.

Furthermore even if the lone mother did not come from a poor family it could still be the case that she comes from a family in which she was poor. Because resources are not necessarily equally divided *within* families it is possible that even in wealthy families there can be individuals living in poverty. In all studies of lone mothers in which comparisons have been made between the financial resources of lone mothers as lone mothers and before they became lone mothers it has been found that a significant minority report that they are 'better-off' as lone parents than they were when married. This finding can of course be interpreted in different ways. Marsden (1973) found that about 'one in three' of his sample of lone mothers said that they were 'better-off' than they had been when married and he comments (p. 62):

> An improved standard of living after separation might merely reflect the former husband's selfishness in keeping his earnings to himself. But . . . there is the very important and more fundamental difficulty for social security planning here, that because many men are paid at rates below national assistance levels separation can bring a financial improvement for the family.

Evason (1981) in her study of lone parents in Northern Ireland found that about a quarter of the divorced and separated lone mothers said they were better-off and concluded (p. 22):

> Thus for many of these women single parenthood represented a movement from poverty as a result of the inequitable division of resources between husband and wife to poverty as a result of the lowness of benefits—not automatically, as is popularly supposed, from adequacy to penury.

Thus while Marsden emphasises the poverty of the whole family before marital breakdown as the main reason why some lone mothers are better-off, Evason emphasises the unequal division of household resources. Both are undoubtedly contributory factors. A recent study of women entering a Women's Refuge in Cleveland (Homer, Leonard and Taylor, 1984 cited in Graham, 1987) looked at both these factors. Measuring poverty by household income against supplementary benefit scale rates then 45 per cent of the women came from poor families (income below supplementary benefit levels); measuring poverty by the women's income against the expenditure for which they were responsible then 71 per cent of the women had been poor during marriage. Thus this group of women included both those who came from poor families and those who had been poor because of an unequal distribution of family resources.

However the most important point about the 'better-off' finding and other recent research on the distribution of resources within households (eg Pahl, 1980 and 1985; Brannen and Wilson, 1987) is that it clearly shows the potential vulnerability of the financial position of women within marriage. Although the traditional view of the breadwinner husband and stay-at-home wife no longer conforms to reality (if it ever did) it is still true that for most women marriage—or more specifically children—means financial dependency on men. Even though today the majority of married women are in paid employment, this employment is secondary in two senses. It is secondary to that of their husbands in that his earnings will usually provide the major component of family income. This means that low wages for women are not perceived to be a particular problem, because the earnings of married women are assumed to be a 'top-up' and not a sole or major source of family income. Women's employment is also secondary in the sense that it takes second place to what is considered to be her primary responsibility—the care of her family and children. The primary role of women is still seen as being in the domestic sphere rather than in the labour market, this means her employment has to be 'fitted in' around her domestic responsibilities. It also means that both employers and the state can ignore the question of these domestic responsibilities—in effect men are assumed not to have them and women are expected to make their own arrangements if they wish to take paid work.

The high risk of poverty among lone mothers can therefore be seen as a fairly direct consequence of gender roles and consequent inequalities in marriage and in access to employment. It has therefore been suggested (eg Weitzman, 1981, 1985; Funder, 1988; Maclean, 1987) that women should be given adequate compensation for their work within the family, as homemakers and mothers. As Maclean (p. 53) puts it 'rather than abandoning alimony claims, ex-wives should in fact seek compensation for the loss of earnings that they have incurred through marriage and maternity'. Such an approach means that, following marital breakdown, a couple would not simply be dividing material property and income, but also seeking to re-pay one another for their respective contributions to the marriage. The problem with this approach is that it accepts the status quo of marriage and of the differentiated roles of men and women within marriage. It seeks to make these roles of equal value rather than equally shared—equal in the sense of 'different but equal' rather than in the sense of 'equal and interchangeable'. But unless women can be financially independent of men marriage is likely to remain unequal. The most promising place to start thinking about equality is in the way in which responsibility for children is organised because this is the basis for the sexual division of labour which creates women's financial dependency on men.

The costs of children are both direct and indirect. At the moment the state makes a (small) contribution to the direct costs of children through child benefit, but the indirect costs are allowed to fall almost entirely on women. These indirect costs include the lost earnings during any period out of the labour market and, perhaps more importantly, the reduced earnings that follow because of part-time employment and lack of seniority and experience. As Cohen and Clarke (1986, p. 3) put it:

> Childbearing has a major and permanent effect on the pattern of women's employment. This effect is both prospective and retrospective, ie it affects both the kinds of training and occupations open to women when they first enter the labour market, in anticipation of future childbearing, and the employment opportunities open to them when they return to the labour market after having a child.

These indirect costs of children can be very substantial. Using data from the DE Women in Employment Survey, Joshi (1987b) has estimated that a 'typical' woman taking an eight year break to have two children and returning to part time employment would lose over her lifetime about £135,000—or almost half of what she would have earned had she remained childless (£293,000). Arguably the reason why these indirect costs fall mainly upon women rather than men is that they would be even higher for men. It is therefore necessary to reduce this differential in order that these costs can be spread more evenly between men and women. This would involve very positive labour market policies with regard to occupational segregation, provision of child care facilities and changes in the organisation of employment to allow both parents to take responsibility for child care. However one very good way to ensure that the indirect costs of child bearing are shared more equally between men and women would be for the state to provide much higher levels of benefit to meet the direct costs of children. If child benefit were substantially higher then there would be no need for the man to earn a 'family' wage and the woman's financial dependency on the man would be reduced. These arguments are not, of course, new but formed a large part of the debate that surrounded the introduction of family allowances (Land, 1975; Macnicol, 1980). Higher child benefit is an essential step to reducing poverty among lone mothers, both in the short term (as was demonstrated in Chapter Five) and in the long term, as part of steps to remove women's financial dependency on men.

Even with higher child benefits however families with only one parent would still require additional assistance with the direct costs of children in order to make up for the absence of the other parent. Variants on the idea of 'advanced maintenance schemes' would be the most appropriate way to do this in order to ensure that both parents contribute financially to the upkeep of their children.

Despite the 'little progress' made over the past 50 years, there are solutions to the poverty of lone-parent families. But the solutions may have to mean fairly radical changes to our views of the duties and obligations of parents and the state towards children. In order to prevent poverty among *lone* parents it is essential to start with the recognition that *both* parents can equally be financial and emotional providers for their children: equal breadwinners and equal carers.

# Bibliography

Abel-Smith B. and Townsend P. (1965) *The poor and the poorest*, London: Bell and Sons.

Abowitz D. (1986) 'Data indicate a feminisation of poverty in Canada too', *Sociology and Social Research*, 70, 3, 209–213.

Anderson M. (1983) 'What is new about the modern family: a historical perspective' in British Society for Population Studies, *The Family*, London: OPCS.

Atkinson A. B. (1984) *Take-up of social security benefits* Paper prepared for the Comptroller and Auditor General, London School of Economics International Centre for Economics and Related Disciplines.

Baldwin S. and Cooke K. (1984) *How much is enough? a review of the supplementary benefit scale rates*, London: Family Policy Studies Centre.

Bane M. J. and Ellwood D. (1984) *The dynamics of children's living arrangements*, USA: Harvard University.

Bartlett C. and Finlay H. (1988) 'Child support in Australia' in M. T. Meulders-Klein and J. Eekelaar (eds.) *Family, State and Individual Economic Security*, Brussels: Story Scientia.

Berthoud R. (1984) *Study of the 1980 reform of supplementary benefit*, Working Papers, London: Policy Studies Institute.

Berthoud R. (1986) *Selective social security: an analysis of the government's plan*, London: Policy Studies Institute.

Beveridge W. (1942) *Social insurance and allied services*, London: HMSO.

Bradshaw J., Cooke K. and Godfrey C. (1983) 'The impact of unemployment on the living standards of families' *Journal of Social Policy*, 12, 4, 433–452.

Bradshaw J. and Beadham R. (1984) 'Housing rebates: their take-up by families with children' *Poverty*, 57.

Bradshaw J. and Morgan J. (1987) *Budgeting on benefit: the consumption of families on social security*, London: Family Policy Studies Centre.

Brannen J. and Wilson G. (eds.) (1987) *Give and take in families*, London: George Allen and Unwin.

Brennan T. (1987) *Child Support Scheme: an update*, Perth, Australia.

Brown A. (1986) 'Family circumstances of young children', *Population Trends*, 43, 18–23.

Bumpass L. L. (1984) 'Children and marital disruption: a replication and update', *Demography*, 21, 1.

Burghes L. (1987) *Made in the USA: a review of workfare, the compulsory work-for-benefits regime*, London: Unemployment Unit.

Burgoyne J., Ormrod R. and Richards M. (1987) *Divorce Matters*, Harmondsworth: Penguin.

Burnell I. and Wadsworth J. (1981) *Children in one-parent families*, University of Bristol: Child Health Research Unit.

Cabinet Sub-Committee on Maintenance (1986) *Child Support*, Canberra: Australian Government Publishing Service.

Campbell B. (1987) *The Iron Ladies: why do women vote Tory?* London: Virago.

Canadian Council on Social Development (1984) *Not enough: the meaning and measurement of poverty in Canada*, Canada, Ontario: Canadian Council on Social Development.

Cass B. and O'Loughlin M. A. (1984) *Social policies for single-parent families in Australia: an analysis and a comparison with Sweden*, Social Welfare Research Centre, University of New South Wales, Australia.

Cass B. (1985) *Poverty in the 1980s: causes, effects and policy options*, Conference Paper, ANZAAS, Monash University, Australia, August 1985.

Castle B. (1980) *The Castle Diaries 1974–76*, London: Weidenfeld and Nicolson.

Charles N. and Kerr M. (1986) 'Eating properly, the family and state benefit', *Sociology*, 20, 3, 412–429.

Charlesworth S. (1988) 'The economic and social position of one-parent families in Australia and France: a comparative view' in M. T. Meulders-Klein and J. Eekelaar (eds.) *Family, State and Individual Economic Security*, Brussels: Story Scientia.

CHES (1982) *First report to the DHSS on the 10 year follow up*, University of Bristol: Child Health Research Unit.

CPAG/Low Pay Unit (1986) *The rising tide of poverty*, London: CPAG/Low Pay Unit.

Clason C. E. (1986) 'One-parent families in the Netherlands' in Deven F. and Cliquet R. L. (eds.) *One-parent families in Europe*, The Hague/Brussels: NIDI and CBGS.

Cockburn C. and Heclo H. (1974) 'Income maintenance for one-parent families in other countries' Appendix 2, *The report of the committee on one-parent families*, Cmnd 5629, London: HMSO.

Cohen B. and Clarke K. (1986) *Child-care and equal opportunities: some policy perspectives*, EOC, London: HMSO.

Commission on Social Welfare (1986) *Report of the commission on social welfare*, Ireland, Dublin: Stationery Office.

Cooke K. (1987) 'The living standards of the unemployed' in Fryer D. and Ullah P. (eds.) *Unemployed People*, Milton Keynes: Open University Press.

Corden A. (1983) *Taking-up a means-tested benefit: the process of claiming FIS*, London: HMSO.

Dale A. (1986) 'Differences in car usage for married men and married women: a further note in response to Taylor-Gooby' *Sociology*, 20, 1, 91–92.

Daniel W. W. (1980) *Maternity rights: the experiences of women*, London: Policy Studies Institute.

Daniel W. W. (1981) *The unemployed flow*, London: Policy Studies Institute.

David M. (1986) 'Morality and maternity: towards a better union than the moral rights family policy', *Critical Social Policy*, 16, 1, 40–57.

Davis G., MacLeod A. and Murch M. (1983) 'Divorce: who supports the family' *Family Law*, 13, 217–224.

Department of Education and Science (1986) *International statistical comparisons of the participation in education and day care of 3 to 6 year olds*, London: DES.

Department of Employment, *Employment Gazette*, January 1981, October 1986, May 1986.

Department of Employment (1986) 'Unemployment figures: the claimant count and the Labour Force Survey' *Employment Gazette*, October, 417–422.

Department of Health and Social Security (1978) *Social Assistance*, London: DHSS.

Department of Health and Social Security (1981) *Low-income families 1979*, London: DHSS.

Department of Health and Social Security (1983) *Low-income families 1981*, London: DHSS.

Department of Health and Social Security (1985a) *The reform of social security*, Volumes 1–4, Cmnd 9517–9520, London: HMSO.

Department of Health and Social Security (1985b) *The reform of social security: programme for action*, Cmnd 9691, London: HMSO.

Department of Health and Social Security (1986a) *Low-income families 1983*, London: DHSS.

Department of Health and Social Security (1986b) *Social Security Statistics 1986*, London: HMSO.

Department of Health and Social Security (1988) *Low-income families 1985*, London: DHSS.

Department of Social Security (Australia) (1986a) *Labour force status and other characteristics of sole parents: 1974–1985*, Social Security Review, Background Paper No. 8, Woden ACT, Australia: Department of Social Security.

Department of Social Security (Australia) (1986b) *Overseas countries assistance to sole parents*, Social Security Review, Background Paper No. 14, Woden ACT, Australia: Department of Social Security.

Deven F. (1986) 'A review of trends in the research on one-parent families' in F. Deven and R. L. Cliquet (eds.) *One-parent families in Europe*, The Hague/Brussels: NIDI and CBGS.

Deven F. and Cliquet R. L. (1986) (eds.) *One-parent families in Europe: conference proceedings*, The Hague/Brussels: The Netherlands Interuniversity Demographic Institute (NIDI) and the Population and Family Study Centre (CBGS).

Dilnot A. W., Kay J. A. and Morris C. N. (1984) *The reform of social security*, Oxford: Clarendon Press/Institute of Fiscal Studies.

Donnison D. (1982) *The politics of poverty*, London: Martin Robertson.

Douglas J. W. B. and Blomfield J. M. (1958) *Children under five*, London: George Allen and Unwin.

Douglas J. W. B. (1964) *The home and the school*, London: MacGibbon and Kee Ltd.

Douglas J. W. B., Ross J. M. and Simpson H. R. (1968) *All our future*, London: Peter Davies.

Duncan G. and Rodgers W. (1987) 'Lone-parent families and their economic problems: transitory or persistent', paper given at the OECD Conference *Lone Parents: the economic challenge of changing family structures*, Paris: OECD.

Economic Advisers Office (undated) *Lone parents: on and off supplementary benefit*, DHSS, Mimeo.

Eekelaar J. and Maclean M. (1986a) *Maintenance after divorce*, Oxford: Clarendon Press.

Eekelaar J. and Maclean M. (1986b) 'The financial consequences of divorce: the wrong debate' in M. Brenton and C. Jones (eds.) *The yearbook of social policy 1986*, London: Routledge and Kegan Paul.

Eldridge S. and Kiernan K. (1985) 'Declining first-marriage rates in England and Wales: a change in time or a rejection of marriage' *European Journal of Population*, 1, 327–345.

Ellwood D. (1986) *Working Off Welfare*, Harvard University, John F. Kennedy School of Government, USA.

Ellwood D. and Summers L. H. (1986) 'Is welfare really the problem' *The Public Interest*, 83, 57–78.

Elton H. D. (1974) 'Estimating entitlement to family income supplement' *Statistical News*, 24.9.

Ermisch J. (1983) *The political economy of demographic change*, London: Heinemann.

Ermisch J., Jenkins S. and Wright R. E. (1987) 'Analysis of the dynamics of lone parenthood: socio-economic influences on entry and exit rates' Paper given at the OECD Conference *Lone Parents: the economic challenge of changing family structures*, Paris: OECD.

EEC (1982) *One-parent families and poverty in the EEC*, Copenhagen: EEC.

Eurostat (1984) *Social indicators for the European Community*, Brussels: EEC.

Evason E. (1981) *Just me and the kids*, Belfast: EOC.

Ferri E. (1976) *Growing up in a one-parent family: a long-term study of child development*, London: NFER.

Fiegehen G., Lansley S. and Smith A. (1977) *Poverty and progress in Britain 1953–1973*, Cambridge: Cambridge University Press.

Field F. (1975) 'How good a model is FIS for a means-tested GMA?', *Poverty*, 31, 17–22.

Finer M. (1974) *Report of the committee on one-parent families*, Cmnd 5629, London: HMSO.

Finer M. and McGregor O. R. (1974) 'The history of the obligation to maintain', Appendix 5, *Report of the committee on one-parent families*, Cmnd. 5629, London: HMSO.

Fogelman K. (1983) *Growing up in Great Britain*, London: Macmillan.

Frey P. (1986) *Survey of sole parent pensioners' workforce barriers*, Social Security Review, Background/Discussion Paper No. 12, Woden ACT, Australia: Department of Social Security.

Funder K. R. (1988) 'The impact of work history factors on post-divorce income and property division' in M. T. Meulders-Klein and J. Eekelaar (eds.) *Family, State and Individual Economic Security*, Brussels: Story Scientia.

Garfinkel I. (1984) *Child support: an addition to our social security menu*, J. W. Geothe Universitat Frankfurt and Universitat Mannheim, Working Paper No. 133, West Germany, Frankfurt.

Garfinkel I. and Wong P. (1987) 'Child Support and Public Policy' Paper given at OECD Conference *Lone Parents: the economic challenge of changing family structures*, Paris: OECD.

George V. and Wilding P. (1972) *Motherless families*, London: Routledge and Kegan Paul.

George V. (1975) 'Why one-parent families remain poor', *Poverty*, 31, 6–12.

Gibson C. (1982) 'Maintenance in the magistrates' courts in the 1980s' *Family Law*, 12, 138–141.

Gittins D. (1985) *The family in question*, London: Macmillan.

Godfrey C. and Baldwin S. (1983) *Economies of scale in large low-income families*, Working Paper No. 166, Social Policy Research Unit, University of York.

Godfrey C. and Bradshaw J. (1983) 'Inflation and poor families', *New Society*, 65, 1083.

Graham H. (1987) 'Women's poverty and caring' in Glendinning C. and Millar J. (eds.) *Women and poverty in Britain*, Brighton: Wheatsheaf Books.

Graham J. and Marshall P. (1983) *Family Finances Survey (NI)* PPRU Occasional Paper No. 1, Belfast: PPRU.

Greif G. L. (1985) *Single fathers* Lexington USA: D. C. Heath and Company.

Griffiths B., Cooper S. and McVicar N. (1986) *Overseas countries' maintenance provisions*, Social Security Review, Background Paper No. 13, Woden ACT, Australia: Department of Social Security.

Hakim C. (1982) *Secondary analysis in social research: a guide to data sources and methods with examples*, London: George Allen and Unwin.

Harris J. (1977) *William Beveridge: a biography*, Oxford: Clarendon Press.

Harrison M., Harper P. and Edwards M. (1984) 'Child Support—public or private' Conference Paper, *Family Law in 1984*, Hobart, Australia.

Haskey J. (1982) 'Widowhood, widowerhood and remarriage', *Population Trends*, 30, 15–20.

Haskey J. (1983a) 'Marital status before divorce and age at divorce: their influence on the chance of divorce', *Population Trends*, 32, 4–14.

Haskey J. (1983b) 'Children of divorcing couples', *Population Trends*, 31, 20–26.

Haskey J. (1986a) 'One-parent families in Britain'' Population Trends, 45, 5–13.

Haskey J. (1986b)'Recent trends in divorce in England and Wales: the effects of legislative changes', *Population Trends*, 44, 9–16.

Homer M., Leonard A. E. and Taylor M. P. (1984) *Private violence: public shame*, Cleveland: Cleveland Refuge Aid for Women and Children.

Haveman R. H. (1987) *Poverty, policy and poverty research*, Wisconsin: University of Wisconsin Press.

Houghton H. (1972) *Separated wives and supplementary benefit*, London: DHSS.

House of Commons *Hansard* written answers, 3rd April 1985, Column 636.

House of Lords Select Committee on the European Communities (1985) *Parental leave and leave for family reasons*, (HL84), London: HMSO.

Hunt A. (1973) *Families and their needs*, London: HMSO.

Hutton S. (1986) 'Low-income families and fuel debt' in Ramsay I. (ed.) *Debtors and creditors: a socio-legal perspective*, London: Professional Books.

Jordan S. (1987) *The Common Treasury* Social Security Review, Background Paper No. 22, Woden ACT, Australia: Department of Social Security.

Joshi H. (1987a) 'Obstacles and opportunities for lone parents as breadwinners in Britain' Paper given at the OECD Conference *Lone Parents: the economic challenge of changing family structures*, Paris: OECD.

Joshi H. (1987b) 'The cost of caring' in Glendinning C. and Millar J. (eds.) *Women and poverty in Britain*, Brighton: Wheatsheaf Books.

Kahn A. J. and Kamerman S. B. (1983) *Income transfers for families with children*, USA, Philadelphia: Temple University Press.

Kamerman S. B. and Kahn A. J. (1983) 'Income transfers and mother-only families in eight countries', *Social Service Review*, Vol. 57, 448–464.

Kamerman S. B. and Kahn A. J. (1987) *Mother—Only Families in Western Europe*, report to the German Marshall Fund, USA, New York.

Kiernan K. (1986) 'Teenage marriage and marital breakdown: a longitudinal study', *Population Studies*, 40, 1.

Knight I. (1981) *Family Finances* OPCS Occasional Papers No. 26, London: HMSO.

Lambert J. and Streather J. (1980) *Children in changing families*, London: Macmillan.

Land H. (1975) 'The introduction of family allowance' in P. Hall et al. (eds.) *Change, choice and conflict in social policy*, London: Heinemann.

Land H. (1983) 'Poverty and gender: the distribution of resources within the family' in M. Brown (ed.) *The structure of disadvantage*, London: Heinemann.

The Law Commission (1980) *The financial consequences of divorce: the basic policy. A discussion paper*, London: HMSO.

The Law Commission (1981) *Family Law: the financial consequences of divorce* Law Com. No. 112, London: HMSO.

Layard R., Piachaud D. and Stewart M. (1978) *The causes of poverty*, The Royal Commission on the Distribution of Income and Wealth, Background Paper No. 5, London: HMSO.

Leete R. (1978) 'One-parent families: numbers and characteristics' *Population Trends*, 13, 4–9.

Leete R. and Anthony S. (1979) 'Divorce and re-marriage: a record linkage study', *Population Trends*, 16.

Lefaucheur N. (1986) 'How the one-parent families appeared in France' in Deven F. and Cliquet R. L. (eds.) *One-parent families in Europe*, The Hague/Brussels: NIDI and CBGS.

Letts P. (1983) *Double struggle: sex discrimination and one-parent families*, London: National Council for One-Parent Families.

Lewis J. and Piachaud D. (1987) 'Women and poverty in the twentieth century' in Glendinning C. and Millar J. (eds.) *Women and poverty in Britain*, Brighton: Wheatsheaf Books.

Maclean M. (1987) 'Households after divorce: the availability of resources and their impact on children' in Brannen J. and Wilson G. (eds.) *Give and take in families*, London: Allen and Unwin.

Macnicol J. (1980) *The movement for family allowances*, London: Heinemann.

Marsden D. (1973) *Mothers alone*, Harmondsworth: Penguin. (Second edition, first edition 1969.)

Martin J. and Roberts C. (1984) *Women and Employment: a lifetime perspective*, London: HMSO.

Millar J. (1985) 'The incomes and expenditure of supplementary benefit recipients', *Poverty*, 60, 41–44.

Millar J. (1986) *Lone-parent families in the Republic of Ireland*, The Organisation for Economic Co-operation and Development, Paris, France.

Millar J. (1987) *Lone parents, poverty and income support*, Unpublished D. Phil thesis, University of York.

Millar J. (1988) 'The costs of marital breakdown' in Walker R. and Parker G. (eds.) *Money matters*, London: Sage.

Millar J. and Cooke K. (1984) *A study of the take-up of one-parent benefit in Hackney*, Social Policy Research Unit, Working Paper No. 227, University of York.

Mitton R., Willmott P. and Willmott P. (1983) *Unemployment, poverty and social policy: a comparative study in the UK, France and Germany*, London: Bedford Square Press.

Moffit R. (1988) 'The effect of transfer programmes on human capital formation' Paper given at IFS Conference *The Economics of Social Security*, London, April 1988.

Moss P. and Lav G. (1985) 'Mothers without marriage', *New Society*, 73, 1180, 207–208.

Mount F. (1983) *The subversive family*, London: Counterpoint.

Moylan S., Millar J. and Davies R. (1984) *For richer, for poorer? DHSS cohort study of unemployed men*, DHSS Research Report No. 11, London: HMSO.

Murch M. (1980) *Justice and welfare in divorce*, London: Sweet and Maxwell.

Murphy M. J. (1985) 'Marital breakdown and socioeconomic status: a reappraisal of the evidence from recent British sources', *The British Journal of Sociology*, XXXVI, 1, 81–93.

Napp-Peters A. (1986) 'One parent families: marginal existence or new family self-consciousness?' in F. Deven and R. L. Cliquet (eds.) *One-parent families in Europe*, The Hague/Brussels: NIDI and GBGS.

National Council for One Parent Families (1982) *Key facts and figures*, Information Sheet Number 5, London: NCOPF.

Nichols-Casebolt A. (1986) *Single-parent families in the United States*, The Organisation for Economic Co-operation and Development, Paris, France.

Nicholson J. (1979) 'The assessment of poverty and the information we need' in DHSS *Social security research: the definition and measurement of poverty*, London: HMSO.

Nixon J. (1979) *Fatherless families on FIS*, DHSS Research Report No. 4: London HMSO.

O'Connor J., Hearne R. and Walsh K. (1986) *Social assistance: experiences and perceptions of first-time applicants*, Report of the Commission on Social Welfare, Background Paper No. 3, Ireland, Dublin: Stationery Office.

O'Higgins M. (1987) *Lone-parent families in the European Community*. European Programme to Combat Poverty, Working Papers, University of Bath.

Office of Population Censuses and Surveys (1981) *General Household Survey 1979*, London: HMSO.

Office of Population Censuses and Surveys (1982) *Census Historical Tables 1801–1981*, London: HMSO.

Office of Population Censuses and Surveys (1984) *General Household Survey 1982*, London: HMSO.

Office of Population Censuses and Surveys (1985a) *General Household Survey 1983*, London: HMSO.

Office of Population Censuses and Surveys (1985b) *General Household Survey Monitor: preliminary results for 1984*, GHS 85/1, London: OPCS.

Overton E. and Ermisch J. (1984) 'Minimal household units' *Population Trends*, 35, 18–22.

Pahl J. (1980) 'Patterns of money management within marriage' *Journal of Social Policy*, 9, 3, 313–335.

198

Pahl J. (1985) *Private violence and public policy: the needs of battered women and the response of public services*, London: Routledge and Kegan Paul.

Pahl R. E. (1984) *Divisions of labour*, Oxford: Basil Blackwell.

Parker H. (1985) 'Off target', *New Society*, 75, 1206, 232.

Parker G. (1986) 'Unemployment, low income and debt' in Ramsay I. (ed.) *Debtors and creditors: a socio-legal perspective*, London: Professional Books.

Pascall G. (1986) *Social policy: a feminist analysis*, London: Tavistock.

Piachaud D. (1985) *Round about fifty hours a week: the time costs of children*, London: CPAG.

Popay J., Rimmer L. and Rossiter C. (1983) *One-parent families: parents, children and public policy*, London: The Study Commission on the Family.

Rainwater L., Rein M. and Schwartz J. (1986) *Income packaging in the welfare state*, Oxford: Clarendon Press.

Raymond J. (1987) *Bringing up children alone: policies for sole parents*, Social Security Review, Issues Paper No. 3, Woden ACT, Australia: Department of Social Security.

Raynsford N. (1985) 'The false hope and the fiasco: housing benefit' in Ward S. (ed.) *DHSS in crisis*, 53–66, London: CPAG.

Richardson A. (1984) *Widows benefits*, Family Income Support Part 4, London: Policy Studies Institute.

Rimmer L. (1983) *Divorce: 1983 Matrimonial and Family Proceedings Bill: a briefing paper*, London: Family Policy Studies Centre.

Rimmer L. (1986a) 'Family employment and welfare' *The Quarterly Journal of Social Affairs*, 2, 3, 243–264.

Rimmer L. (1986b) 'One-parent families in Great Britain: financial and social aspects' in F. Deven and R. L. Cliquet (eds.) *One parent families in Europe*, The Hague, Brussels: NIDI and GBGS.

Robins P. K. and Dickinson K. P. (1984) 'Receipt of child support by single-parent families' *Social Service Review*, 622–641.

Robinson J. and Griffiths B. (1986) *Australian families: current situation and trends, 1969–1985*, Social Security Review, Background Paper No. 10, Australia, WODEN ACT, Department of Social Security.

Roll J. (1988) *Family Fortunes: parents incomes in the 1980s*, London: Family Policy Studies Centre.

Rowntree S. (1901) *Poverty and town life*, London: Macmillan.

Saunders P. and Whiteford P. (1987) *Ending Child Poverty: an assessment of the government's family package* Social Welfare Research Centre Reports and Proceedings No. 69, The University of New South Wales, Australia.

Schwarz K. (1986) 'One-parent families in the Federal Republic of Germany' in F. Deven and R. L. Cliquet (eds.) *One-parent families in Europe*, The Hague/Brussels: NIDI and GBGS.

Smart C. (1984) *The ties that bind: law, marriage and the reproduction of patriarchal relations*, London: Routledge and Kegan Paul.

Smeeding T., Torrey B. and Rein M. (1988) 'The economic status of the young and the old in eight countries' in J. Palmer, T. Smeeding and B. Torrey (eds.) *The Vulnerable: America's children and elderly in an industrial world*, Washington DC: The Urban Institute Press.

Smith J. E. (1984) 'Widowhood and ageing in traditional English society', *Ageing and Society*, 4, 4, 429–449.

Snell K. D. M. and Millar J. (1987) 'Lone-parent families and the welfare state: past and present', *Continuity and Change*, 2, 3, 387–422.

Statistical Office of the European Communities (1986) *Labour Force Survey 1984*, Luxembourg: office des publications officielles des communautes europeenes.

Statistical Reports of the Nordic Countries (1987) *Social security in the Nordic Countries: scope, expenditure and financing 1984*, Copenhagen: Nordic Statistical Secretariat.

SBC/DHSS (1977) *Supplementary Benefits Handbook*, Fifth edition, London: SBC/DHSS.

Svenne-Schmidt T. S. (1988) 'Advance payment by the state of maintenance to children' in M. T. Meulders-Klein and J. Eekelaar (eds.) *Family, State and Individual Economic Security*, Brussels: Story Scientia.

Tarpey T. (1985) *Explaining the increasing dependence of lone-parent families on supplementary benefit*, Unpublished MA thesis, University of York.

Thane P. (1978) 'Women and the Poor Law in Victorian and Edwardian England', *History Workshop*, 6, 29–51.

Townsend P. (1975) 'Problems of introducing a GMA for one-parent families', *Poverty*, 31, 29–39.

Townsend P. (1979) *Poverty in the UK*, Harmondsworth: Penguin.

Trost J. (1987) 'One-parent families after cohabitation' in Deven F. and Cliquet R. L. (eds.) *One-parent families in Europe*, The Hague/Brussels: NIDI and CBGS.

Unemployment Unit (1987) *Unemployment Unit Briefing June/July 1987*, London: Unemployment Unit.

Veit-Wilson J. (1985) *Supplementary benefit: what is to be done*, Newcastle upon Tyne: School of Applied Social Science.

Walker C. (1984) *Changing social policy*, London: Bedford Square Press.

Walker C. (1986) 'Reforming supplementary benefit: the impact on claimants' *Social Policy and Administration*, 20, 2, 91–102.

Walker R., Lawson R. and Townsend P. (eds.) (1984) *Responses to poverty: lessons from Europe*, London: Heinemann.

Walsh A. and Lister R. (1985) *Mothers life-line: a survey of how women use and value child benefit*, London: CPAG.

Ward S. (1975) 'One-parent poverty—the trap closes', *Poverty*, 31, 26–28.

Weale A., Bradshaw J., Maynard A. and Piachaud D. (1984) *Lone mothers, paid work and social security*, London: Bedford Square Press.

Werner B. (1984) 'Fertility and family background: some illustrations from the OPCS Longitudinal Study', *Population Trends*, 35, 5–10.

Wicks M. and Hutton S. (1986) *The use of electricity by families with children*, Research Report 15, London: Electricity Consumers' Council.

Wicks M. (1987) *A future for all: do we need a welfare state?* Harmondsworth: Penguin.

Wietzman L. (1981) 'The economics of divorce: social and economic consequences of property, alimony and child support awards' *UCLA Law Review*, 28, 6, 1181–1268.

Wilson E. (1977) *Women and the welfare state*, London: Tavistock.

Wilson P. (1981) *Free school meals*, OPCS Occasional Paper No. 23, London: HMSO.

Wynn M. (1964) *Fatherless families*, London: Michael Joseph.

# Index